The Science and Art
of Interviewing

The Science and Art of Interviewing

KATHLEEN GERSON AND
SARAH DAMASKE

OXFORD
UNIVERSITY PRESS

OXFORD
UNIVERSITY PRESS

Oxford University Press is a department of the University of Oxford. It furthers
the University's objective of excellence in research, scholarship, and education
by publishing worldwide. Oxford is a registered trade mark of Oxford University
Press in the UK and certain other countries.

Published in the United States of America by Oxford University Press
198 Madison Avenue, New York, NY 10016, United States of America.

Library of Congress Cataloging-in-Publication Data
Names: Gerson, Kathleen, author. | Damaske, Sarah, author.
Title: The science and art of interviewing / Kathleen Gerson and
Sarah Damaske.
Description: New York : Oxford University Press, 2020. |
Includes bibliographical references and index.
Identifiers: LCCN 2020017680 (print) | LCCN 2020017681 (ebook) |
ISBN 9780199324286 (hardback) | ISBN 9780199324293 (paperback) |
ISBN 9780199324316 (epub) | ISBN 9780197533857
Subjects: LCSH: Interviewing. | Interviewing in sociology. | Interviewing—Technique.
Classification: LCC H61.28 .G47 2020 (print) | LCC H61.28 (ebook) |
DDC 001.4/33—dc23
LC record available at https://lccn.loc.gov/2020017680
LC ebook record available at https://lccn.loc.gov/2020017681

3 5 7 9 8 6 4

Paperback printed by LSC Communications, United States of America
Hardback printed by Bridgeport National Bindery, Inc., United States of America

Contents

Acknowledgments   vii

1. Depth Interviewing as Science and Art   1

2. Getting Started: Pinning Down the Questions and
   Research Design   30

3. Interviews with Whom? When a Big Question Meets a Small
   Sample   45

4. Constructing an Interview Guide: Creating a Flexible Structure   66

5. Conducting Interviews: Seeking Discoveries That Matter   100

6. Analyzing Interviews: Making Sense of Complex Material   143

7. Pulling It All Together: Telling Your Story and Making
   Your Case   172

Appendix A: Examples of Recruitment Documents and Procedures   195
Appendix B: Examples of Consent Forms   199
Appendix C: Examples of Interview Guides   203

Notes   235
Bibliography   255
Index   269

Acknowledgments

One reward of finishing a book is to finally get the chance to thank the people who made it possible. Yet this is a daunting task, not only because the village it takes to write a book is so large but also because words are so inadequate to express the gratitude we owe our fellow villagers. To start at the beginning, it is especially difficult to convey the depth of our appreciation to James Cook, our editor par excellence. He supplied the original impetus for this project when, in a classic case of "be careful what you say," Kathleen casually mentioned that there is a method to the madness of interviewing as a social research endeavor. James then convinced us to spell out that method in written form and provided the steadfast support and wise counsel needed to get us to the end. It is no exaggeration to say that this book would not exist without him.

James also recruited a large and remarkably devoted group of outside reviewers, whose thorough, incisive feedback helped us transform several (very rough) drafts into a much better final product. Our deep appreciation thus goes to Allison Pugh and the other anonymous reviewers who gave so generously of their time and wisdom.

We have been exceptionally fortunate to receive sustained support from a widespread network of colleagues, friends, and relatives. Over many years of teaching and mentoring, our students have provided inspiration and taught us lessons as valuable as the ones we have endeavored to teach them. To mention only a few by name, we are grateful to Eman Abdelhadi for research assistance and inspiration above and beyond the call of duty and to Eliza Brown, Lauren Clingan, Sabrina Dycus, Ananda Martin-Caughey, and Marie Mercier for their helpful and insightful feedback on earlier versions of the manuscript.

We have also benefited from the many treasured colleagues who read chapter drafts or otherwise engaged with our ideas as we developed them. Among these colleagues, NYU's Lynne Haney, Ruth Horowitz, Colin Jerolmack, Iddo Tavory, and May Al-Dabbagh (at NYU Abu Dhabi) as well as alumnae Ellen Lamont, Alexis Merdjanoff, Josipa Roksa, and Stacy Torres are especially appreciated. At Penn State, Sarah thanks colleagues Michelle

Frisco, Jennifer Glick, Valarie King, Kate Maich, Molly Martin, Susan McHale, Léa Pessin, and Jenny van Hook. Kathleen's writing group, which over the years has included Lynn Chancer, Ruth Horowitz, Tey Meadow, Arlene Skolnick, and Cynthia Epstein, offered a steady source of support and constructive observations, its members always expressing enthusiasm for the project while never pulling their punches about needed improvements. Sarah's writing groups, whose members include Jessica Halliday Hardie, Carrie Shandra, Heather Jacobson, and Kristen Schultz Lee, offered insightful comments and critiques as well as much needed moral support as Sarah navigated both pre- and post-tenure academic life. Eviatar Zerubavel's belief in the need for a book like this, as well as his conviction that we were the people to write it, provided critical encouragement that convinced us to add this project to our already crowded to-do list.

We also thank the generative communities found on #soctwitter, #poliscitwitter, and #academictwitter more broadly. Although there are far too many contributors to name here, we are thankful for the numerous colleagues who replied to our queries about people's favorite interview-based books (many of which were our favorites as well), who posted thoughts about depth interviewing and qualitative methods that inspired our thinking, and who became members of our broader community of scholars and researchers. We thank everyone for their vision and inspiration.

Last, though very, very far from least, we thank our families and especially our life partners and children (and, for Kathleen, grandchildren), all of whom supported us and enriched our lives immeasurably during the time it took for this book to gestate. In addition to keeping Kathleen well fed, intellectually energized, and remarkably sane and happy, John Mollenkopf believed in the value of adding this book to our crowded writing agenda and then gave his own valuable time by reading every page and editing every line. No one could ask for an editor and intellectual confidant with a better sense of what it takes to conduct important, high-quality research or with a better ability to convey this importance with elegance and verve and as little jargon as possible. Paul Damaske nurtured both this project and the Damaske household. His contributions—via conversations, editorial comments, and co-parenting—were given with good-natured cheer, patience, and generosity. Sarah's daughter, Charlotte Damaske, gave Sarah the chance to see the world anew again (a gift for an interviewer). Charlotte was born near the start of this project, and Kathleen's grandchildren, Charlie and Dot, joined the world soon thereafter. It's impossible to exaggerate the joy, laughter, light, and meaning that they—along with Kathleen's daughter, Emily; Emily's partner, Scott; and Sarah's parents, Frankie and Steve—have brought to our lives. We are exceptionally fortunate and feel immensely grateful.

We dedicate this book to our children, Emily Gerson Mollenkopf and Charlotte Lucille Damaske, and to the generations of researchers now at work, in the making, and yet to come.

1

Depth Interviewing as Science and Art

Qualitative interviews form the basis for countless books and articles, yet these accounts rarely offer an insider's view of how they were produced. Most researchers, including interviewers, generally strive to present their findings seamlessly. An extended discussion of method would interrupt the narrative flow and take up space better left for presenting the arguments that emerged from the interviews. Yet it is both theoretically and practically important to demystify the process that leads to these findings and arguments in order to make clear the unique—indeed, irreplaceable—empirical and theoretical contributions qualitative interviews offer. Our goal in this book is to make that method visible and, in doing so, to offer our approach to maximizing interviewing's power.

Qualitative interviews are unique because they place each participant's voice at the heart of the research. In this way, interviewers give people an opportunity to tell their stories with their own words and, as we explore in later chapters, encourage them to think more deeply about their experiences than is usually possible with other methods. Yet interviews do not stop with the first story a person tells. Through techniques that stress careful questioning, listening, and probing, interviewers invite each person to delve into that story by inviting them to share their experiences, their accounts, their motivations, their aspirations, and their efforts to make meaning out of their experiences, social contexts, life trajectories, and social ties. Then, through careful analysis, each component of an interview takes its place in relation to all the other information shared by that participant, amid the social and historical setting in which their experiences take place, and in the context of all the other interviews. Finally, interviewers return to their original question(s)—or perhaps to new questions that emerged during the research process—and use their findings (especially unanticipated discoveries) to provide answers and contribute new theoretical insights about the social world. While inspiration, interpersonal skills, and even luck matter in this process, we argue that good interviews do not just happen. Instead, collecting interview material and making insightful breakthroughs with it depend on taking steps that

The Science and Art of Interviewing. Kathleen Gerson and Sarah Damaske, Oxford University Press (2021). © Oxford University Press. DOI: 10.1093/oso/9780199324286.001.0001

create the fertile ground in which inspiration can emerge, develop, and be confirmed.

We develop this position by building on classic works, old and new, that have offered pioneering approaches to conducting qualitative research, but we also offer our own perspective. Like Barney Glaser and Anselm Strauss's *The Discovery of Grounded Theory*, we stress the ways that theory building is integral to interview research.[1] Like Robert Merton and his colleagues' *The Focused Interview* and Robert Weiss's *Learning from Strangers*, we recommend interviewing techniques that rely on careful listening, deep probing, and striving to see the world through the participants' eyes.[2] And like Kristen Luker's *Salsa Dancing into the Social Sciences*, we argue that good qualitative research adheres to the logical principles that also apply to other methods.[3] While taking off from these themes, we draw on our experiences as well as selected examples from the work of others to present a distinct framework. In our approach, interviewing becomes an especially powerful research tool when it employs a set of strategies that include:

- Combining careful preparation before entering the field (in formulating questions and crafting the research design) with mental flexibility and openness to unexpected findings in the process of conducting interviews and analyzing the findings
- Developing a theoretically informed research design to select an appropriate sample of participants and place them in their proper social-historical context
- Organizing the interview experience to emphasize dynamic processes and trajectories—including the developmental paths of individuals, groups, and organizations—thus helping participants provide meaningful answers in a time-ordered, narrative sequence
- Asking questions that tap the multiple dimensions of human experience, including *what* happened (that is, descriptions of important events and the social contexts surrounding them), *how* interviewees experienced these events (that is, what meaning they held for each person), and the *responses* these experiences evoked (that is, the cognitive, emotional, and behavioral consequences going forward)
- Taking contradictory responses seriously, not as an indication of inauthenticity but rather as an opportunity to explore socially embedded structural and cultural conflicts that pose dilemmas and conflicts for social actors

- Taking advantage of the ability to collect sequential information on the various dimensions of human experience as an unfolding, interactive process between structure and agency[4]
- Paying attention to the distinction between the accounts people draw on to explain their experiences and decisions and the often hidden social forces—contextual, institutional, and interactional—that contribute to these outcomes

By following these principles, we argue, interviews can and do make unique and necessary contributions to knowledge not just about individuals but also about social relationships, institutions, and whole societies. The key is knowing when and how to enact each principle throughout the research process, from the earliest ideas that spark the research questions through the final efforts at answering them and reporting the conclusions. Whether your goal is to conduct an interview-only study, to include interviewing in a mixed-method project, or simply to know more about the principles and practices that structure this kind of research, we offer a step-by-step approach to formulating, conducting, analyzing, and reporting on interview-based research. First, however, let us consider some basic issues: What is a qualitative—or depth—interview?[5] What do interviews contribute, and how are those contributions distinct from the evidence gathered by other methods? And what are the common misunderstandings about interviewing as a method, and how should we address them?

What Is a Depth Interview?

What makes an interaction a depth interview? The answer may seem obvious, but interviewing can take many forms. It can be free-flowing or highly structured. It can involve one interviewee at a time, a couple together, or even a small group. It can take place in-person or at a distance via a video-conference program such as Skype, or Zoom, or via the telephone. It can seek personal information about numerous realms and periods of a person's life, focus on discrete periods or areas of a person's life, or gather insider knowledge from an informant about a group or organization or large-scale event.

All of these interviewing formats share an open-ended, probing, and discursive structure, but they do not seek the same kind of information. Focus groups gather only the information that people are willing to disclose when they know others, who may be friends or strangers, will hear what they say. Couple interviews make it possible to observe dyadic interactions, but they cannot assess what each would say were the other not present. One-on-one interviews between an interviewer and interviewee encourage the disclosure of highly personal information, including experiences and views people may be reluctant to share with even their closest confidants. Such one-on-one interviews can take place with a sample of people who have no connection to each other, but they can also involve interviews with people who are connected in some way, such as intimate partners, co-workers, or participants in the same social movement. In any case, participants provide information not only about themselves but also about the social contexts and relationships in their lives.[6]

While many of the issues we consider are relevant for all of these formats, we focus on interviews with one interviewee at a time. This format is "deep" in several ways. First, one-on-one interviews can be lengthy—typically two hours or more. Taking time makes it possible to establish trust, create an atmosphere of comfort, give participants the space to consider their responses, and ask (and get answers to) probing follow-up questions. In this context, an interview can elicit highly personal information and span wide areas and periods of a person's life. Each interview can create its own tempo, letting participants move at a pace that works best for them. Some people will speak quickly and briefly, while others will offer expansive details and may wander off track. Even the briefest interviews need to be long enough to allow people to provide in-depth knowledge of themselves, their life experiences, and their social worlds. Unlike ethnographers, who maintain sustained contact with the people in their chosen sites, interviewers typically rely on one or two interviews with the same person and must gain as much information as possible in each session.[7] Establishing sufficient rapport so quickly may seem unrealistic, but we consistently find that most people welcome the chance to tell their story to an interested, supportive listener and become engaged in the process to a remarkable degree.

Second, qualitative interviews ask people to reveal matters they may never have thought about in depth or revealed to others. Whether discussing the course of their lives, a particular period in the past, their current situation, or views about the future, interviews probe beyond participants' initial responses with follow-up questions that allow them to pause, reflect, and respond more fully. Interviews about personal life may prompt them to consider their experiences in a new light, while interviews about the roles people play in social or organizational processes may prompt them to consider in new ways contexts they have taken for granted. Interviews thus gather far more detailed and intimate knowledge than a survey or observational study can uncover.

Third, interviews ask people to consider multiple aspects of the same experience. Participants can recount an event, the circumstances surrounding it, and the ensuing consequences. They can discuss the social contexts that shaped an experience and the responses this experience evoked. They can report how and why they tried to shape that experience, what they did (or failed to do) about it, and what they thought or felt or did afterward. Interviewing is thus a method for charting and explaining the unfolding links between broader social structures and norms, on the one hand, and the beliefs, emotional states, and actions of individuals, on the other.

All interviews are "deep," but interview studies can rely on a range of formats. They can take place in a variety of settings, from the privacy of a home or an office to a public setting, such as a coffeehouse, restaurant, or park. Although nothing equals meeting in person, new technologies have made it possible to virtually connect over longer distances, thus expanding the options for selecting a sample and gaining participation. The ideal location is the one each participant prefers because that enhances comfort and trust. No setting is perfect, however. When the ideal is not possible, the second-best option is always better than none at all. The key is to create an atmosphere where participants feel free to share insights about matters that some may never have thought about or discussed with anyone.

Flexibility in an interviewing study extends to decisions about sampling size. As long as the chosen format gathers multi-leveled information from enough participants to allow the researcher to discover patterns, make key comparisons, include a range of different perspectives, and draw convincing conclusions, there are no rigid rules about sample size.[8] It is possible to extend or change the sampling strategy as the research unfolds and new findings suggest adaptations. This ability to include numerous participants and to make adjustments as the study proceeds complements interviewing's ability to gather a wealth of information from each individual. What sets interviewing apart from other methods is that it strikes a balance between breadth and depth. Interviews can delve far more deeply than any survey, even if the survey is administered in person. They can include a larger and more diverse group of participants than an ethnography, which typically focuses on one, two, or at most several research sites. By combining the search for in-depth knowledge with the ability to learn from a diverse range of people, interviewing offers a unique lens through which to discover and explain the shape and dynamics of the social world.

What Do Interviews Do?

Interviews offer a range of evidence that is difficult—potentially impossible—to gather in other ways. They can uncover social and mental processes that cannot be observed. They can discover social patterns and trends that are hidden or poorly understood. They can trace dynamic processes that develop through time. They can highlight differences in the ways people experience and interpret complex events. They can explore the link between macro-structural arrangements and micro processes such as the formation of individual identities, worldviews, and action strategies or meso-level processes such as how individuals participate and interact in collective processes or decisions. They can provide insight into the inner life of individuals and place these insights in a social and historical context. And, finally, they can use these insights to build theoretical explanations about how social and cultural arrangements shape human experience and how human actors create and potentially change social and cultural frames.

Uncovering the Unobservable

Interviews provide a window on the vast array of human experiences that we cannot see or easily measure. They make it possible to map and analyze mental processes, private activities, and social arrangements so taken for granted that they remain imperceptible. The private nature of interviewing encourages participants to disclose views and experiences they may never have shared with others or even taken the time to think about. Even though interviews take place with one interviewee at a time and rely on individual reports, the sum of their multiple reports—and in the context of careful analysis—offers a picture of dyadic interactions, collective activities, and broader institutional arrangements. To understand various "invisible" structures of the workplace, for example, Adia Harvey Wingfield interviewed African American professional men to discover how institutional racism structures opportunities in professional organizations and work settings, while interviews with African American mothers allowed Dawn Marie Dow to uncover how these mothers' parenting practices were shaped in part by their attempts to provide their children with a sense of racial safety, particularly when they lived in mostly white neighborhoods.[9] Interviewing Sierra Leonean contractors allowed Kevin Thomas to discover how high unemployment rates and a lack of information about global trends led young migrant workers to take jobs as service workers in Iraq despite the dangers of exploitation.[10] These are just a few examples of how interviewing can be used as a tool that allows us to metaphorically "see" what is literally invisible.

Many of a person's most important experiences occur at times and places that are beyond an investigator's reach, including events that took place in the past and activities that are too private to allow others to observe. Past events cannot be observed, but they can be recounted. In doing so, the interviewer needs to take care to distinguish between past experiences that are relatively straightforward to recall and verify—for example, major life events such as marriages, childbirth, and educational and job histories—and the meaning people impart to such events and experiences. Yet acknowledging the challenges involved in gaining meaningful and accurate information about the past does not mean it is impossible to do so or that doing so is not a worthwhile endeavor. Instead, the job of a good interviewer is to face these challenges, and we offer a set of strategies to meet and overcome them.

Just as interviews offer a window onto the past, they also offer a window onto private interactions. To take an obvious example, sexual behavior remains largely beyond the realm of observable social activity. Even in those rare instances when it might be possible for a disengaged researcher to observe this and other forms of intimate activity, doing so would necessarily change the nature of what is being observed. Engaging in sex with another person is inherently performative, but it is quite different for sexual partners to perform for each other than it is for them to perform for a nonparticipant. What's more, simply observing sexual interactions offers little in the way of self-evident information. Does the observed behavior represent the authentic expression of genuine sexual pleasure or, alternatively, does it reflect a process of "faking" pleasure or camouflaging discomfort? And if expressions of sexual pleasure (or discomfort) are meant to mislead, is the motive to make a partner feel better (or worse), bring things to a close more quickly, and/or protect oneself from any negative consequences that revealing one's true feelings might provoke? Since sexual activity necessarily involves performance, observation alone cannot answer these questions.

Sexual behavior may provide an especially vivid example of why discovering and exploring the unobservable dimensions of social life matters, but it points to a universal principle. Since the causes, meaning, and consequences of virtually all human behavior are rarely self-evident, investigating the human actions and experiences that are unobservable is essential to understanding and explaining social and personal life. We would not want to exclude information about past experiences, private activities, or mental processes simply because an outsider cannot directly observe them.[11] We can only ascertain the meaning people impart to their behavior and the motives that inform it by asking probing questions that explore both the meaning of actions and the ways they emerge from past experience and shape future behavior.

Private acts are important not just in themselves but also for what they tell us about society. Feminist researchers have demonstrated how the private sphere is a site where social inequalities are produced and displayed. Interviews can shed light on the dynamics that take place within households, including the relationships between paid domestic workers and their employers as well as the relationships among family members. In her interviews with domestic workers, for example, Pierrette Hondagneu-Sotelo discovered how employers of domestic workers failed to acknowledge their status as "real" employees, justifying decisions to keep wages low and withhold benefits.[12] Interviews like these help us investigate how gender, race, and class structure unequal relationships in private settings, which may go unnoticed but have profound consequences. In this way, interview findings have provided much of what we know about the experiences of both marginalized and privileged groups.[13]

Beyond the private sphere, it is also difficult to observe many of a society's most entrenched institutional arrangements and processes. Structures of opportunity and constraint—for example, the "glass elevator" that white men enjoy in professions where women and minorities predominate, or the "ideal worker" ethos that penalizes involved parents at the workplace—are powerful precisely because they are hidden.[14] Observation alone cannot tell us how institutional actors make decisions or why bureaucratic processes produce systematically biased outcomes. In their studies of social service bureaucracies, for example, both Sharon Hays and Michael Lipsky relied on interviews to understand not just what they observed but also how the participants, including service providers and clients, viewed these interactions.[15] By asking probing questions, interviews can uncover the invisible structures and processes that shape people's options and outcomes and then explore how people perceive their consequences.

Even when it is possible to observe an event or outcome, interviews can reveal how participants seek to influence, process, and respond to these occasions—not just in the moment but also as they look back at a later time. Interviews allowed Diane Vaughn to move beyond conceptualizing a relationship breakup as a static "life event" to identify the stages in a lengthy process she calls "uncoupling."[16] Ethnographers, too, rely on interviews to find out how participants make sense of the events they have observed or in which they have participated.[17] Miliann Kang supplemented ethnographic observations with interviews to understand how Korean immigrants found and managed their work as nail salon technicians, while Iddo Tavory and his research team used interviews to explore why advertising executives sought meaning in their jobs by adding pro bono work to the work they were paid to perform.[18]

Whether the focus is on past events, private activities, or invisible institutional structures, interviewing provides access to crucially important information that would otherwise remain hidden. What's more, interviews offer discretion and flexibility about when and how to gain this information. Not only do they allow us to investigate and make sense of the vast realm of human experience that cannot be observed; they also allow us to uncover the nuances that questionnaires with predetermined question wording and pre-coded answer categories cannot. They make it possible to explore and explain both the largely invisible but highly consequential dimensions of social experience and the diverse meanings people impute to these experiences.[19]

Discovering the Unknown, Explaining the Known

By bringing the invisible into focus, interviews are especially adept at exploring social patterns and processes that have been ignored, understudied, or not yet identified; at clarifying the underlying factors producing them that we know exist but do not yet clearly understand; and at reorienting prevailing theoretical approaches that may be misleading, incomplete, or even wrong. In short, interview-based research searches for answers to empirical and theoretical puzzles. It poses questions rather than testing hypotheses, and it pursues a logic that emphasizes discovery rather than a logic that emphasizes verification.

First, interviewing facilitates the exploration of new social developments and understudied groups. Some populations are too small and others too recently formed to be studied by—or even located for—survey methods. In these instances, interviewing, like ethnographic research, provides an especially apt way to study such groups, social developments, or organizational fields. Mignon Moore, for example, investigated relationship dynamics and parenting practices among Black lesbian couples, a group she describes as "invisible families."[20] By doing so, she uncovered a power dynamic not typical among heterosexual couples: among these same-sex couples, the biological parent exercised more power in the household regardless of who earned more. In a similar way, by combining an ethnographic study of a start-up developing AI programs for music composition with depth interviews of composers employed in a variety of settings, Kevin Lee found that the rise of digital technologies is reshaping composers' views about what it means to compose music as they grapple with the age-old tension between rationalization and creativity in a new technological age.[21]

For larger social groups or well-documented trends, interviews offer a method for explaining why they have emerged and how they persist. Quantitative studies can ascertain the size and characteristics of a social group and the statistical relationships that link a specified set of variables for the group, but they can only guess at the reasons for these relationships and the mechanisms that link them. Interviews can help solve those mysteries by investigating the individual actions, personal motivations, and social contexts that produce well-established relationships. Take Kathryn Edin and Maria Kefalas's study of poor single mothers, which begins by acknowledging a rise in the proportion of single mothers among poor women and then relies on interviews to reveal why this has happened.[22] In contrast to the common view that poor, unmarried women are acting irrationally and irresponsibly, the interviews reveal they have little incentive either to wait for a steady partner who is unlikely to arrive or to postpone motherhood—the one meaningful relationship they can create on their own.

Interviews can also help reorient widely accepted theories that nevertheless provide partial, misleading, or even erroneous explanations. In an effort to explain why many low-income African Americans cannot find satisfactory employment, Sandra Smith (in coordination with Alford Young Jr.) conducted interviews that challenge the common explanations, which posit their reluctance to work, discriminatory practices, or some combination of the two.[23] While she finds that discrimination plays an important role, she adds a nuance to the explanatory story by focusing on the role of networks. Although her participants wished to find a job, they were reluctant to use their own networks to search for a job or offer their network contacts to others—a process she calls "defensive individualism." By delving into the motivations and strategies of job seekers, she was able to correct a partial and misleading picture of how marginalized groups contend with discrimination and the lack of social and economic resources.

Interviewing also provides a method for addressing empirical puzzles that prevailing theories either do not address or cannot solve. Sarah's research on women's work paths began with such a puzzle: if financial "need" impels working-class and poor women to work while middle-class women can "choose" whether or not to seek a paid job, then why are middle-class women *more* likely to join the labor force than are their working-class and poorer peers?[24] To unravel this paradox, she interviewed women in a variety of class positions. Rather than simply asking why each woman was or was not currently employed, however, she inquired about their employment histories. These interviews revealed that women with more job opportunities and domestic supports were also more likely to work steadily, while those with fewer opportunities and supports were more likely to pull back from paid employment. A third group, consisting of those who were disproportionately poor and lacking both in supports at home and in labor market opportunities, followed an "interrupted path" in which they alternated between periods of employment and unpaid labor, and unemployment. By specifying the public and private circumstances that shaped diverse life paths, these interviews were able to explain why financial need alone cannot explain women's employment commitments.

In addition to explaining puzzles that emerge from larger studies, interview studies can also create new concepts, frameworks, and questions that larger studies can then address. David Pedulla and Sarah Thébaud, for example, were able to build on a finding Kathleen detailed in *The Unfinished Revolution*: that the majority of the young adults she interviewed expressed aspirations for an egalitarian relationship but also held "fallback positions" that diverged from these ideals, with most men planning to fall back on a more traditional, gender-based division of earning and caregiving and most women planning to avoid the perceived dangers of economic and social dependence in marriage by seeking self-reliance.[25] To explore whether this framework would help explain the views and actions of a wider population, Pedulla and Thébaud conducted a vignette study with a nationally representative sample that found similar results: most Americans say they prefer egalitarian work/family arrangements, but only if supportive social policies make that a realistic option.

In all these ways, interview studies can shed light on what we do not know and on what we know but do not understand. By emphasizing a logic of discovery, interviews can uncover patterns of thought and action that are not yet recognized; can clarify social patterns, groups, and trends that are recognized but poorly understood; can provide explanations for known relationships that remain puzzling; and can formulate new concepts and frameworks that reorient theoretical approaches. Depth interviews seek surprises and then use them to develop new ways of conceiving and explaining the social world.

Charting Dynamic Processes and Links Between Structure and Action

Interviewing is also a powerful tool for mapping macro-micro links and dynamic processes of change and stability, especially when it uses a "life history" format to gather time-ordered information. While not all depth interviews use this form, it provides a structure that is adept at capturing trajectories of stability and change as they emerge over time. Life history interviews can collect multi-layered information, such as participants' encounters with institutions and the reactions these encounters evoke, as their lives develop through time. In this way, time-ordered interviews can cast a bright light on the interplay between structure and agency as institutional arrangements shape options and people devise strategies in response.

Since everything has a life history, time-ordered interviews are not confined to the life course of individuals. They can focus on almost any arena of social life, including families, relationships, social movements, and organizational processes, to name only a few. They can as well focus on any period or life stage, from childhood through old age. Regardless of the substantive focus, the key is to obtain a timeline of important events and critical turning points and then probe for the responses these events engendered.

A life history format also makes it possible to investigate how diverse institutional spheres interact—such as how people's lives intersect with government agencies, the workplace, the neighborhood, or the household. Do different institutional arenas complement each other, converging to render some options irresistible and others nearly impossible? Or do they conflict, making any course of action problematic? Like intersectional analysis, which focuses on how multiple identities such as race, class, and gender intersect in people's lives, detailed life histories can examine how different institutional spheres intersect to shape people's experiences and options.[26] In our research, we focus on exploring how rising structural and cultural conflicts between family and work institutions have created dilemmas with no unambiguously "correct" resolutions. Since these institutional conflicts make it increasingly difficult to conform to preexisting norms, individuals and families must choose between traveling well-worn but eroding paths and pioneering new ones.[27]

Time-ordered life histories make it possible to explore the shape of changing pathways and to compare them with more stable ones. In a study of undocumented youth, Roberto Gonzales found that their trajectories diverged from those of their documented peers as they moved from childhood through adolescence to young adulthood. Both groups shared a high level of stability and a strong sense of social belonging in childhood, but members of the undocumented group were more likely to face blocked opportunities during the transition to adulthood, which made it difficult for them to sustain a stable trajectory and avoid involvement in illegal activities.[28]

A life history format can also cast light on the significance of events that do *not* occur. By asking questions about *potential* experiences, it is possible to discover how *lack* of exposure to a consequential event—for example, an opportunity to move ahead at work or a supportive environment for coming out as gay—shapes life paths and life chances. It is not possible to measure a "non-event" taken on its own, but putting it in a comparative context can reveal its significance. Kristen Schilt's life history interviews with transgender men found important differences in their perceptions before transition and after transition. Although they had not perceived discrimination when classified as women, their shift to a new gender status revealed what had once been invisible—that men enjoy privileges women do not.[29]

A carefully conceived interview study that asks about alternative options and makes comparisons with those who followed other paths can thus avoid a "hindsight bias" by comparatively examining the reasons for the paths not taken.[30] In a similar way, by charting the interaction between social contexts, life events, and individual responses, it can avoid both an "agency bias" that overemphasizes the role of individual choice and a "determinist bias" that reduces individual action to the sum of external forces. Interviews thus make it possible to map dynamic processes and place them in a larger social context. They can chart exposure (or lack of exposure) to consequential social contexts and life events and explore the reactions these settings and experiences do and do not provoke. With a carefully developed interview guide and a theoretically grounded sample selection, they can reveal the social factors that can prompt conformity to prevailing norms and structures or, alternatively, set the stage for resistance to them.

Building Theory

Because depth interviewing can address such a wide range of analytic tasks—that is, reveal mental states and social activities that cannot be observed, examine the links between structural processes and individual actions, discover unexpected social patterns, shed light on empirical puzzles, chart dynamic processes, and place all of these findings in their social and historical context—it can do much more than provide what Clifford Geertz has termed "thick description."[31] Producing nuanced descriptions is surely an essential contribution, but interviewing also offers techniques for building social theories that explain why and how these descriptions take the form they do.

To draw on a distinction made by the demographer Andrew Cherlin, interviewing encourages "explanatory" rather than "predictive" analysis.[32] Conducting a predictive analysis means searching for two or more factors that are highly correlated so that knowing the value on one will increase the chances of predicting the value on another. An explanatory analysis, in contrast, requires discovering how and why such factors are correlated. As Cherlin points out, knowing the state of the economy shortly before an election is helpful in predicting the outcome of the voting, but as useful as that information may be, it cannot reveal mechanisms that link these two factors. Interview material can illuminate what correlations cannot— that is, how structural and cultural forces interact with individual acts of meaning-making and decision-making to produce a range of outcomes. Approached in this way, interviewing nurtures both the development of new conceptual categories and the discovery of the relationships among them. It illuminates processes of social reproduction and change by mapping developmental trajectories as they unfold through time.[33] In all these ways, interviews provide the raw material for building potent explanatory frameworks.

Facing the Challenges

If interviewing is a powerful methodological tool, it also poses some unique challenges. How can we be confident about the validity of findings from such a relatively small sample? How can the meaning of wholly self-reported answers be deciphered rigorously? And how can we overcome our own conscious and unconscious biases in order to see the world as participants do? It is necessary to acknowledge these challenges and consider how to tackle all of them to achieve the full potential of interviewing as a reliable research method.

What Can Small Samples Tell Us?

Interview studies rarely include enough people to satisfy the tests of statistical significance that survey research uses to establish validity and reliability. Not only would it be too labor-intensive, costly, and time-consuming to complete depth interviews with such large samples, but trying to manage the resulting information would be overwhelming. In our experience, an interview that lasts two to two and a half hours typically produces a transcription of 70 to 120 double-spaced pages. A sample of 80 to 120 people would thus produce between 5,600 and 14,400 double-spaced pages. Though coding and analyzing this much text may seem challenging, it is quite feasible (and we provide a strategy for doing so in Chapter 5). It is not feasible, however, to do so with a sample large enough to subject it to complex statistical analysis. The smaller sample sizes of interview projects thus involve a trade-off that offers greater depth of knowledge in exchange for forgoing the larger numbers needed to perform advanced statistical manipulations.

Numbers do matter, however. The challenge of interview studies is not to reach a size large enough to permit statistical analysis but rather to include enough strategically selected participants to have confidence in the findings and to demonstrate they are not idiosyncratic or the product of selection bias. Sample sizes need to be large enough to reach what Glaser and Strauss call "saturation"—the point at which each ensuing interview confirms previous findings and does not evoke new and surprising ones.[34] We would add another criterion: the number needs to be large enough to recognize variations, patterns, and relationships, to make strategic comparisons among participants, and to demonstrate the validity of these patterns. The goal is not to estimate the *percentage* of each pattern in a wider population but rather to discover the *reasons* such patterns exist and the ways they are connected to each other. This requires ensuring that interviewees vary across potentially theoretically important characteristics. As Arthur Stinchcombe argues in *Constructing Social Theories*, it is just as important to discover what explains a social trend as it is to estimate the size of that trend.[35]

Smaller studies can find the explanation for a pattern, but they need not (indeed, they cannot) establish the overall proportion of people who represent that pattern. They should also contain the full range of potential diversity for the topic or social setting of interest. For a study of outcomes in a social service agency, for example, it would likely be important to include front-line workers, clients, managers, regulators, funders, and other relevant actors in the agency environment. While interview studies may not include enough participants to generalize to a larger population, they offer a key ingredient that surveys cannot: sufficient depth and breadth to discover the factors, mechanisms, and processes that create broader trends. Through systematic analysis, interviews can identify the underlying institutional structures and social norms that shape the patterns identified in larger surveys.

What Do Self-Reports Reveal?

Like respondents who answer closed-ended survey questions, interview participants may be prone to say what they believe the interviewer wants to hear rather than what they really believe. As fundamentally social animals, we humans are inclined to present ourselves as we think others would like us to be. This risk, called "social desirability bias," means that some answers may reflect socially acceptable views rather than the ones an interviewee actually holds.[36] Of course, not all interviewees wish to please. Some may prefer, consciously or unconsciously, to present themselves as rebels who do not conform to what others consider politically or socially correct. Still others may not have given much thought to what they believe or how they see themselves. And interviewees may not share interviewers' notions about what is socially acceptable. Yet social desirability bias is nevertheless an ever-present possibility in any human interaction.

Some take this critique of self-reports even further. Colin Jerolmack and Shamus Khan declare that interviews and other findings based on what people "say" have little to offer because they bear little relationship to what people "do." Only by observing behavior, they argue, can researchers avoid what they term an "attitudinal fallacy" that conflates words and actions.[37] In a contrasting critique, John Levi Martin and Stephen Vaisey argue that interviews cannot measure the unconscious attitudes, tendencies, and snap judgments that presumably guide action.[38] Vaisey makes a distinction between "cold cognitions," which require deliberation, and "hot cognitions," which reflect unconscious reactions to real-life circumstances. Using this bifurcated model, he argues that surveys with closed-response categories do a better job of tapping hot cognitions that more closely align with people's immediate responses than do open-ended, probing questions, which ask people to reflect more deeply about what they think and feel.

Needless to say, we emphatically disagree with these critiques, which in different ways vastly oversimplify the interview process. No interviewer would presume to claim that what people say is a direct measure of what they do—at least beyond the recognition that speech itself is a specific form of action. Similarly, interviews can and often do include closed-ended as well as open-ended questions. Yet the open-ended follow-ups and probes are essential to reveal the meaning of closed-ended responses. Both critiques thus misunderstand what interviewers do and what interviews can offer. Yes, careful interviewers need to acknowledge and respond to the ever-present possibility that social desirability bias will influence the interview process, but this does not mean that all of the information collected is biased.

Moreover, as many feminists or other critical theorists have pointed out, such critiques of depth interviewing place the stance, viewpoint, and voice of the researcher over that of the participants. From Dorothy Smith to Joyce Ladner to Bonnie Thornton Dill, feminists have noted ways that bias in social research often stems from a researcher's own position rather than from bias on the part of the researched, thus further marginalizing individuals and groups who have historically been discounted or dismissed.[39] By denying the power of research that allows participants to discuss their own experiences and consider their significance in their own words, we risk silencing the very voices we most need to hear.[40] In a context that enhances thoughtful cooperation and mutual respect, depth interviewing offers an opportunity to center the voices of those who have been ignored, silenced, or misunderstood.

What, then, is the analytic status of a self-report, and how can interviewers minimize the risks and discover the deeper significance of what people tell them? To begin, it is helpful to view the human tendency to present ourselves

in a positive light as one aspect of a complicated and unfolding interview interaction. The goal is to create a safe space where a desired self-presentation
marks only the starting point for sharing deeper levels of disclosure and self-
knowledge. Each interview question, posed appropriately and followed by
pertinent probes, should signal that any answer is acceptable (and we provide examples about how to do this in Chapter 4). When the initial questions
are incisive and the follow-ups encourage further reflection, the interviewer
can develop a partnership that invites interviewees to share more and extend their insights well beyond an initial answer. A collaborative interaction
can delve into the reasons for a response that may seem rote and identify
the deeper views and feelings that lie beneath it. In this way, interviews can
address the challenge of desirability bias head-on by seeking to distinguish
between "authentic" and "socially desirable" answers and then exploring the
meaning of each.

Yet even when interviewees resist presenting themselves in anything but
a positive light, such responses need not be dismissed as uninformative. To
the contrary, socially desirable answers tell us a great deal about cultural
norms and social scripts. In *Labor of Love*, for example, Heather Jacobson
found that many women are quick to deny the role of money in their decision to become a surrogate mother—an understandable response when
cultural norms stress women's selflessness and stigmatize those who use
their bodies for financial reward.[41] Probing further, however, Jacobson discovered the central importance of financial incentives and then explored
why women are reluctant to acknowledge the role of money. This interactive
process made it possible to identify the cultural scripts that some women
draw on to account for their decisions, the reasons other women feel less
constrained to do so, and the range of circumstances that led to the decision
among both groups.

With careful probing, interviews can also capture both after-the-fact
rationalizations people offer to explain their actions and the less obvious
factors that motivate action but remain beyond the grasp of consciousness. Such justifications provide the interviewer with "accounts"—that is,
the stories people tell themselves and others to explain why they make
the choices they report.[42] Rather than dismissing these accounts as "mere"
justifications (or false consciousness), interviews explore their meaning
by asking, first, about the social contexts that give rise to these choices
and, next, about how social actors make sense of their actions within these

contexts. Taking this approach, Sarah discovered that women from all classes use a language of "family need" to explain their work decisions, even though those with work opportunities used it to explain why they work for pay and those who lacked such opportunities used it to explain why they do not, while Enobong Hannah Branch found that many Black women said their husbands should be the breadwinner even though they lived in households with a much less traditional division of paid labor.[43] Similarly, in interviews with activists on both sides of the abortion debate, Kristen Luker found that both groups believed their views stemmed from their ethical and moral precepts, even though contrasting experiences at work and in the home led them to develop opposing views about the morality of motherhood.[44] In each of these studies, careful interviewing made it possible to uncover the accounts people offered for their views and life choices *and* the social forces that shaped *both* their actions and their accounts.

How can interviews capture the often hidden forces that shape outlooks and behavior and the justifications people construct to explain them? This can be accomplished by asking "what" and "how" questions first, emphasizing specific events, experiences, and examples, and then following up with "why" questions that give people a chance to offer their own explanations (as Chapter 5 explains in detail).[45] This structure allows participants to tell their stories as they have experienced them, while also gathering specific details about the events and social contexts that shaped them. Paying close attention to questionnaire design allows studies to uncover the reasons people offer for their outlooks *and* the social factors and psychological processes that gave rise to them. Rather than confusing justification with motivation, interviewing seeks to distinguish between them, analyze how they are related, and explain why they may diverge.

How people talk about themselves and others provides a window on the nature of cultural norms, how people construct accounts to explain their actions and beliefs, and the social contexts that shape these accounts. Hans Gerth and C. Wright Mills refer to this process as constructing a "vocabulary of motive."[46] For Allison Pugh, it means that interviews "can access different levels of information about people's motivations, beliefs, meanings, feelings, and practices—in other words, the culture they use—often in the same sitting."[47] In this way, interviewers can learn not just how accounts emerge but also why they take the forms they do.

What Is the Significance of Contradictory Accounts?

Interviewees' descriptions of important life experiences may be subjective, but they are nonetheless valid and highly consequential. Despite some skepticism that "talk is cheap" and that what people say offers little insight into what they do, the relationship between actions and mental states is itself a crucial dimension of social life that interviews can explore.[48] Interviewers are in an especially good position to recognize this distinction and investigate whether (and why) actions and mental states are discrepant or congruent. As William Thomas and Dorothy Swaine Thomas long ago declared, "It is not important whether or not the interpretation is correct—if men [sic] define situations as real, they are real in their consequences."[49] What people (of any gender) believe can and does guide action, and any discrepancy between the two alerts us to areas where people may be prone to offer conflicting accounts. Rather than assessing the "accuracy" of such contradictory statements, interviews can discover their meaning and chart their consequences. Doing so requires granting validity to each response while also attending to its place amid the pattern that emerges over the course of an interview and in comparison with the other interviews.[50]

It is not unusual for an interviewee to offer inconsistent responses as the interview proceeds. Michael Burawoy has noted, "The focused interview offers an opportunity for closer interrogation, but discrepancies remain between what people say they do, what they say they should do, and what they actually do."[51] Rather than treating such inconsistencies as evidence of a lack of authenticity in the answers, it is more theoretically useful and empirically accurate to see them as a window into the ways structural and cultural arrangements create ambivalent and even contradictory reactions. In *The Cultural Contradictions of Motherhood*, Sharon Hays found that women's ambivalent statements about their mothering practices reveal a cultural landscape that pressures women to engage in "intensive mothering" even as they are increasingly likely to hold a paid job.[52] Ellen Lamont found that middle-class young adults tend to profess strong support for gender equality, yet they are nevertheless likely to follow a traditional gender script in which men initiate a date or a marriage proposal.[53] Similarly, Natasha Warikoo's interviews with white students at elite universities uncovered a conflict between their expressed support for "diversity" on campus and their more ambivalent or even resentful views about classmates whom they perceive as having benefited from affirmative action policies.[54] And in interviews with Muslim

Americans, Eman Abdelhadi found that many participants professed a pref-
erence for a mosque with a diverse membership while also wishing for one
with members who shared their background.[55]

While it might be tempting to conclude that at least some of these expressed
views are false statements, the more revealing explanation is that conflicting views reflect an inner tension between two (or more) social ideals or
pressures. In each of these cases, the interviewers used inconsistent accounts
to explore the cultural and structural contradictions people face. Holding
several opposing ideas at the same time not only is integral to the human experience but also illuminates the socially constructed dilemmas that prompt
people to speak and act in inconsistent ways.[56] Interviewing enables us to
uncover such inconsistencies, probe for their nuances, and explore their
sources and consequences. Rather than rejecting the validity of contradictory statements, the use of interviews allows researchers to pay attention to
these points of ambiguity, seek to discover the social, emotional, and mental
conflicts they reflect, and explore the ways people respond to them.

How Can We Limit Interviewer Bias?

Interviewees are not the only group whose responses may be subject to bias.
Researchers, too, are socially embedded actors whose conscious and unconscious biases may affect their findings. All researchers, regardless of their
chosen method, face this challenge. Just as interviewers need to pay attention to participants' efforts to present themselves in a positive (and, for some,
negative) light, they must also attend to their own "positionality"—that is,
their social position in relation to the interviewee.

Attending to the implications of positionality is especially pertinent when,
as is often the case, there is a significant social difference or power imbalance between the researcher and the research subject. The history of social
research is replete with studies that were ultimately proven wrong because
their designers made misleading presumptions based on their own social
advantages. To take one example, recent research has upended the once
widely accepted conclusions from a study known as the "marshmallow test,"
which purported to demonstrate that young children who "delay gratification" (as measured by being willing to postpone eating a marshmallow or
similar treat) become more successful adults.[57] New research has found that
the original study neglected the role of social class by failing to realize that

poorer children are more inclined to take the treat immediately because they are (quite rationally) less confident it will still be available at a later time.[58]

The marshmallow test vividly illustrates how a researcher's unconscious bias can lead to misleading interpretations of the results. It is a cautionary tale about the perils of research designs that fail to attend to how a researcher's social position may influence the research design and the conclusions that are drawn.[59] While social differences between an interviewer and inter-viewee can arise in any context, including those involving interviews with superiors as well as subordinates, feminist and critical race theorists point out that this danger is especially acute when members of a dominant group turn their attention to studying members of less advantaged ones. Dorothy Smith, for example, contends that "feminist scholarship forces us to recog-nize that the oft labeled 'unbiased observer/outsider' is often a white man looking at a community that is not his own."[60] Added to this danger, margin-alized groups are likely to be particularly skeptical about a study's value or a researcher's motives. Unequal positioning can thus not only lead to flawed results but also further marginalize those who are already marginalized and discourage them from participating at all.

Whether the challenge is whites studying people of color, professionals studying the less educated, or members of one gender or ethnic group studying members of another, researchers cannot simply presume to put their biases aside—especially since they may not be aware of their existence. Some, such as Joyce Ladner, have questioned whether it is desirable to claim objectivity when studying issues of great moral weight, such as racism or pov-erty.[61] And Howard Becker has pointed out that when it comes to studying human actions and social patterns, it is simply not possible to avoid "taking sides."[62] Any interaction, he argues, involves a "hierarchy of credibility"— that is, a system of ranked groups in which a member of the higher-ranked group is more likely to be believed.

Yet recognizing this conundrum does not require us to limit our research focus to only those who are most like us, even if we could identify who that would (and would not) include. To understand the full range of human expe-rience, we need to cast our research gaze well beyond the confines of our own social worlds. Responsible interviewing requires instead that we pay atten-tion to our own socially embedded biases and take steps to minimize the in-fluence they might exert on our perceptions about the experiences of others. Interviewers who are sensitive to the ever-present dangers of positional bias are in a better position to address them. Rather than isolating research subjects from their social worlds (as is the case of experiments) or limiting respondents to pre-coded, closed-ended answers (as surveys require), the interviewer's job is to discover as much as possible about the interviewee's social world and search for the reasons underlying their reported outlooks and choices. And unlike ethnographic observation, interviewers can gather information about the diverse ways that their participants view the world. Interviewers do not just report the story they see in the field; they also gather, report, and analyze the many stories their participants tell them.[63]

Creating the trust so crucial to success requires sensitivity to differences of race, gender, culture, social class, and more. This sensitivity, in turn, requires reflexivity—a self-conscious awareness of one's motives for conducting the research. In the chapters to follow, we offer concrete strategies for integrating a reflexive ethos at every stage of the research process. It is fine, for example, to let personal passions guide the choice of a research topic, but a careful reading of the literature will help generate questions that reach beyond one's own predispositions about the answers. Orienting questions need not—and generally cannot—be value free, but we can strive to take account of the different values that pertain beyond our own preoccupations.

It is also important to adopt a sampling strategy that does its best to avoid skewing the results. A carefully selected sample reduces the chances a researcher will find only what they are looking for. The interview guide should include questions that allow for a range of possible answers without signaling that one is more "correct" or "desirable" than another. The same vigilance is integral to conducting interviews. Personal passions should not bias the way the interviewer asks questions or receives answers. The interviewer's job is to listen and learn, not pass judgment, and that can happen only when interviewees feel free to discuss controversial views and actions without fear of reproach.

Finally, reflexivity means actively looking for surprising and potentially disconfirming results rather than focusing on the findings that were expected or hoped for. Indeed, seeking counterfactuals that disconfirm research expectations not only helps to guard against imposing one's personal values but also encourages the discovery of the unexpected and helps build a stronger case for whatever argument ultimately emerges. Regardless of the task at hand, all of these strategies require acknowledging that while we may have a stake in the research (which is why we chose to do it), we can take active steps to limit its influence. After the research is complete and the findings and theoretical implications are clear, it is once again appropriate to take a personal position—a position that can now carry more weight because it flows from careful research rather than from preconceived ideological commitments.

No strategy can remove all bias. As Becker has noted, we need to acknowledge our personal and political outlooks, use our analytical tools to rise above them, and offer ideas that others can seek to confirm. Yet using these approaches increases the chances of recognizing and minimizing whatever biases we bring to the task of interviewing others and making sense of their responses. Unlike quantitative studies, where collecting information from large numbers of people often masks the potential for bias, depth interviewers can address the possibility directly by acknowledging our position relative to the research questions and participants. If interviewers remain sensitive to the dangers of imposing their own views on the groups they study, they may be able to give voice to whomever they interview, including those who are different from them in important ways and those who have been ignored, marginalized, or misunderstood.[64]

The Whole Truth and Nothing but the Truth?

The issue of truth is among the most controversial and misunderstood aspects of interviewing. How is it possible to learn about a person's life in a span of several hours? How likely is it that a participant will or can provide accurate information? How does an interviewer distinguish between truth and falsehood or take account of matters that are left unsaid? Indeed, what does "truth" mean in the context of an interview? Does "telling the truth" mean being accurate or only being sincere? Does it require completeness, or will a partial truth do? And to what degree and in what ways should interviewers accept a person's answers when they have reason to be skeptical about their authenticity?

Since the word "truth" is a slippery term that has many meanings, these questions have no simple answers. The first step is to clarify what this means in the interview context. A student of Sarah's once insisted she could tell whether an interviewee was being "truthful," by which she meant she could decide whether the interviewee was fabricating or omitting parts of the story. The fallacy of this position—in addition to how it dismisses the participant's answers—rests with two unstated presumptions: first, that it is possible and necessary to know everything about a person's life and, second, that there is only one "true" version of a person's experience.

Even if it were possible to observe people closely as their lives proceeded, we could not guarantee that this strategy would collect "truer" information, especially about such unobservable matters as motivations, perceptions, and views. It is neither feasible nor desirable to use a single measure to gauge a person's truthfulness. In interviews as in life, people construct narratives that are neither strictly true nor strictly untrue; instead, these accounts reflect various understandings of people's life experiences at specific moments in time, including when such events occurred and how they appear looking back at the time of the interview.[65] Kristen Luker has thus argued that depth interviewers "are not so much interested in the veracity of the interviews, in some cosmic sense of the word, as we are in the deep truth of them."[66]

To find the "deep truth" in an interview, we need to hear people's narrative accounts and also explore how additional information—gathered not only within the interview but from other interviews as well—provides broader and more hidden layers of understanding. Allison Pugh suggests that interviews can tap four kinds of information: the honorable, where people strive to present themselves in a favorable light; the schematic, in which language reveals frameworks or worldviews; the visceral, which taps feelings and emotions; and meta-feelings, which reveal how people feel about what they feel.[67] Alongside this list, we would add a somewhat different one, emphasizing that interviews can explore the paths people (or organizations and institutions) take over a given period, the social contexts in which layers of meaning surrounding these events are embedded, the tensions created by competing types of meaning, the accounts people construct to understand the sources of these meanings, the ways these accounts change in response to new experiences, and the visions of ideal and expected futures that arise from multiple meanings.[68]

Depth interviewing opens the door to pursuing these approaches. It provides a method for depicting the various components of social life and then asking how they are linked to social structures and strategic actions. It is, moreover, not necessary to view any one approach as preferable to another. Instead, taken together, they reveal the range of options interviewers possess for designing and conducting interviews that seek to illuminate through both accuracy and authenticity. All these possibilities illustrate that, far from being "just talk," interviews can evoke a layered narrative that provides a powerful tool for theorizing the links between worldviews, structures, and actions.

Interviewing as Science and Art

Depth interviewing occupies an ambiguous place in the research toolkit. The "qualitative" component conjures images of research driven by intuition and instinct, while the "methods" side suggests the need to master a clearly defined set of scientific rules. Yet there is no inherent conflict between following a systematic method and doing creative work. To the contrary, combining logical principles of inquiry with creative inspiration enhances interviewers'—indeed, anyone's—ability to make significant breakthroughs.

Creative insight is integral to the interviewing process. As C. Wright Mills noted, it takes a sociological (or, more broadly, social) "imagination" to understand the links between the individual and society—between "personal troubles" and public issues.[69] This imaginative spirit helps us fashion a theoretically trenchant set of questions out of a general topic of importance. It also fosters the empathy necessary for us to hear stories from participants that may challenge our own values and presumptions. Inspiration provides the mental flexibility needed to search for surprising findings in an unexplored empirical terrain. And it is integral to the quality we call "a feeling for the data," which helps in the search for order amid the seeming disorder of qualitative material. At every stage, creative imagination helps guide decisions about which theoretical and empirical leads to follow and which to set aside.

Yet while necessary, creative inspiration is rarely sufficient. Waiting for insight to strike, without the benefit of a carefully designed plan to facilitate that quest, is a risky strategy at best. To paraphrase Branch Rickey, the legendary Brooklyn Dodgers general manager who broke baseball's color line by hiring Jackie Robinson and famously declared that "luck is the residue of design," we argue that—in interview-based research as in life—insight is the residue of forethought and planning.[70] Following the basic principles of the logic of inquiry, which is rooted in the scientific method, enhances the chances we will make a creative breakthrough and also lends credence to any creative arguments that do emerge. Two logical rules of inquiry are especially useful: first, pose questions that seek to explain as well as to describe, and second, build comparisons into the study design and analysis. This approach not only makes it possible to build theoretically incisive arguments but also provides support for such arguments by seeking disconfirming evidence and addressing counterfactual possibilities.

Interviewing makes its strongest contributions by posing questions that ask "how" and "why" as well as "what"—an approach that requires taking theory into account at the outset and keeping it front and center to the end. Like the "grounded theory" approach, this means using inductive techniques to build theory as discoveries emerge in the field. Interviewers must always seek the unexpected. Yet inductive reasoning alone does not offer a workable strategy for interviewers, who first need to decide what "the field" will contain before entering it. Interviewers must determine who the appropriate members of the field are and what information needs to be gathered from them. It is not possible to make these decisions with a clean theoretical slate.

Launching a project thus requires a deductive approach that uses theory to identify appropriate groups and questions. Thinking through the relevant theories and theoretical debates, including how well or poorly each theoretical approach is able to shed light on the core questions you wish to pose, makes it possible to recognize and explain important discoveries as they emerge in the field. Early theorizing, however inchoate, provides a starting point for building a better explanation during and after the collection of interview material. As Michael Burawoy puts it, "We start with theory, we end with theory, and evidence drives the mediation between the two."[71] Yet, as Burawoy's words remind us, these early decisions are not set in stone. It is both acceptable and common practice to tweak the criteria for selecting participants and to adjust the interview guide at a later time, especially in response to insights that emerge during early stages of interviewing.

The second logical principle that strengthens interviewing's analytic power is building comparisons into the research design and analysis. In addition to any implied comparisons with groups not included, it is important to build two direct comparisons into any study: the comparative context that develops *within* an interview and the comparative context found *among* the interviews. Placing each answer in the context of all the information elicited in the entire interview gives each specific piece of information its particular meaning. And placing each interview in the context of all the other interviews reveals patterns that only a bird's-eye view can show.

Building in comparisons within and across the interviews requires a systematic approach to both sample selection and questionnaire construction. The interview guide, as we will show, should seek the full range of information needed to answer the core "what," "why," and "how" questions. This means developing questions that tap the various outcomes deemed relevant along with the full range of factors, processes, and mechanisms that might explain them. The sampling strategy also needs to zero in on the groups that will foster strategic comparisons. No interview stands alone; its significance becomes clear only in comparison to the others. Sample comparisons thus provide analytic leverage to decipher the theoretical meaning of each interview, reveal patterns of similarity and difference, and tease out which factors do or do not help explain them.

At its best, depth interviewing combines the rigor of science, with its stress on systematic rules of inquiry, with the creative spark of art, with its stress on inspiration and intuition. Having a theoretically focused question and research design sets the stage for discovery and explanation. By combining attention to the logic of inquiry (and its stress on theory building) with the search for unexpected findings, interviewing can solve unresolved empirical puzzles and offer new ways to make sense of the social world.

The following chapters offer a road map for navigating the path from conception to completion of research that relies, either in whole or in part, on interviewing. We move through all the steps in the research process, from the initial stage of formulating a question to the final one of pulling everything together and writing it up. We address the routine but rarely discussed challenges interviewers encounter at each stage. What are the core empirical and theoretical questions? What research design is "good enough," and is a better one possible? Whom should be interviewed, and what questions asked? What kind of interview structure will help guide the participants through a process that is meaningful and informative for both interviewer and interviewee? Once interviewing begins, what are the most effective ways to create the right atmosphere for thoughtful self-disclosure and to adjust in real time to surprising findings and new insights? When has the time arrived to stop conducting additional interviews and focus intently on analyzing the full range of collected material? What analytic strategies will help wrestle the large amounts of seemingly chaotic information into a clear, powerful, and theoretically focused argument?

To address these questions, we draw on our own work and that of others to offer a set of analytic tools and user-friendly strategies. Although we trace the sequential steps of the research process—from developing a research question to designing and conducting interviews to analyzing the rich material they provide—it is not necessary to read the chapters in order. Those who wish to consider each step in the process may prefer to start at the beginning, while those with specific questions may prefer to skip to the sections that address their concerns.[72] Whether you are a student beginning to learn about interviewing, an experienced researcher who wishes to know more about how and why to use this method, or even someone who uses other methods yet would like to find out what interview findings have to offer, we invite you to consider the ways interviewing adds a unique and indispensable method that helps us understand not just individual experience—as important as that is—but also the institutions, social structures, and social processes that shape both individual experience and collective life.

2

Getting Started

Pinning Down the Questions and Research Design

At the outset, any research involves formulating questions and constructing a design for gathering evidence to answer them. For research that relies primarily on interviewing, this is the moment of maximum choice. Unlike research that relies on the analysis of already collected data, interviewers enjoy wide latitude as they consider what questions to ask and decide how best to go about answering them. This discretion is one of interviewing's noteworthy advantages, but it also can pose a range of bewildering choices—a degree of freedom that can spark anxiety as well as excitement.

How can interview-based research make the most of these early challenges? While those doing other kinds of research can decide to add interviews at a later time, those who rely on interviewing as their primary method need to start with a substantial amount of forethought and planning. Ethnographers, for example, may begin observing a research site without knowing what they may wish to ask in interviews (should they choose to conduct them). Survey researchers who decide to follow up at a later time with open-ended interviews need not decide what questions to ask until the initial data is in. Interviewers, in contrast, must first decide whom to interview and what to ask them before they can take any further steps. These decisions depend on, first, formulating the core research questions and, next, understanding the relevant theoretical debates and empirical state of knowledge needed to answer them.

The core question or set of questions will shape the project in myriad ways, both large and small. While these questions are sure to evolve in response to unanticipated findings in the field, new insights cannot emerge until the questions and their implied research design specify which "fields" to enter.[1] While projects centered on ethnographic observation also use interviews, such projects typically begin with immersion in a specific site (or sites) and then select appropriate interviewees after spending time in the field. Projects

The Science and Art of Interviewing. Kathleen Gerson and Sarah Damaske, Oxford University Press (2021). © Oxford University Press. DOI: 10.1093/oso/9780199324286.001.0001

that rely primarily on interviews are rarely tied to a single location and thus require a different kind of advance planning.

Even before deciding whom to interview and what to ask, it is first necessary to assess whether interviewing is the right method for you and your project. This decision rests on the answers to a series of prior questions: What are the core research questions? Can they be answered through depth interviews (either in person or long distance through a variety of remote-enabled technologies)? Is this strategy doable with the resources available? Is interviewing an appealing method that will sustain your commitment? While answering yes to these questions does not guarantee a smooth journey, *not* asking them will greatly complicate the research process. The place to start, then, is to consider if interviewing is the right method for the questions you wish to answer and an appealing way to go about answering them.

Is Interviewing the Best Fit?

The answer to this question may seem straightforward. After all, shouldn't the main criterion be whether interviews are appropriate for addressing a study's substantive and theoretical questions? In practice, however, the answer may be tricky. It is vital to choose a method that engages your talents and sustains your interest. When the going gets tough and the work gets tedious—which will surely happen at some point in the long journey from research design to data collection through analysis and writing—finding your method enjoyable can make all the difference. For this reason, shaping your research question to fit the method you prefer raises the chances you'll enjoy the process of conducting the research and will consequently be able to make significant contributions. As with any endeavor, it is wise to go with your strengths.

Choosing a method that fits your talents and interests sparks engagement and sustaining commitment, but this need not mean interviewers must "naturally" possess exceptional interpersonal skills. Such skills are surely an asset, but they can be learned along the way. Not only can you develop interviewing skills, but you can also use a set of techniques that help create rapport. Laura Robinson and Jeremy Schulz, for example, propose an "iterated questioning approach" that depends less on interpersonal skills than on using a systematic procedure for questioning and probing—one that resembles our technique (discussed in Chapters 4 and 5) of asking a series of "nested questions."[2] Of course, most who choose to interview are likely to enjoy human interaction, especially in one-on-one situations, but it does not follow that interviewers must be especially adept in all social situations.

Another misconception is that interviewing is "easier" than other methods. For better or worse, every method has its own distinct challenges. Historical research requires spending hours in archives searching for material that may not have seen the light of day in decades or even centuries. Quantitative research requires preparing large data sets and teasing out statistical relationships among closed-ended responses to preselected questions. Interviewing, by contrast, involves finding a pool of potential participants, soliciting their participation, engaging in lengthy interactions with strangers, and searching for order in the complicated responses they provide. To carry out these tasks, you will need to endure rejections (during the recruiting process), ask people to share some of the most private parts of their lives (in the interviewing phase), and live with the uncertainty that comes with making sense of complex information that requires frequent rethinking and theoretical readjustment (especially during the analysis stage). For all these reasons, deciding to conduct interviews is not simply a matter of asking a question that interviewing is best suited to answer. It also means deciding that this is an appealing method for you.

Formulating the Questions

Once you are committed to interviewing, the work of research design begins. This starts with formulating a good question—a more difficult task than it may initially seem. While it may be easy to identify a topic that interests you, a topic is not a question. Formulating a question requires focusing on a specific set of empirical events and/or relationships and asking what forms they take, how they emerge, and why they take the forms they do. It may seem premature to do this so early in the process, but you will have future opportunities to reframe the questions as the interviewing proceeds. Since interviewing yields surprising findings more often than not, the chance to reframe early questions in response to unanticipated findings is one of its strengths.

The flexibility to reformulate the core questions does not, however, lessen the need to start with one or more organizing research questions. Without a beginning research question, you cannot move forward with a research design, including deciding on an appropriate sample and creating an interview guide that will gather the specific information you need. Even when the original questions change, as they are likely to do, the reformulated ones can only emerge from the process of pursuing an original project design.

So what makes a question "good" for interviews to answer, and how do you go about developing one? First, your research question needs to pass the "so what?" test. If the answer seems trivial or obvious—if we already know the answer or don't particularly care what the answer might be—there would be little need to devote significant effort to answering it. This apparent truism hides a more complicated challenge. Researchers, like everyone else, bring their own conscious and unconscious perspectives to their work. Our personal experiences, passions, and proclivities will shape what we study just as they do for any other choice. And because passion for a topic fuels the desire to understand it, this "fire in the belly" can be an advantage. Yet others may not share your passion and will need to know why they should care. So once you have found a question, the next step is to consider its significance for colleagues and even the wider public.

In addition to passing the "so what?" test, a good question should not presuppose an answer. It is common and even useful to draw on personal biography when choosing a topic, yet you should never presume to know the answer to the questions based only on your own experiences. Interviewers, like all social researchers, first need to acknowledge that we are embedded social actors with the same impulse to make biased presumptions that every social actor possesses.[3] We then need to recognize that our job is to seek to understand the social world beyond our immediate—and often misleading—experiences. Doing so depends on posing questions that can have a varied range of potential answers, including ones that would disconfirm our "preferred" answers. A good question is thus one for which neither you nor others know the answer. It addresses a puzzle that needs solving rather than a point you wish to "prove." Interviewing invites us to explore the power of a favored explanation and then seek to develop one that does a better job of accounting for whatever we may find.

Kristen Luker summarizes the core components of a good research question in this way: First, it should identify the relationships under investigation. Second, it should help us understand how that relationship "explain[s] something important about social life." Third, it should allow for a "range of possible answers." And fourth, it should contribute to existing debates in the relevant research fields.[4] These are the components of a good research question for *any* method, but there are certain kinds of questions that interviewing is especially well equipped to answer.

What Kinds of Questions Can Interviews Answer?

Just as different methods tap different skills, different methods also address different types of questions. Interviewers thus need to pose questions that in-depth conversations with a limited number of people can answer. Depth interviewing is not appropriate if the goal is to verify hypotheses statistically, specify the strength of relationships among pre-established variables, or assess the prevalence of a pattern in a large population.[5] Unlike quantitative research, which often aims to verify (or reject) existing arguments and explanations, interviewing seeks to discover patterns and relationships that remain puzzling or open to substantial disagreement. Interviewing is thus a powerful tool for exploring complex social dynamics, investigating their possible causal structure, resolving empirical puzzles and theoretical debates, discovering the links between micro- and macro-processes, and developing new ways of conceiving and explaining poorly or incompletely understood trends and relationships.

Even when studies with large samples have established strong statistical relationships within a set of variables, interviews can explore the processes and mechanisms that create these relationships, revealing how and why they exist. At the other end of the explanatory spectrum, interviewing is also an especially potent method for gathering the information needed to construct questions for a large-scale survey. In each of these ways, qualitative interviews complement quantitative studies. They provide tools to discover new ways of understanding social processes and relationships.

Crafting an interview project starts with a question that neither presupposes an answer nor lends itself to a simple yes or no. While you might begin with a question that seeks to establish whether (or not) important concepts are related to each other, the heart of interviewing is to follow that up with questions about why this relationship exists (or why not), how it came to be, and what its consequences are. These questions focus attention on discovering the factors (the "why") that contribute to outcomes (the "what"), along with the processes (the "how") that link those factors and outcomes in an interactive chain. The questions can change once interviewing begins, and the open-ended nature of interviewing encourages a tacking back and forth between early ideas, new discoveries, and reformulated questions. Yet you must begin with a clear question that takes account of gaps in established knowledge and allows you to recognize surprising findings when they emerge. That is most likely to happen when you ask questions that interviewing is especially, even uniquely, suited to answer. Though hardly an exhaustive list, here are some fruitful approaches.

Addressing Empirical Puzzles

Addressing a puzzling "social fact" (to use Emile Durkheim's term) has produced some of the richest and most illuminating interview findings.[6] Such questions increase the chances of making a breakthrough by taking into account the theoretical debates that surround them. Puzzles can take various forms. They can address conflicting findings from a given set of social trends and practices or different explanations for the same trends and practices. In other words, you can begin by locating and describing an empirical "fact" that either lacks an explanation or has prompted conflicting ones. If others have failed to notice, address, or adequately explain the puzzle, so much the better.

Jennifer Reich's study of parental decisions about their children's medical care, for example, asked why well-educated parents reject the vaccines that science has conclusively demonstrated are safe and effective.[7] Her interviews with parents and doctors discovered that parenting pressures, especially on mothers, led these parents to adopt a language of expertise and to develop a resistance to big pharma and the broader medical community. Her findings not only explain the rise of resistance among modern parents but also point to policy changes that might convince skeptical parents to vaccinate their children.

As Lisa Wade began to investigate the increasing concern about hooking up on college campuses, she noticed another puzzle: despite the "moral panic" about the practice described in countless popular outlets, college students reported "no more sexual partners than their parents did at their age."[8] Instead, Wade argued, a "hookup culture" so dominates discussions of campus social life that other patterns of sexual behavior get much less attention and the recognition of students who don't engage in hookups "fades in comparison." Only through careful interviews with a diverse range of students was Wade able to disentangle the realities of sexual partnerships on campus from the myths of rampant hooking up and to investigate the worlds of those not attending hookup parties as well as those who did.

These two examples of research both addressed empirical puzzles and found a deeper truth beneath the popular discourse.[9] Such puzzles offer an opportunity to turn common wisdom on its head, making them, in Murray Davis's words, more "interesting" to a general readership as well as an academic audience.[10] Interview studies that investigate empirical puzzles can refute common assumptions and discover the "complicating social factors" that contribute new knowledge and offer new ways of thinking about what we think we already know.

Investigating Poorly Understood Groups, Practices, and Institutions

Interviewing is also a potent tool for examining social groups and practices that social researchers have barely recognized or understood. In these instances, the interviewer's focus on a relatively small sample size becomes an asset rather than a disadvantage. It provides you with a window for focusing on a small but nevertheless important segment of the population. It can also trigger a theoretical reframing by turning assumptions about large groups into questions about smaller group variations within and departures from these general patterns.

Dawn Marie Dow and Riché Daniel Barnes, for example, investigated the work-family choices and strategies of middle-class Black mothers and career women, a group that scholars had largely overlooked despite the burgeoning research on women professionals.[11] Their separate studies revealed a pattern of choices that grow out of the tension between the historical "collective memory" of Black communities about the need for women's paid work and newer cultural pressures for women to safeguard their marriages by relinquishing some independence. In a similar way, Angie Chung studied how the grown children of Asian and white immigrants to the United States negotiate their family and work responsibilities amid two conflicting myths—one that praises Asians as hardworking "model minorities" and another that demonizes behavior associated with "tiger moms."[12] Chung finds these myths take a great emotional toll on the children of Asian immigrants, a toll the children of white immigrants do not pay.[13] And by interviewing cisgender women partnered with transgender men, Carla Pfeffer discovered the numerous social and legal challenges these families face and the ways they learned to "perform and co-create" identities. By investigating family dilemmas and reactions to them among a diverse group of understudied households, each of these studies has broader implications that expand our understanding about how gender and race are negotiated within American families as a whole.

Interviews in these cases demonstrate how to transcend earlier paradigms that may not adequately explain the experiences and practices of newly emerging or demographically outnumbered social groups. In doing so, they also provide new insights about the social norms and practices of more thoroughly studied groups. By illuminating the social and mental practices of groups that have been ignored or understudied, these interviews cast light on the structures and processes that shape social life more generally.

An added complication is that members of poorly understood and/or socially marginalized groups may be understandably reluctant to participate in an interview or even to be asked to do so. As Catherine Connell points out, a simple invitation may inadvertently "out" someone who has been recommended by another participant (via snowball sampling, a method we discuss in Chapter 3).[14] While there may be no straightforward way to overcome the heightened skepticism that occurs among vulnerable groups, she emphasizes the importance of recognizing, understanding, and preparing for these dilemmas and working even harder to address them in ethical and theoretically appropriate ways.

Exploring Macro-Micro Links and Interactive Processes

Interviewing can also answer questions about the unfolding interaction and reciprocal connections among micro-, meso-, and macro-structural arrangements and the processes that link them to one another. Because interviewers can gather information about both social contexts and internal states, they can explore how these contexts affect individual experiences and how individuals react to these experiences and potentially alter the social contexts that give rise to them. By investigating how people wittingly or (more often) unwittingly respond to the cultural and structural forms of their time and place, interviewing thus promotes a focus on the intersection of biography, history, and social structure, which C. Wright Mills called the "orienting framework" of the sociological imagination.[15] One way to focus on social change processes is to interview members of a strategically placed cohort (or cohorts) and investigate how its members respond to their social contexts by either reproducing or changing the patterns and practices they have inherited.[16]

These investigative devices leave interviewers well positioned to un-
veil the mechanisms that explain the relationships found in quantitative
studies. While large-scale studies can document large-scale social trends and
measure the strength of relationships between various factors and outcomes,
they typically leave quantitative analysts with educated guesses about why
these trends and relationships exist. Interviews can explore how and why
such trends unfold in the lives of individuals, thus discovering the micro-
processes that are both driving and being driven by the trends.

Countless studies use interviews to augment quantitative findings. In one
case, after finding in an audit study that men who either worked part-time
or were not employed were less likely than other groups, including women
who either worked part-time or were not employed, to receive an offer for a
job interview, David Pedulla followed up by interviewing the people charged
with making decisions about whom to interview, of whom 70 percent were
women. Their interviews revealed that gendered assumptions—specifically,
that an ideal male worker should work full-time with no interruptions—
led employers to sift out men whose applications demonstrated a record of
spotty or part-time employment.[17]

Another mixed-methods project, conducted by Tressie McMillan Cottom,
used depth interviews with students enrolled in for-profit colleges to find out
why such schools have expanded so rapidly. Combining the analysis of national trends and ethnographic tours of for-profit campuses with interviews
of students enrolled in them, she learned that low-wage workers believed
these schools would confer a degree more quickly and conveniently, despite
their higher price tag compared to traditional, nonprofit educational options.
Her mixed-methods approach made it possible to explain how large-scale
economic and social trends, such as increasing labor market insecurity and
the scheduling constraints facing time-squeezed families, induced disadvantaged groups—particularly the financially marginal, women, and people of
color—to participate in a risky new industry.[18]

In another study, Carla Shedd combined interviews with survey data to investigate how schools either reinforced or ameliorated inequalities in urban
neighborhoods.[19] She discovered that the African American and Latinx
youth who traveled farther to attend better-resourced and more racially diverse high schools became more attuned to issues of social injustice than
either their white and Asian schoolmates or their African American and
Latinx peers who attended less well-resourced, majority-African American
and majority-Latinx schools. Drawing on prior research pointing to the

importance of neighborhood contexts, she discovered the deeper meaning and less apparent consequences of race, place, and educational experience in the lives of urban teenagers.

Pedulla, McMillan Cottom, and Shedd all bridged the macro-micro divide by combining interviews with other sources of information, including large-scale data and ethnographic immersion. Each in their own way was able to explain the emergence of new and not-yet-understood social trends. Their studies exemplify how integrating interview findings with other kinds of information illuminate the processes that happen on the ground and provide a look into the "black box" of quantitative and ethnographic findings.

Developing Theory

Another approach to framing a question is to address a theoretical debate or puzzle. What limits existing theories? How well or poorly do they account for the outcomes you wish to explain? Do competing theories represent debates within a discipline, across subdisciplines, or between different disciplinary approaches (such as assessing the relative power of economic, psychological, or sociological explanations)?

Addressing a theoretical debate need not conflict with seeking to understand a new or poorly understood social development. To the contrary, the rise of a new trend and social group calls on us to revisit prevailing theoretical frameworks to see how well or poorly they explain these new empirical "facts." Interviewers can advance both substantive and theoretical knowledge by posing questions that focus on current theoretical insufficiencies or disagreements as well as a lack of knowledge about important social developments and practices.

A good way to start is to ask which current theoretical perspectives purport to explain the issues you wish to understand. The next step, then, is to ask how well or poorly each explanatory framework performs. Both the academic literature and popular debate can provide relevant perspectives, and you are likely to find popular counterparts to the scholarly perspectives. Kathryn Edin and Timothy Nelson's study of poor fathers living in the inner city, for example, interrogates whether popular culture and conservatively oriented social science explanations are correct in depicting such men as deadbeat dads who are psychologically disinclined to care for their children.[20] They began by asking, "Is it true that these fathers simply don't care for the children they conceive?"[21] Their research then moved beyond this framing to explore the nature and experience of fatherhood under conditions of poverty and its attendant constraints, asking, "What does fatherhood mean in the lives of low-income, inner-city men?"[22] Existing arguments that ring false when oversimplified can thus provide an excellent starting point for posing a question that will make a meaningful theoretical contribution even as it shatters misleading stereotypes and commonly accepted but misleading beliefs.

Theoretical debates between disciplines also provide fertile ground for depth interview studies. Louise Roth's study of women and men on Wall Street asked why women earned far less than comparably employed men.[23] Economic theories typically say that differences in human capital—such as education, work experience, and individual commitment—explain such disparities, while sociologists place more stress on structural and institutional barriers. Starting with these contrasting perspectives, Roth conducted interviews that would assess both perspectives and search for a more supple account. She found that, in contrast to human capital approaches, the workplace culture in Wall Street firms rewarded men's interpersonal styles and connections, while penalizing women (and some men) who were unable or unwilling to develop them. Her interviews revealed how gendered occupational niches dominated by men created unconscious biases and exclusionary cultures that disadvantaged women despite their individual qualifications.

Interviewing can also advance theory by expanding or complicating an existing theoretical approach. The goal here is less to assess the relative power of competing theories than to interrogate, complicate, refine, and/or extend a particular theoretical frame. Michael Burawoy recommends an "extended case method" to refine or adapt a theoretical tradition in light of new historical and analytic developments.[24] Following this tradition, Lynne Haney's interviews with women in the Hungarian welfare system after the fall of the Soviet Union extended theories of the state to encompass the active strategies of welfare workers and recipients.[25]

Another option is to use interviewing to develop an original theoretical framework. You can build on empirical findings that existing approaches have ignored or failed to adequately explain. Such empirical lacunae can arise in a variety of ways. Improved research methods can uncover new findings, historical trends can undermine existing paradigms, or researchers can bring new sensitivities and perceptual lenses to the study of classic research arenas. In all of these instances, your focus shifts from providing an alternative explanation for the same outcome to arguing that the emergence of new outcomes requires a new approach to explaining them.

The rapid diversification of family forms in the late twentieth and early twenty-first centuries provides a good example of how historical trends can undermine existing theory, evoke new theoretical questions, and require innovative exploratory approaches to make sense of a new social landscape. The reigning functionalist theory of "sex roles," which argued that the homemaker-breadwinner family represented an ideal "fit" with the requirements of modern societies, might have seemed adequate to explain the predominance of two-parent, heterosexual, gender-divided households in the 1950s, but it could not account for the rise of a new and far more diverse mix of family forms today. Any convincing theory must now recognize the variety of family arrangements, including dual-earner couples, single-parent households, same-sex couples, and single-individual homes, and explain their growth and popularity. Such historical moments call out for exploratory studies that reconsider fundamental theoretical questions. It is difficult to imagine where theoretical thinking about family life, sexuality, gender relationships, workplace dynamics, and political movements—to name only a few of the many social transformations of the last half century— would be today had it not been for the countless studies that have relied on interviews to discover and map the full range of new social forms and the reasons for their emergence.[26]

The various approaches to posing a question are not mutually exclusive. To the contrary, interviewing, like most research, typically begins with both empirical and theoretical questions. By focusing on unexplained empirical developments, interviewing can not only clarify a theoretical debate but also, and perhaps more important, nurture the construction of new theoretical frames that transcend existing debates. If paradigm shifts occur when existing theories can no longer account for a mounting number of new empirical findings, as Thomas Kuhn has argued, then interviews are an ideal vehicle for making these discoveries.[27]

Whether assessing the explanatory power of diverse theoretical frames (within or between disciplines), expanding the boundaries of a specific theoretical perspective, or replacing a dominant but inadequate approach, the research process begins with posing a theoretically informed question. Once the interviewing commences, you need a theoretically grounded research design to pave the way for gathering information that will help you make theoretical breakthroughs. Since feedback loops between findings and theory are integral to the interview method, you will have many future opportunities to expand, rethink, and even upend your own and others' theoretical thinking.

Turning to Research Design

Once developed, the core questions set the stage for constructing a research design that maximizes your chances of answering them. This moment poses two paramount challenges—grounding the research theoretically and formulating an appropriate design. Assuming you wish to explain as well as describe a puzzling social development—that is, finding out "why" and "how" in addition to "what"—then theory should guide your next steps. Yet how? You can ground a project theoretically in several ways. The most straightforward is to frame the research to weigh in on the relative power—or usefulness—of various theoretical approaches to explain the puzzling outcomes your research seeks to address.[28]

Using Theory to Guide Design

This process begins with a critical overview of relevant theories. Rather than summarizing the literature, the key is to explore how the relevant theoretical perspectives bear on the specific empirical questions you want to ask and assess how well or poorly they answer them. This will tell you which theoretical frames are problematic and which are promising (as well as why and how), which in turn will help you clarify the questions that need asking. Identifying what may be missing or misleading in prevailing theoretical arguments also helps to justify your project and encourages creative thinking by pointing to the ways your research can correct or expand current ways of conceiving the problem and providing answers to it. Identifying the relevant theoretical and substantive puzzles thus guides research design by pointing to the individuals and groups to interview and the information to collect from them.

Thinking About Outcomes

Since interviewing seeks to discover the contours of poorly understood social patterns and processes, you may be tempted to conclude there is no need to specify an expected outcome. Although you need not know in advance what forms your outcomes will take—and your educated guesses may prove incomplete or off the mark—you must nevertheless think carefully about what outcomes you seek to find. Even though you are likely to adjust and change course, it is better to consider the range of possible outcomes—however vaguely conceived—than to avoid the task of thinking about them. This exercise will draw your attention to the analytic task: to explain as well as to describe. It also sets the stage for noticing surprises when the interviewing begins. Indeed, it is difficult to identify a finding as a surprise unless you start with some sense of what current theories or conventional wisdom would lead us to expect. Thinking about outcomes raises the chances that you will notice the interview details that upend expectations and point toward theoretical breakthroughs.

Outcomes must also vary in some way. Though it may seem obvious, this is why we call outcomes dependent variables. A central task in getting started is thus to conceptualize your outcomes and their possible variation in degree or type. While it may not be possible to know what the interviews will tell you, it is essential to know what to look for. To the extent that the initial formulation proves correct, it will guide your voyage of discovery. To the extent that the initial formulation is misleading, incomplete, or incorrect, interview evidence will suggest how to reframe and refine your original conceptions.

Since interviewing studies seek answers to questions about which little is known, the chances are high that unexpected findings will emerge and prompt you to adjust the empirical and theoretical questions. In the long, unpredictable trek through the stages of research, your best chance to get to the finish line is to start with a question that addresses an empirical puzzle, to conceptualize the range of possible outcomes, and to engage with a theoretical debate about what might drive their variation. This prior planning should ignite your desire to find answers, help you navigate the next steps, and sustain your commitment when the going gets tough.

The Next Steps

Once you have clarified potential outcomes, it is time to specify a research design that grounds your interviews in the empirical puzzles and theoretical debates that motivate the project. Identifying outcomes and relevant theoretical frameworks will guide your decisions about whom to interview and what to ask them. The goal is to develop a design that increases your chances of discovering new ways of charting and explaining the "social facts" you will investigate.

As you begin to construct a research design, it is reassuring to remember—one more time—that you will have opportunities to make changes going forward. Interviewing is a flexible method that allows—and usually requires—shifts of focus when unexpected findings lead to new theoretical insights, which then lead to new questions, sample groups, and analytic frames. Whether you view these feedback loops as an opportunity or a drawback depends on your comfort with letting go of earlier assumptions. Even if the process feels disorienting, this is how breakthroughs take place and why interviewing provides such a fertile method for making them.

3

Interviews with Whom?

When a Big Question Meets a Small Sample

There is no such thing as a perfect sample. Every research effort, including those with large samples and generous funding, faces practical limits that make it impossible and/or undesirable to include everyone who might be considered relevant. Even the U.S. Census, which is constitutionally required to count every resident and draws on the enormous resources of the federal government, routinely undercounts hard-to-find groups such as the homeless and the undocumented. Like all researchers, depth interviewers must make compromises in the search for an appropriate sample. It is nevertheless essential to carefully consider and diligently work to develop a strategy that offers the best chance of finding a sample that is valid for your purposes and lends credence to your findings. Given how much effort you will need to devote to collecting and analyzing the interviews, it is more than worthwhile to devote a similar level of attention to finding the best possible sample.

The main challenge is to find a sample that will lead others to have confidence in the soundness and importance of your findings. Given that the sample will necessarily be small, you cannot rely on the standard techniques that survey research uses to establish validity and representativeness. Instead, you need to devise a sampling strategy tailored to interviewing's unique challenges. The first step is to use your core questions and research goals as a guide for outlining the contours of an ideal sample. Once you have envisioned such a sample, you'll be able to think through the challenges of finding it and consider the realistic options. Developing a creative way to find a sample that approximates your ideal increases the likelihood that the findings will be convincing and your arguments can make lasting contributions.

The Science and Art of Interviewing. Kathleen Gerson and Sarah Damaske, Oxford University Press (2021). © Oxford University Press. DOI: 10.1093/oso/9780199324286.001.0001

What Kind of Sample Do Interviewers Need?

The gold standard for large-scale studies is to draw a sample that randomly selects participants from a given population, so that all members have an equal probability of being chosen. This approach presents the sampled subset as representing the whole group accurately enough to produce valid generalizations about that larger population.[1] When demographers want to ascertain the racial distribution in the United States, for example, they typically rely on estimates drawn from the American Community Survey (a survey that annually samples about 1 percent of the U.S. population). In this way, systematic random probability sampling allows quantitative researchers to draw statistically valid conclusions about the population at large by relying on a carefully selected large sample.

Rarely can interviewers select a statistically representative random sample. You may be able to select participants randomly from a specified list (as both of us have done and as we discuss later in the chapter), but the small sample sizes that lend themselves to depth interviewing mean your findings are not, strictly speaking, statistically "representative" of a wider population. This does not, however, prevent you from developing generalizable theoretical insights. As Mario Small points out, statistical representativeness is not—and should not be—the goal of qualitative research.[2] Instead, interviewers can and should seek a sample that Kristen Luker describes as "reasonably representative of the larger phenomenon" with, in the words of Barney Glaser and Anselm Strauss, "generality of scope."[3] The key is not to commit selection bias by choosing only the participants who fit your expected pattern. Rather than claiming representativeness, your goal is to select a sample capable of yielding theoretically generalizable insights—an approach we call theoretical sampling.[4]

Theoretical sampling focuses on finding a variety of participants who are well positioned to reveal the practices, mechanisms, and relationships your research seeks to explain. Rather than estimating the *rate* at which a finding occurs in the general population, the objective is to explain the *reasons* it occurs (or, alternatively, does not).[5] Whether your goal is to explain the reasons for a demographic pattern, an institutional arrangement, or a cultural practice, the key is to find a sample that includes the full range of participants who are integral to providing the answer. You can then decipher the shape of a specific demographic, cultural, or institutional pattern within the sample and also illuminate the conditions under which similar patterns are likely to emerge among other groups or at other times and places.

Theoretical Sampling for Controls and Comparisons

Since it is never possible to interview everyone who might provide pertinent information, you must carefully define the criteria by which to select interviewees. This decision is inescapable and highly consequential, since it shapes the kinds of questions your study can address and how you can answer them. The place to begin is by asking what kind of sample is most likely to generate substantive and theoretical breakthroughs. This may seem obvious, but doing so depends on first clarifying your study's core questions and theoretical aspirations. This sets the stage for deciding which groups are best positioned to help answer the questions and adjudicate the theoretical debates. Even though practical considerations will likely put your ideal sample out of reach, thinking through the contours of an ideal sample helps you develop a realistic strategy for approximating it.

Deciding on controls and comparisons is integral to the process of theoretical sampling for any method. For interviewers, this involves deciding who is—and is not—a member of the group of interest. Put another way, it requires drawing a boundary between whom to include in the sample and whom to exclude. When selecting criteria for inclusion and exclusion, you will also need to decide which key subgroups you wish to compare. The criteria for inclusion represent sample controls, since they will define the limits beyond which you will not be able to draw theoretical conclusions. If, for example, you choose to focus on members of the middle class and exclude working-class participants (however defined), you will not be able to draw conclusions about class differences or similarities. Selecting key subgroups within the sample, in contrast, makes it possible to analyze differences and similarities among these groups on the outcomes you seek to understand. If you include participants with a range of class positions, for example, you will be able to investigate whether or not those differences are linked to differences in your outcomes of interest, and if so, why.[6]

Sampling for controls and comparisons may seem more appropriate for quantitative studies with large samples, but these are logical principles and integral to any systematic analysis, regardless of the numbers involved. The distinction between large-scale and small-scale studies is not *whether* they should apply the logic of controls and comparisons but *how*. Analysts with large samples can use statistical procedures to control for respondent attributes and compare groups within a sample. Since interviewers do not have the luxury of applying statistical controls after compiling a data set or making comparisons among the many subgroups that a large sample can contain, the challenge is to determine which sample controls and variations are central to answering the substantive and theoretical questions you wish to pose. The essence of theoretically grounded sampling is to develop principles for including (and excluding) participants and systematically varying the attributes of the people whom you include. These rules help you select a sample for theoretical reasons that are tailored to answer your study's questions and increase its explanatory power.

Setting Sample Boundaries

Deciding on the criteria for including or excluding someone in your sample is typically less straightforward than it may appear. Take Eric Klinenberg's study of the consequences of living alone.[7] The criteria for inclusion may seem self-evident, but what does it mean to live alone? Should your sampling universe include single-room-occupancy hotels and dormitories or only fully outfitted domiciles? Should it include only those who do not share any living space with another person or extend to singles who share some common space but little else with a temporary roommate? And do people of all ages qualify or only working-age adults? Even a study of an apparently clearly defined group involves drawing boundaries that leave some in and others out, and it must do this in a way that advances the study's goals and purposes. Klinenberg's research included a variety of "solo" forms—from young singles to middle-aged adults to the poor and elderly occupying single-room living quarters—making it possible for him to analyze across a variety of subcategories. Living alone provided a sampling control, while casting a relatively wide net within this general category made it possible to explore general patterns of similarities and differences among a variety of the "solo" forms.

Caitlyn Collins's cross-national research on employed mothers also demonstrates how the strategic use of sample controls can increase a study's explanatory leverage.[8] Although she wished to understand how diverse national contexts shape mothers' experiences, she limited her sample to middle-class mothers with paid jobs, excluding working-class and poor women and all nonemployed mothers. While controlling for the participants' class position, parental status, and employment situation narrowed her sample, doing so provided analytic clarity about the role of national context by ruling out a number of alternative explanations (such as a mother's economic resources or work commitments) for her findings. Had her sample included women of all classes and work statuses, it would have been difficult—perhaps impossible—to disentangle the effects of national context from the socioeconomic attributes of individual mothers. By confining her sample to women who shared important traits, Collins could analyze the ways political, policy, and cultural differences shaped the differences she found in the degree and type of support reported by middle-class, employed mothers in Sweden, Germany, Italy, and the United States.

Building in Strategic Comparisons

Alongside sampling controls that limit variation, interview samples also need to build in enough comparisons to discover and analyze the key dimensions of potential variation in the causes and consequences of interest. Comparisons make it possible to ascertain which conditions do and do not give rise to the outcomes you wish to understand. Without building strategic comparisons into your sampling strategy, it will be difficult (and in some cases impossible) to tease out whether and why specific patterns emerge and why they take the form they do.

Building on prior studies, Jessica Calarco wished to understand why middle-class children, on average, do better in school than poor children.[9] The obvious starting point was to interview middle-class children and their parents about their educational resources and strategies, but confining the interviews to the middle class would limit her analytic options.[10] If the goal is to discover why middle-class backgrounds bestow privileges that working-class backgrounds do not, it is necessary to include working-class children and parents to ascertain why they are not able to secure similar advantages. Building class comparisons into the sample enabled Calarco to discover that working-class students are more prone to "learn to follow rules and work through problems independently," which paradoxically left them disadvantaged compared to their middle-class peers, who felt more comfortable interrupting teachers, asking questions, and demanding assistance.

Deirdre Royster's study of African American men's labor market experiences provides another good example of how building comparisons into your sample increases interviewing's explanatory power.[11] Setting out to understand what happens to young Black men who heed the advice to "get a trade," Royster wished to assess the power of explanations that focus on skill differences to explain why this group of job-seeking men are more likely to fare poorly in the labor market. Since these market-based arguments implicitly assume that young white men do better because they possess more marketable skills, Royster interviewed both Black and white men who graduated from vocational high schools. By comparing men who vary in their racial identity but share similar levels and types of training and work attitudes, she found that more effective social networks—not human capital attributes— accounted for the white men's more successful employment trajectories, and she was thus able to develop an explanation that did a better job of accounting for racial disparities in the job market.

The good news is that there are myriad ways to build systematic variation into your sampling strategy. In a study of single motherhood in Russia, Jennifer Utrata augmented interviews with single mothers by also including grandmothers, married mothers, and disengaged fathers.[12] The scope of Utrata's sample enlarged as early interviews revealed the importance of these other groups. It allowed her to compare mothers and grandmothers and to chart generational change as single motherhood became more prevalent among contemporary Russian mothers.

In another case, Annette Lareau, Elliot Weininger, and Amanda Cox, much like Calarco, wished to understand why middle-class children enjoy educational advantages, but they took a different approach by sampling various groups of school officials. Their strategy of interviewing diverse educational decision-makers revealed that lobbying by elite parents helped secure advantageous school districts for their children.[13] There are many ways—and no one "right" way—to build variation into an otherwise clearly bounded sample. The key is to do so in any way that increases the odds of answering the questions you deem most central. Building explicit comparisons into your sample design is the generally preferred option, but there may be good reasons to forgo that strategy. Some studies may be so exploratory that interviewing needs to begin before you can know which comparisons are most important. Some studies may rely on comparisons between the group being investigated and other groups that are not in your sample.

Whether the focus is on a group that is quite small, never before investigated, or some combination, your sampling strategy may rely on making comparisons with groups that are not in your sample but about which we already know a great deal. Anthony Abraham Jack's study of the "privileged poor" and the "doubly disadvantaged" on college campuses includes African

American, Latinx, and white students who fall into either of those two categories, but when it came to those in the upper-income group, he interviewed only African Americans.[14] Since we already possess voluminous comparative information from prior studies about elite whites on college campuses, Jack was able to leverage that previously collected data when discussing his own findings. Rather than reducing the number of privileged poor or doubly disadvantaged interviewees by including members of an advantaged group, he maximized the number of interviews he could conduct with the groups of interest and relied on prior research to draw key comparisons with other groups.

Similarly, Steve Viscelli's study of long-haul truckers did not include truckers who had left trucking or workers who chose occupations other than trucking.[15] Although he could not explain why some truckers stayed while others sought jobs elsewhere, the combination of interviews with ethnographic immersion and historical analysis allowed him to compare truckers' early work experiences with their experiences after regulatory control increased, union power declined, and a transformed labor market eroded their work conditions. While Viscelli did not explicitly seek variation within his target sample, he ultimately found variation by making comparisons that emerged within the target sample and with other groups outside its scope.

Interview studies also routinely target narrow sampling sources that exemplify large social patterns. Heather Jacobson wished to understand how mothers of adopted children negotiate racial and ethnic differences, but the analysis would become unmanageable if she included the full range of parent-child differences.[16] To limit the range while preserving sufficient variation, she focused on adoptions from China or Russia, the areas from which U.S. parents are most likely to pursue adoptions. In order to study the immigration experiences of highly skilled youth—a topic that encompasses a very large global population—José Soto-Márquez selected one sending source (Spain) where educated young adults are leaving in large numbers and then compared their immigration trajectories in the three main receiving locations (Buenos Aires, London, and New York).[17]

While Jacobson and Soto-Márquez both wished to understand large global trends, it was neither practical nor analytically useful for them to seek a random sample from the entire pool of the relevant population. Instead, they sampled from groups who can be considered good exemplars of the larger phenomena—in Jacobson's case, two countries providing the largest percentage of foreign adoptees in the United States, and in Soto-Márquez's, a country with one of the largest exoduses of highly educated youth. These narrowed samples provided analytic controls but remained wide enough to ensure variation in the outcomes each study sought to understand.[18]

All of these examples highlight how the logic of systematic controls and comparisons guides the work of finding a sample that can answer an interview study's core questions. Regardless of the topic, this is the key to theoretical sampling and the best way to enhance your analytic leverage. Paradoxically, while it is important to specify your sampling criteria before interviewing begins, it is also important to remain open to modifying the criteria going forward. Since you will conduct the interviews one at a time, there will be opportunities to use early findings to assess original sampling decisions. Practical obstacles may require adjustments, and findings in the field may point to tweaks that take your sample in new directions. These uncertainties do not, however, decrease the importance of forethought. Rather, they make it all the more important to start with a plan based on theoretical principles so that the need for change will be apparent if and when it arises.

Size Matters

Theoretical sampling also has implications for sample size. The time- and labor-intensive nature of interviewing limits how many interviews you can realistically conduct and analyze. (Indeed, the added time it takes to analyze a greater number of lengthy interviews can be just as large as the added time it takes to conduct them, as we discuss in Chapter 6.) Yet you also want to collect enough interviews to develop an insightful explanation and defend it convincingly. This trade-off makes it tricky, at best, to calculate an appropriate sample size. The standard advice is to aim for what Glaser and Strauss call "theoretical saturation," which they define as the point at which "no additional data are being found whereby the sociologist can develop properties of the category."[19] This standard provides a worthy abstract goal, but it is often difficult to discern in practice.

Why is it difficult for interviewers to know if or when they have reached saturation, and what does this difficulty imply for your sampling strategy? Since interviews are conducted one at a time, in the early stages it is hard to know what kind of information the next interview might yield. The first twenty interviews might produce similar findings, but the next one may still lead in a new direction. The next twenty interviews may also turn out to be quite similar to each other but notably different from the first twenty. The findings from a small number of interviews may reflect the vagaries of who is interviewed *first* far more than they reflect the discovery of a generalizable pattern. If saturation means having enough information to draw convincing conclusions about patterns and relationships, such a small number is rarely sufficient, even if these early findings are consistent.

At any point in the interviewing process, from conducting the early interviews to conducting the hundredth, one more interview always holds the possibility of adding something new. If the goal is to reach a point when no "new" information—generally defined—is likely to emerge, the search for saturation can become an endless journey. As an abstract principle, it does not solve the problem of deciding how many interviews are enough. To settle on a minimum necessary sample size—including the minimum number needed in each subgroup within the sample—you first need to know what *kind* of saturation to seek.

The only way to identify the kind of saturation you need to achieve is to devote enough forethought to research design to recognize what type of new information would be central. This requires, as Mario Small proposes, "sampling for range"—that is, treating each interview as a single case and asking if this case reveals anything new that helps answer the research question or questions.[20] In this "sequential" fashion, repeatedly returning to the research question to ask what each new interview adds to the emerging insights eventually leads to saturation. The early interviews may well produce discoveries that reshape the sample design (and alterations to the interview guide, which we discuss in Chapter 4), but careful early planning reduces the chances that new information will emerge in late interviews that will be central or even pertinent to the research goals.

Saturation is a minimum standard because it reminds interviewers not to leave the field prematurely, but it cannot substitute for prior planning. Indeed, you cannot define what achieving saturation means unless you are clear about your study's theoretical goals. This means asking how many interviews you need, at a minimum, to draw theoretically relevant conclusions and have confidence in their validity. The answer depends on the degree and type of variation you built into the research design, for doing this points to the minimum number of participants you need in each designated subgroup.

To calculate these numbers, it is helpful to create a table that depicts ideal (or at least minimally acceptable) target sizes for each sampling category. A visual schema not only clarifies the sampling goals; it also helps guide decisions about where to find good sample sources. Table 3.1 outlines the

Table 3.1 Proposed Sample for Damaske's Unemployment Study (n = 100)

	Men	Women
White working-class	15	15
African American working-class	10	10
White middle-class	15	15
African American middle-class	10	10
Total	50	50

comparison groups for Sarah's study of workers' experiences with job loss and unemployment.[21]

Sarah's ideal sample controls for job history by targeting only those people who have experienced unemployment and then seeks gender, racial, and class variation within this group. To ensure that men and women held similar workforce commitments prior to losing their jobs, she also limited the sample to those people who had been full-time workers. And since a study goal was to examine the influence of economic changes since the Great Recession, she also targeted people who had lost a full-time job after 2009. Finally, since cohort position shapes exposure to changes in women's and men's opportunities, she decided to restrict the sample to people ages twenty-eight to fifty-two, an age group old enough to have begun building families and accruing work experience but not yet facing retirement.[22] Although this sampling strategy excludes large swaths of the working population, it enhanced her focus on the core research questions. Controlling on work experience, cohort location, and life stage made it possible to explore the influence of gender, race, and class on the experience of job loss.

Creating a visual depiction of the key sample groups will help assess how much variation your study can sustain and how many people you will need in each category of variation. To reiterate, the goal is not to achieve statistical representation of a larger population but to make sure your sample includes people from all relevant backgrounds. Outlining this ideal sample provides a map of the groups you need to target and clarifies how many you need to include in each category. The higher the number in every cell, the easier it will be to identify what the members of each group have in common and what distinguishes them from other groups. It also allows you to assess whether the subgroups share similarities you did not anticipate or other theoretical frameworks would not have predicted.

Since the designated subgroups will still likely contain noteworthy variation despite their shared attributes, you need to set a minimum size for each group, with the possibility of adding more if that proves possible or necessary. Sarah set a minimum of ten people in each cell so that she could explore if and how gender, class, and race—either alone or in combination—shape unemployment trajectories. She also anticipated that participants would vary on other notable attributes, such as marital and parental status. Even though it was not possible to take account of all the consequential ways in which interviewees may differ, the outlined sampling targets specify the comparisons deemed most theoretically important at the outset while also allowing for adjustments if other sources of variation prove to matter at a later time.

Just as Sarah varied the target number for designated subgroups, other studies may call for oversampling in some categories. In Klinenberg's research on living alone, for example, the inclusion of more African American women made sense because they are more likely than others to live alone.[23] For Collins's cross-national study of middle-class employed mothers, the high level of racial, ethnic, and cultural diversity in the United States suggested the need for including more American mothers than mothers from Sweden, Germany, and Italy, where such dimensions of diversity are less pronounced.[24] D'Lane Compton notes that studies with queer populations often face high recruitment barriers, but such studies share similar expectations— both practical, in terms of publishing, and theoretical, in terms of study aims—about how to recruit participants (as well as heteronormative bias about what the sample should include). As we do, Compton recommends that sample sizes must be considered alongside research questions and study goals, rather than matching a singular gold-standard number.[25]

Deciding how many people you need in each designated group and the sample as a whole depends on knowing and applying your project's empirical and theoretical goals. Keeping in mind the goal of theoretical saturation, your sample should never be too small to discover trends and relationships. The wider the range of your theoretical categories, the larger the sample you will need. Beyond the goal of reaching saturation, however, you also need to conduct enough interviews to build a case that others will find convincing, and that number may exceed the minimum number needed to discover patterns. Since the standards held by others may vary by topic, methodological style, and publishing venue, it is worthwhile to survey the relevant books, articles, and journals to see what they have to say not just about substantive matters but also about research design. What do journals, and especially those that publish a variety of qualitative work, say about their standards for sample size? Among book publishers, how many interviews are typical for a monograph, and what appears to be a minimum number to warrant publication? Do the methodological appendices of books and articles provide guidance for sampling strategies and sizes? Surveying the publishing terrain not only is likely to provide guidance for developing a sampling strategy but also offers an opportunity to find inspirational models among the work that others have done.[26]

Unplanned and Emergent Variation

As important as it may be to designate sample controls and comparisons, you cannot know every potentially consequential source of variation in advance. No matter which ones you choose to include, other important comparisons will almost surely come to the fore once interviewing is under way.[27] Indeed, the ability to discover unexpected variation (as well as unexpected similarity) is one of interviewing's assets. Annelise Hagedorn, for example, interviewed a group of childcare workers with largely homogenous demographic profiles—almost all were white married women who lived in rural areas and provided home-based care.[28] Yet she found consequential variation in how they viewed professional development, with about a third embracing continued training, another third tolerating it, and the final third actively resisting it. While Hagedorn had not originally planned to investigate these differences, she was able to explore their significance because she had originally interviewed enough participants. Their demographic similarities made it possible to discover other consequential forms of variation and to analyze the other social factors that explained these differences.

Discoveries often emerge after all of the interviews have been conducted and it becomes possible to decipher the significance of each interview in the context of all the others. It is, of course, too late to add to the sample at this point, but that is also not likely to be necessary. Assuming you have developed a thoughtful sampling design and conducted careful interviews, the chances are high that you will have enough information from the appropriate group of people to pursue a wealth of emerging ideas.

The search for consequential variation continues through every stage of research. You may think you have achieved saturation, only to find new discoveries that shift the meaning of "how many are enough." Thinking through the contours of an ideal sample provides a practical blueprint for using theoretical principles to select a sample. It is reassuring to know that this early blueprint is nevertheless flexible enough to allow changes—such as increasing the sample size, expanding criteria for inclusion, or changing the contours of variation within it—at a later time. Indeed, it is better to make adjustments than to settle for a sample that omits a theoretically important group or is too small to answer the emergent questions.

Finding a Good Sample

In sampling as in life, the ideal must ultimately give way to the possible. After thinking through the controls, comparison groups, and minimum size that characterize your ideal sample, the next challenge is to find an acceptable approximation. All research faces such constraints as money, time, or location that put the "perfect" out of reach. Indeed, you may discover that what appears to be "perfect" at the outset looks quite different after you complete a number of interviews. Finding appropriate interviewees can be costly (although not as costly as conducting a large-scale survey), and few among us have the funds to support a limitless design. The good news is that a good sample need not be perfect. The challenge is to find the best possible sample while remaining attentive to its limitations (and taking comfort in its strengths).

Since the best interviews take place face-to-face, location is often the most obvious constraint. It is usually impractical as well as costly to draw a small sample from a large geographic area. Instead, your sampling strategy can draw broad locational boundaries and then seek as much diversity as possible within them, while remaining mindful of what groups this strategy will be likely to exclude. Samples drawn from one region of the country, for example, can strive to include social groups that are more plentiful in other regions. A good way to address locational constraints is thus to include areas that have as much diversity as needed to answer your research question and provide grounds for arguing that your insights apply in other places. To find a demographically diverse group that more closely resembles the U.S. population, both of us have drawn portions of our samples from areas that are more rural and suburban as well as more politically and culturally conservative than most other places in the New York metropolitan area.

When the ideal sample meets the reality of a limited budget and a regional location, you need not let the perfect be the enemy of the good. A "perfect" sample is neither realistic nor necessary. Creativity, careful planning, and persistence will help produce a theoretically focused sample that can provide answers to big questions. With these principles in mind, let's consider some strategies for finding a good sample and for deciding which one to use.

Random Sampling

If and when it is possible, the gold standard for finding an interview sample is random selection. Unlike the rationale for random sampling in survey research, however, the goal of random selection in interview research is not to claim the sample represents a wider population. Rather, it helps ensure that the process of selecting participants does not bias the ultimate findings. Although interview studies need not claim statistical representativeness, they do need to provide assurance that the participants fairly represent the range of variation within the specific group you wish to understand. The best way to avoid building in systematic, if unknown, bias is to avoid personally selecting participants or, alternatively, depending on volunteers who select themselves. Random sampling among members of an identifiable group lowers concern that interviewer bias (by choosing who participates and who doesn't) or self-selection bias (by relying on people to enlist) has systematically excluded people who differ from your participants in unknown but potentially consequential ways.

To select a random sample, the first line of attack is to seek a source that provides a list of potential participants from which you can select a subset that to the extent possible resembles your ideal sample. Since most interview studies focus on a specific segment of the population rather than the population as a whole, you can often find an appropriate source from which to select people randomly, thus efficiently targeting the relevant group while avoiding the self-selection biases associated with asking for volunteers. The challenge is to find a list that provides sufficient information—such as name, address, age, gender, and phone number or email address—to select and then contact an appropriate group of interviewees.[29]

Elaine Howard Ecklund's study of religion among American scientists exemplifies this approach.[30] Ecklund identified twenty-one elite American universities and then randomly selected scientists from the rolls of seven natural and social science disciplines to participate in a quantitative survey. After receiving survey responses from almost 1,650 respondents, she randomly selected a subset of this group to interview in depth. Ecklund decided to exclude scientists at non-elite institutions or teaching colleges and research centers not associated with academia. Among the universities selected, she built in comparisons by including scientists in selected disciplines (such as biologists, physicists, and social scientists). Even though a study of this breadth required several grants and a team of researchers, it provides a model for those with fewer resources about how to conceive and implement a sampling strategy that uses targeted random sampling and builds in systematic controls and comparisons.

Not all studies lend themselves to this approach, of course. Since most universities provide public listings of their faculty, along with a wealth of information about their professional affiliations, personal history, and how they can be reached, professors are more accessible than most groups. Yet even if a list of names and contact information is not readily available, there are other options that can approximate this approach. A slight adjustment in the sample criteria might make it possible to select randomly from a group that bears a close resemblance to the ideal sample.

If it is not logistically or economically feasible to select interviewees from a national list, as Ecklund did, a local or regional list of the target population will more than suffice. To find participants for *Hard Choices*, Kathleen selected a sample of young women from lists of university alumnae and community college attendees across the region.[31] Relying on these sources had several advantages. Lists from two different sources made it possible to investigate similarities and differences among a diverse group of women who varied in their class positions, educational backgrounds, and economic resources. Yet both lists provided critical information such as gender and birthdates, which also made it possible to select from the targeted age and gender groups. Equally important, using lists from educational institutions— rather than workplaces or neighborhoods—ensured the participants would vary in their work and family commitments, the core outcomes to investigate and explain.

If a reasonably appropriate list (or set of lists) can be found, randomly selecting participants is the most straightforward route for finding a sample that is not self-selected but is well positioned to answer the core research questions. Sampling in this way also helps ensure enough diversity to build relevant controls and comparisons into the research design. Yet it can be difficult to find and gain access to a list of this kind, and even when one is available, it can be challenging to procure a high participation rate from its members. Although we have both enjoyed success with this recruitment strategy, it requires patience and persistence as well as the availability of the necessary information. The payoff is that contacting potential participants directly and personally buoys participation rates to levels that far exceed the rates surveys typically yield.[32]

Theoretical Sampling from a Known Universe and Prior Knowledge

For many studies, it is simply not possible to find a list from which to randomly select appropriate interviewees. If the focus is on a "hidden" population—such as workers in the underground economy, undocumented immigrants, or women seeking abortions—a list either is unlikely to exist or would likely be inaccessible if it did. Similarly, for many social groups and organizations—such as a social movement or political campaign that contains a diverse mix of paid staff, volunteers, clients, and other interested parties—lists of identifiable members do not exist. In such cases, creativity and persistence will go a long way. To find out how immigrant-serving nonprofits in San Francisco were responding to rising challenges from politicians, citizens, and immigrant groups, Els de Graauw had to not only find a broad array of organizational actors but also convince them to take the time to meet with her and discuss an array of sensitive and controversial matters.[33] Kristen Luker sought to understand why women who did not wish to have a child and knew how to use contraception nevertheless became pregnant. Although gaining access to a list containing such confidential information was clearly not possible, she was able to volunteer at a clinic and interview women seeking an abortion for an unplanned pregnancy about how and why they became pregnant.[34] By inviting everyone who fit the study criteria to participate, she not only enlisted a group of hard-to-find participants but also gained their trust and support.

Even when a group is not especially difficult to find, it may nevertheless be difficult to select from it randomly. Deirdre Royster initially planned to select a random sample of young Black and white men who had graduated from a vocational high school (a procedure similar to Kathleen's sampling of women college graduates and community college enrollees). When she found that only half the graduates had up-to-date contact information, she decided to rely on the accurate phone numbers and then ask the people she interviewed to provide updated information for their classmates.[35] By using a theoretical sampling strategy that began with random selection and then added a snowball technique, Royster was able to find a sample that, though not exclusively random, carefully selected the young men whose lives she sought to understand.

Some research begins with ethnographic immersion and then augments these observations with depth interviews. The interviews provide deeper insights about the experiences and perceptions of the observed participants, and the ethnographic immersion opens avenues for finding and building ties with interviewees. In these studies, the original ethnographic setting provides the information to guide sample selection. To understand the world of nursing, Daniel Chambliss conducted case studies of nurses in carefully selected hospitals.[36] Based on extensive observations in these hospital settings, he extended the study's scope by interviewing 110 nurses about the construction and implementation of ethical standards in medical care. Since the standard of practice is relatively similar across hospitals (even though they differ in numerous other ways), Chambliss was able to gather in-depth information about the medical system by combining observations of each hospital setting with interviews of a rigorously selected group of people who worked there.

A related approach is to use theoretical sampling principles by relying on prior knowledge about the research issues. Cynthia Miller-Idriss wished to conduct research on far-right youth movements in Germany, but she knew she could not speak with everyone involved in these movements and also did not want to confine the sample to only those involved.[37] Selecting participants based on their participation in a far-right youth movement—the outcome she wished to understand—would make it impossible to discover why some youth joined these movements and others did not.[38] To address these challenges, she drew her sample from two Berlin vocational schools that served the type of youth who are disproportionately involved in such far-right movements. From these schools, Miller-Idriss and her research team oversampled students in trades known to have higher rates of movement participation, while also sampling from students in trades known to have lower participation levels. By focusing her sampling design in this way, she was able to find enough students involved in far-right movements while also including students who were not involved. These are just a few examples of the diverse ways interviewers can draw on prior knowledge and emergent insights to sample from a known universe.

Snowball Sampling

When circumstances call for it, snowball sampling is both a useful way to augment other strategies and a reasonable strategy in its own right. If a study focuses on members of groups who are difficult to find—such as the parents of children with disabilities, transgender men and/or women, or gang members, to name only a few—it simply may not be possible to find a list, an organization, or an identifiable place from which to select participants. In these situations, snowball sampling may be not only the best option but also the only possible one.

Finding a sample via snowball techniques involves identifying an initial group of participants who then provide you with links to additional ones. In Adia Harvey Wingfield's study of Black professional men's experiences working in predominantly white occupational settings, she asked people she knew "personally and through professional contacts to refer me to Black men who fit the criteria for the study."[39] After this first step, she asked the people who agreed to participate for others who might also take part, a process she repeated for each link in the chain until the sample was complete. This strategy ultimately yielded a group who worked in a variety of professional fields, including "thirteen lawyers, twelve doctors, ten engineers, and seven bankers." Yet Mignon Moore notes that it is not always possible to find informants who can help expand the sample through snowballing, a difficulty she encountered in her research on Black sexual-minority women and on Black LGBTQ seniors.[40] When this happens, gaining access to the social spaces where relevant participants spend time offers another route for building a network and creating trust in hard-to-find or marginalized communities.

The biggest drawback of snowball sampling is its reliance on the social networks of a small number of original interviewees. Since birds of a feather tend to flock together, these social networks are likely to be more homogenous than a random sample of a similar group.[41] This tendency toward network similarity means snowball sampling is more prone than other methods to built in selection bias. Fortunately, there are ways to minimize this challenge and keep it to an acceptable level. First, these circumstances make it more important to carefully articulate the composition of an ideal sample and know what comparison groups and range of variation you need to find. Next, you should begin with as many starting points (or nodes) as possible. Finally, you should reach out as far as possible from the original participants by asking them to recommend distant acquaintances and "friends of friends" rather than close friends and relatives (unless these closer connections are part of what you wish to study). The more original recruits the sample contains and the further the reach in recruiting others, the lower the chances of building bias into the sample.

Roberto Gonzales's study of young adult Latinos and Latinas who are undocumented exemplifies how beginning with multiple nodes can enhance snowballing. He spent time getting to know "respondents and community stakeholders" and becoming embedded in their communities.[42] Meeting people in a variety of local settings made it easier for him to identify and recruit participants and then ask them to suggest additional ones. By drawing his initial respondents from schools, community organizations, college campuses, and churches, Gonzales decreased the likelihood his sample would be too homogenous. He then sought additional diversity by selecting a relatively equal number of men and women and a relatively equal number of people who did and did not attend college.

Some studies target a group so small that one source cannot provide enough participants. In her study of transgender men, Kristen Schilt recognized it would not be possible to select a random sample among a group with so few members, many of whom would feel understandably reluctant to disclose their identity to a stranger.[43] Knowing that she needed multiple sample sources, she recruited participants from online discussion groups, support groups, and personal contacts. To overcome selection bias, she sought variation in several ways—by including people living in California and Texas, two states with vastly different labor laws regarding LGBTQ workers; by selecting from cities known to differ in their political environments, including those with conservative and liberal reputations; and, finally, by seeking to interview both "out" and "stealth" transgender men. These efforts limited the danger of drawing conclusions based only on those who actively participated in "trans" forums and ensured she would be able to make comparisons among men residing in different cultural and institutional milieus.

Selecting Participants or Letting Them Select You

Why invest so much time and effort in selecting a sample when it would be faster and easier to rely on volunteers (a practice commonly called convenience sampling)? The answer is simple: to produce results that you and your audience can confidently believe are reliable. People who actively choose to participate in a study are likely, on the whole, to do so for reasons that differ in some consequential way from the motives of those who do not. They may have more free time, possess a special interest in and strong opinions about your subject, or see an opportunity for personal gain (financial or otherwise).[44] It is impossible to know what might motivate a participant to volunteer, but that is the heart of the problem. It is better, to the extent possible, to avoid an unknowable and immeasurable bias. For this reason, we recommend explaining to skeptics who may resist the invitation to participate that speaking with them matters precisely because they are in the best position to offer information that would otherwise remain buried and ignored.

While interviewers should do whatever possible to reduce sampling bias, turning to volunteers is certainly preferable to giving up altogether when there is no viable alternative. One of the volunteer method's great strengths is its ability to learn about groups whose members are difficult to find. Less-than-ideal sampling options should never prevent gathering this knowledge. Since the interviewing method seeks to discover new social patterns and develop new explanations (which can be tested and refined in larger-scale studies), using an imperfect sample is decidedly preferable to not conducting the research at all.

Next Steps

Whether the sampling strategy involves recruiting randomly selected participants, snowball sampling, seeking volunteers, or some combination, a good sample contains the core controls and comparisons needed to answer the study questions and develop an explanation for the outcomes. Any thoughtful strategy will involve painstaking efforts not just to find suitable participants but also to clarify the theoretical rationale for interviewing them. Devoting the time and effort to define and find a sample as close to the ideal as possible paves the way for you to make noteworthy discoveries that prompt others to take notice and believe.

Finding an interview sample may be challenging, but it also offers oppor-tunities that working with preexisting data collected by others cannot. Rather than relinquishing key decisions, interviewers retain control over whom to speak with and what to ask. You have the autonomy to tailor the sample to your research goals, even if that means selecting participants who are espe-cially difficult to find. And since your sample need not be large (at least by the standards of survey research), it need not be costly to procure. Even sources that allow the random selection of participants, such as voter registration, polling, and enrollment lists, are often available at little to no cost. Finally, because depth interviewing seeks to discover rather than verify theoretical insights, the depth and breadth of the information it allows you to gather more than offset the limitations of sample size. The only way to take advan-tage of these opportunities, however, is to think through your research goals and decide what kind of sample will enable you to achieve them.

Whatever specific strategy you choose, using theoretical sampling techniques (such as attending to proper controls and comparisons and lim-iting selection bias) clarifies why you have chosen to include each possible interviewee. When the time comes to reach out, knowing who belongs in your target group (and why) makes it easier to confidently ask for everyone's participation and explain to them why it matters.

It is also reassuring to remember that your initial sampling decisions need not be set in stone. If early findings suggest a need to expand or tweak the scope of your sample or if later findings make it advisable to increase the size (and both of these events have happened to us), you will be able to modify your sample accordingly. Starting with a carefully developed sam-pling strategy is, nonetheless, unequivocally the best place to begin. Not only will this forethought point the way to finding a good sample, but it will smooth your transition to one of the crucial next steps: explaining to poten-tial interviewees why their participation is important and worthwhile.

4

Constructing an Interview Guide

Creating a Flexible Structure

A successful interview (and series of interviews) depends on first designing a thoughtful interview guide or questionnaire.[1] For those who doubt the value of creating a structure for the interview process, it may be tempting to conclude that a formal guide is unnecessary and may even obstruct the interview process. Yet the alternative—such as striking up an unstructured conversation and waiting to see what happens—lacks procedures for evoking meaningful responses, fully covering all areas you deem important, and collecting comparable information across the interviews. A well-developed guide ensures that each area of interest will receive the coverage it needs and that it will do so for every participant. Equally important, the forethought that goes into constructing an interview guide forces you to decide what information is crucial, what is useful but discretionary, and what is not useful or irrelevant. And finally, if paradoxically, when the time comes to conduct the interviews, prior design makes it easier to recognize when important new lines of inquiry emerge that take the interview in unplanned directions.

Imposing Rigor While Protecting Participants

Constructing and using an interview guide allows interviewers to impose rigor on a process that can seem (and all too easily becomes) haphazard while also protecting the privacy of interviewees. To take an example, Alice Goffman's ethnographic account of the daily lives of a group of young African American men living in a poor inner-city neighborhood, reported in her book *On the Run*, received both high praise and high-profile suspicion.[2] Critics such as Steven Lubet, a Northwestern University law professor, and Philip Cohen, a sociologist who oversees a popular blog called *Family Inequality*, have questioned the accuracy and even the veracity of important details.[3] Though difficult for those involved, this controversy brings attention

The Science and Art of Interviewing. Kathleen Gerson and Sarah Damaske, Oxford University Press (2021). © Oxford University Press. DOI: 10.1093/oso/9780199324286.001.0001

to an important tension in the conduct of qualitative research: how can researchers reassure skeptics that their findings are accurate and their analysis valid while also respecting participants' right to privacy?

Some ethnographers have suggested that the best answer is to provide full disclosure, including identifying not only the research sites but also the individual participants. This call has emerged as well in the fields of psychology and management, where concern is rising about a "replication crisis" in experimental designs.[4] Yet even if institutional review boards (IRBs) did not require confidentiality, it is far from clear that sacrificing confidentiality would, in itself, offer much additional assurance about the accuracy of ethnographers' descriptions or the trustworthiness of interviewers' findings. As management scholars Michael Pratt, Sarah Kaplan, and Richard Whittington point out, these debates conflate transparency with research soundness and credibility.[5] Requiring full disclosure of the identity of interview participants offers few benefits while raising the risk of doing unnecessary harm to the participants' lives and the quality of research (especially if it discourages participation, undermines trust, and dampens forthrightness). There is, instead, the need for a broader discussion about how to establish trustworthiness in all types of research settings, including ethnography, where researchers craft field notes that represent a written account of their personal impressions.

Providing confidentiality is crucial—even essential—to creating the trust, openness, and safety needed to recruit and interview participants. Moreover, if a researcher did not intend to maintain confidentiality, many institutions might refuse to grant access to research sites or research participants, and most university institutional review boards would refuse to grant permission to conduct research. Interviews often capture deeply personal information about participants that we have ethical obligations to protect from public consumption.

For all these reasons, we believe making confidential information public risks substantial harm without demonstrably adding rigor to the research process.[6] Instead, by building rigor into the process of data collection, a well-developed interview guide can instill confidence in your interview findings while also protecting confidential information and upholding other ethical standards. Constructing such a guide thus lays the foundation for supporting your evidentiary claims. Collecting comparable information across multiple interviews, for example, allows you to find, measure, and describe patterns (as well as detect departures from expected patterns) that make your evidence more convincing. Providing a clear explanation of how you collected and analyzed this evidence further signals that readers can trust your data.

The framework of a structured questionnaire also helps your interviewees understand what you want to know so that they can provide the pertinent information. Although a free-flowing conversation has appeal, interviewees cannot provide the information you seek unless they (and you) know what that is. This does *not* mean telegraphing or even hinting at the answers, but it *does* mean knowing what questions to ask and when to ask them. Participants need—and a questionnaire offers—a road map that focuses their thoughts and directs their journey.

While a depth interview needs to be organized and systematic, it is also not a rigid set of questions, always to be asked the same way and in the same order. Rather than posing identically worded questions with predetermined answer categories, interviewing provides room to revise your questions and probe in new directions if the original wording or order does not reliably evoke the information you seek. Especially during the pre-test interviews, we do not yet know exactly which questions to ask, how to ask them, or what range of answers to expect. Indeed, one major goal of pre-test interviews is to ascertain what the right questions *are* and how best to phrase them. Even during the early interview phase, you will find new avenues to explore, new questions to add, and some questions to discard as less useful than anticipated.

The interview guide needs to be supple enough to discover serendipitous findings and follow where they lead, but it should not be so haphazard that each subsequent interview is an uncertain journey. A good questionnaire has enough structure to guide the interview experience, yet enough flexi-bility to allow you (and the interviewee) to reach new insights. It is always a challenge to construct the right balance between structure and flexibility.[7] Yet, paradoxically, structure and flexibility are inextricably connected. Your open-ended questions must be able to lead you in unexpected directions, but you have to know what to expect in order to notice that a finding *is* un-expected. For all these reasons, thinking through the content and structure of your interview guide is as essential as developing the core questions and finding a good sample. Put in more abstract terms, this process involves first proceeding deductively—that is, by developing a set of abstract concepts and categories to guide the construction of concrete questions. These con-crete questions, linked in an organized format, form the basis for proceeding inductively—that is, using the interview answers to develop new concepts and explore the relationships between them.

Developing Analytic Concepts and Categories

The first step in constructing an interview guide is to translate your study's central questions—and the full range of factors that might provide answers to them—into down-to-earth queries that make sense to the interviewees. This process starts by asking several questions: What are the core concepts and ideas I wish to measure? What kind of information—such as a person's experiences, actions, perceptions, emotional states, and plans—can best concretize these abstract categories? And what strategy will enable and motivate people to provide useful information? Addressing these challenges involves thinking through the relevant theoretical debates and assessing the current state of empirical knowledge, which in turn will point you toward the outcomes and possible explanatory factors you wish to measure. Assembling this overview sets the stage for identifying the necessary questions, developing wording for each, and organizing them into a sequence that promotes a good conversational flow.

You may be tempted, particularly at the outset, to take a shotgun approach and ask every question you think might be relevant. Yet this is neither practical nor analytically viable. Whatever the topic, the range of possible questions will always outstrip the time you have available to ask them or to analyze the answers. Prioritizing the essential information (and deciding what is peripheral) will allow you to impose order. Just as taking a photograph requires choosing what to focus on, constructing a questionnaire requires deciding what belongs at the center, what belongs at the periphery, and what does not belong in the frame at all.

Although an admittedly difficult task at such an early stage, your best approach is to specify the core variables, including the outcomes (the dependent variables) and the range of factors, forces, and processes that potentially affect them (the possible independent and intervening variables). It may seem antithetical to the wide-ranging, exploratory character of qualitatively oriented research to use technical terms such as "independent variable," "intervening variable," and "dependent variable"—the lingua franca of quantitative analysis. Yet even if these terms do not appeal to your sense of what qualitative research involves, the underlying principles are just as fundamental in interviewing as they are in most other research methods. They remind us to pay attention to the logic of the analysis we wish to pursue. Thinking systematically about factors, processes, mechanisms, relationships, and outcomes will enhance your ability to provide rich descriptions of important social phenomena and then develop nuanced explanations of how and why these outcomes come to be and take various forms in different social contexts.

For those who worry that this prior analytic work might unnecessarily narrow your focus, impose too much structure on the interviews, or foreclose the discovery of new findings and insights, we repeat what we have already argued: conceptual thinking at the outset will increase your chances of identifying unexpected findings and crafting innovative explanations. Everyone carries their own implicit assumptions into the field. If left unexamined, your biases, hunches, and expectations are more likely to stand in the way of recognizing an unanticipated (and perhaps unwanted) result or crafting a new theoretical approach. At some point you will have to reconsider your own presuppositions and those of others. Postponing that work delays the inevitable and will make it more difficult to recognize the theoretical significance of the findings to come.

Beginning at the End

Because interviews have a linear structure, your natural inclination may be to start constructing questions in the same way—that is, beginning with the early ones and moving forward in sequence. This approach works well when it is time for you to organize the *order* of questions (as we will discuss shortly), but the process of *formulating* questions works better if you reverse this order. Instead of thinking from left to right, try thinking from right to left by starting at the end—or, at least, near it. This means being clear about the end states you wish to understand, then moving backward to consider the range of various possible antecedents that may help you make sense of them. With this approach, the first task is to specify the outcomes you wish to describe, understand, and ultimately explain, and develop questions to measure them. After doing this, you will be in a better position to do the same for the preceding measures. Interviewers may possess wide discretion about what information to collect, but this freedom also complicates the process of making analytic choices.

Formulating your own questions gives you the opportunity to think outside the box, pursue original lines of inquiry, and create new conceptual categories, but it also requires considerable conceptual forethought along with careful pre-testing to find out if your concepts make sense and your questions work well enough to measure them. Some of the most important questions you need to consider include: What are the key outcomes—or destinations, as we prefer to think of them—that matter to you? What are the factors and mechanisms that you think and/or others have argued shape these outcomes? How will you translate these abstract concepts into effective measures? How will you construct questions that are flexible enough to make sense to a diverse group of interviewees yet are sufficiently standardized to produce comparable answers? These are the challenges to tackle when you construct your interview guide.

Conceiving Outcomes

Developing questions that measure outcomes begins by clarifying the conceptual categories. It pays to take an expansive approach. Depth interviews can explore many dimensions of human experience that other methods may downplay or miss altogether, such as mental processes and complex views that cannot be reduced to multiple-choice options. They can measure the destinations people have reached (at the time of the interview) and the meaning they impart to these destinations. Rather than assuming that behavior and mental states are consistent or that one can measure the other, your interview structure should focus on each as distinct and equally consequential aspects of a person's life.

Tapping these various dimensions requires developing a detailed set of questions that first asks people to describe the behaviors and commitments you wish to explain and then asks a series of follow-up questions that seek to ascertain the meanings people attach to these activities. By asking first about concrete actions and plans and then delving into the ways each person perceives and evaluates these activities, you can explore if and how mental states and actions are linked. Kathleen has found, for example, that people often express preferences that are at odds with the options they face and the choices they make—a finding that casts doubt on the assumption (sometimes explicit and sometimes implicit) in much economic research that behavior serves as a measure of preferences.[8] It also focuses analytic attention on the social and cultural constraints that might prevent people from enacting their preferences.

This is just one example of how building comparisons among various dimensions of a destination into the interview process provides you with the leverage to assess theoretical approaches and develop alternative explanations. An interview's capacity to measure complex, multi-dimensional outcomes makes it important to think carefully about the variety of outcomes—behavioral, emotional, and ideological—you wish to investigate. Constructing the interview guide with these goals in mind sets the stage for addressing theoretical debates and answering theoretical questions.

Identifying Potential Variation

Once you have conceptualized a set of outcomes, it is time to consider the potential range of variation for each. Although it is not likely nor even desirable to know exactly how each outcome will ultimately vary among your interviewees, it is still important to consider the full range of possibilities. If surprises emerge later, so much the better. In the meantime, each outcome must be able to vary in some way to be analytically useful, and the questions you construct need to be able to measure that range.

Given the limits on sample size and the complexity of the information you will collect, it is better to conceive of variation in terms of diverse "types" rather than as a position on a numerical scale. If you wish to study political outlooks by interviewing a hundred people, having more than three or four types of outlooks is likely to leave you with too few cases in at least one category. Yet even given these limits on how to conceive of the range of variation, the richness of the material you will collect makes it possible to develop categories that are more nuanced than a point on a numerical scale. Instead, you can conceive of substantive outcomes in multi-dimensional ways.

In Allison Pugh's study of children's consumption patterns, for example, children are not simply overconsumers or underconsumers, nor are their consumption styles simply a matter of their class position—two dimensions that could easily take the form of a fourfold cross-tabular table.[9] Instead, Pugh finds that children hold on to their dignity by either consuming at rates comparable to their peers, claiming to consume at such rates, or denying the importance of such consumption. By asking questions that focus on the *meaning* of a child's consumption activities in addition to questions about the amount and content of these activities, her analysis can reach far deeper than survey findings about the amount of their consumption.

Returning to the Beginning

After you have thought through the potential outcomes, their possible range of variation, and how to ask questions about them, it is time to construct the rest of the interview. Although this can be a daunting prospect, your efforts to conceptualize outcomes provide you with a good starting point for deciding what additional information you need to gather. Keep in mind that while you are ultimately seeking to discover and describe specific aspects of social life that remain puzzling or poorly understood, the core empirical challenge is to explain how and why they occur. That means asking about the factors that might have contributed to each interviewee's current place in your conceptual typology as well as the processes and mechanisms that led them to that outcome. Now that you've settled on a preliminary set of outcomes, the relevant theoretical terrain is much easier to identify.

Surveying the Theoretical Landscape

After conceptualizing and concretizing your outcomes, the process of conceptualizing how to ask about their antecedents begins. The best place to start is by considering the explanatory approaches that others have brought to bear on the topic. Whether you believe an existing approach is right or wrong, sufficient or incomplete, on the right track or misguided, the only way to establish its usefulness and/or limitations is to include questions that explore how well or poorly that approach explains the outcomes you wish to understand. Considering the limits of contending explanatory approaches also helps you locate what you think the missing elements are likely to be. The structure of your interview guide will then enable you to assess the strengths and inadequacies of existing approaches as you pursue new theoretical avenues that build on, tweak, or replace them.

To take two related examples, Adia Harvey Wingfield and Christine Williams studied the usefulness of Rosabeth Kanter's analysis of the consequences of "tokenism" in organizations.[10] Kanter's landmark study of a large corporation with few women in leadership positions found that being a token created barriers for anyone else to enter an arena dominated by another group. Rather than studying women in men-dominated fields (as Kanter did), Wingfield looked at Blacks in white-dominated professional settings and Williams investigated men who entered fields where women predominate. Both studies were able to explore the uses and limits of Kanter's analysis by asking how tokenism works for other groups. Williams found that men in women-dominated occupations are more likely to benefit from a "glass escalator," while Wingfield found that Black professional men face a mixed package of constraints and opportunities that make them "invisible no more." By incorporating questions that paid serious attention to a prevailing framework, they were able to discover both its staying power and some of its limitations, thereby expanding and specifying the theoretical terrain.

Identifying Possible Explanatory Factors and Processes

After surveying the theoretical landscape, the next step is to create measures for all the factors these theories deem important. If your goal is to understand adult outcomes, relevant theoretical perspectives might include those emphasizing early childhood factors and experiences growing up as well as experiences in adulthood. Your questions need to gather information that might be important in each of these broad areas. The challenge is to identify all the potentially consequential factors while not overcrowding the interview guide with tangential questions that may prevent you from learning what you conclude is most important.

Decisions about the kind of information to collect will depend on the domain of social life that is your focus, whether that is aspects of a person's life, an organization, a social movement, or a government policy. For any conceived outcome, the task is to identify what is relevant for your purposes. Rhacel Parreñas, for example, consulted the wide-ranging research on domestic workers' migration patterns to develop a set of questions about whether workers hoped to stay in the country to which they migrated, planned to migrate somewhere else, or wished to return to their home country.[11] To investigate why and how some dual-income couples relocate in the face of employment insecurity, Elizabeth Whitaker drew on prior research suggesting that when couples consider who should be a family's primary breadwinner, they base their decisions on social expectations in addition to concerns about achieving financial security.[12] These prior findings alerted Whitaker to focus on the potential role of changing gender norms as well as the experience of economic vulnerability in order to understand when and why some middle-class households choose to follow a woman when she finds a new job. Even if only a fraction of the information collected to address the existing literature ultimately turns out to be useful, it isn't possible to know beforehand *which* fraction that will be. It is thus important to include questions that draw on the full range of currently prominent explanations.

Similarly, most studies will include questions about relevant social contexts, events, experiences, outlooks, and action strategies at other life stages, including the present one. It is thus wise to gather information on the full range of influences that you and others may presume to be consequential so you can adjudicate among them and make comparisons with your own explanation. To the extent that time allows, it is better to err on the side of learning too much rather than too little. An inclusive approach ensures that you will be able to develop and defend your argument and make a case for its value in comparison to those proposed by others.

Theorizing Links and Relationships

Once you have thought through possible outcomes, considered how they might vary, and surveyed the range of approaches to explain them, the next step is to ask how all of these concepts might be linked. Do your outcomes of interest interact, and if so, how might they be connected? What form might the potential relationship among them take? What links—or lack thereof—do you expect to find between the factors that various theories single out as important and the outcomes you wish to explain? When the research question is "big," it will likely contain many subquestions. An outcome in one part of your analysis may, for example, become a starting point for another portion. We often focus first on the circumstances, processes, and paths that lead to various outcomes (such as life commitments to paid work, intimate relationships, and children) and then on the consequences of these outcomes for other aspects of a person's social and personal life (such as political ideologies, plans for the future, and the strategies people construct to cope with the difficulties their current circumstances pose).

This is also a good time to pause and consider the timing and placement of your questions. The process of learning about the factors, processes, and paths that lead to an outcome involves asking questions about "what," "when," "where," "who," and "why." It is generally best to ask these questions in that order, so that interviewees can provide the concrete details of an event or experience before moving on to more speculative questions, such as why the interviewee thinks this event occurred, how they responded, and what consequences the experience had for their lives. Collecting reliable information about specific events and experiences takes careful questioning—another good reason to develop a thoughtful interview guide. The good news is that most interviewees are able and willing to accurately depict personally meaningful experiences, even if they took place a long time ago. As James Comey, a former FBI director, once put it, "Agents know that time has very little to do with memory. They know every married person remembers the weather on their wedding day, no matter how long ago. Significance drives memory."[13]

Once people tell you *what* happened, the stage is set to delve into broader aspects of meaning-making, such as *why* they responded in a certain way, and what consequences the experience had for their life. Answers to questions that seek to learn details about "what," "when," "where," and "who" may form a narrative structure, as life events take place in a sequence, but these questions ask interviewees to describe rather than interpret that narrative. After participants answer a "why" question, they have committed to an account they may feel reluctant to modify or overturn. We thus recommend nesting questions to focus first on ascertaining what happened and then following up with questions that seek interviewees' thoughts on why this happened and what consequences it held for them. By encouraging participants to provide descriptions before offering more subjective information, this format minimizes the chances an interpretive account will unduly influence the depiction of factual details.[14]

For similar reasons, it is also advisable to leave questions that ask people to speculate about the future or express opinions about controversial issues to the later portions of the interview. It is fine for people to offer information of this sort spontaneously in earlier sections, but if they don't, it is better to wait. Since the beliefs and opinions people hold may conflict with their self-image and daily practices, by placing such questions toward the end of the interview you will minimize the chances that interviewees will shape their accounts of the past to conform to their current outlooks.

After clarifying your central concepts and substantive areas, it may help to compile a list of all the information you now wish to collect. Creating this kind of list may reveal areas you have omitted; once compiled, it can guide the process of constructing questions and pulling them together into a coherent and comprehensive whole.

From Concepts to Measures

The time has come to construct your questions and link them together so that each participant can understand your phrasing and format. This means deciding how to word questions, how to sequence questions and their appropriate follow-ups and probes, and how to weave clusters of questions into an organized interview process.

Wording Questions

The wording of questions is crucial for a number of reasons. First, the questions need to make sense to the interviewee. Just as important, if less obvious, is that the wording should help establish trust and create a collaborative atmosphere. And to avoid biasing the findings, the questions need to be neutral. They should allow for any and all logically possible responses. They should never convey a value judgment from you or signal that they have "right" or "wrong" answers.

Any question can meet some of these criteria and fail to meet others. Surveys often face such trade-offs because the questions need to be simple, be uniform, and contain a limited range of answer categories. This can be seen in the examples of questions on the General Social Survey (GSS). To measure attitudes toward women's employment, these questions ask people whether they strongly agree, agree, disagree, or strongly disagree with the following statements:[15]

- A preschool child is likely to suffer if his or her mother works.
- It is much better for everyone involved if the man is the achiever outside the home and the woman takes care of the home and family.
- A working mother can establish just as warm and secure a relationship with her children as a mother who does not work.

These questions have clear and straightforward wording, but giving a respondent the option to either agree or disagree (whether strongly or less strongly) does not allow them to express a more nuanced view. Perhaps more problematic, the phrasing of each question presents only one view, with the first two stressing potential disadvantages when mothers hold paid jobs or households adopt nontraditional gender arrangements. The respondent must disagree with these statements to express a more progressive view.[16]

Depth interviewing invites a more thorough discussion of the complexities and contradictions in people's experiences, actions, and opinions. Rather than presupposing the answer categories, interviews ask open-ended questions that let all possible answers emerge, including many that the researcher could not have predicted or even imagined before the interviewee expresses them. Evoking full, honest, and insightful disclosure, however, requires you to phrase questions so that they do not signal "right" or "wrong" answers or suggest that you find some answers more acceptable than others. The wording and expression of a question must put personal opinions aside and convey genuine curiosity about how your interviewees, who have different life experiences, perceive the world and account for their actions. Consider how you could reformulate the standard survey question presented earlier:

- Do you have an opinion about how women and men divide paid work and taking care of things inside the home? For example, do you think it is better for one partner to work outside the home and the other to care for the home and family, or is it better for couples to share equally, or is there another arrangement that you think is better?
- FOLLOW UPS:[17] Why do you say that? Have you always held these views, or have your views changed over the years? When do you think they [changed/stayed the same]? What happened to change your mind?

Note that these questions replace an "agree or disagree" format with one that presents a range of possible answers and invites respondents to consider where their own views fall on this spectrum. This format also includes follow-up questions that ask people to think about the reasons for their views today, how those views did or did not evolve, and the experiences that contributed to shaping them. They provide a window into the ways people arrive at their positions, and they invite people to think more intently about why they believe what they do.

By rejecting "either/or" response categories in favor of seeking more complicated and diverse responses, open-ended questions can help us to develop more sophisticated survey questions. Building on findings from qualitative interviews, David Pedulla and Sarah Thébaud constructed questions for a vignette survey that found Americans are more likely to prefer egalitarian gender arrangements when they are told that childcare and parental leaves will be available.[18] Similarly, Kathleen worked with Jerry Jacobs to develop vignette questions that substituted more supple measures (gleaned to some extent from Kathleen's interviews) for the "agree or disagree" format used by the GSS. These new measures found that Americans' support for employed mothers and caretaking fathers depends more on whether the parent has a satisfying job and good childcare than on the gender of the parent.[19] The large sample sizes of surveys make it difficult to pose questions with a wide range of possible answers, to encourage open discussion, or to take account of the differing ways people interpret a question's wording and format. Depth interviews can and should strive to do all three. When they do, they can make discoveries that also contribute to constructing better survey questions.

Interviews, unlike surveys, also allow you to alter the question wording if and when circumstances warrant. Sticking to a pre-set wording for everyone can actually undermine the goal of receiving comparable answers among interviewees. Especially when your sample varies by class, race, ethnicity, gender, sexual orientation, or some other socially consequential criterion, your question wording needs to be sensitive to their differences. Accordingly, the phrasing of your questions should be flexible enough to adapt as needed to each participant's linguistic and cultural style.

It is also essential to create a space—literally and figuratively—where interviewees feel free to say they do not understand your question or believe that you have misunderstood their answer. Julie Bettie warns that ethnographic "subjects are not empowered to talk back."[20] Carefully conducted interviews should provide participants with the opportunity to express disagreement and discomfort, but they may be reluctant to do so if they do not feel empowered in the interview situation. Those who perceive the existence of a significant social difference or status inequality between the two of you may resist speaking up when a question seems puzzling or especially sensitive. Those who feel, in Nadirah Farah Foley's words, "marginalized by racism and/or sexism" may perceive a greater power imbalance, creating an even wider gulf.[21] An important way to encourage participants to express any concerns they may harbor and to do so in their own words is to adapt your questions to better fit the specifics of each interview. This responsiveness helps participants see themselves as collaborators rather than as subjects or outsiders—a major reason we conceive of interviewees as "participants" rather than "respondents." It may take longer to build rapport and trust and may even require returning to earlier questions after the comfort level improves. Yet rephrasing questions or asking them at a later point does not sacrifice comparability. To the contrary, it recognizes the diverse meanings any specific wording may convey and respects the diverse ways people express comparable views. Each interview creates a unique relationship, and the key is to take the time needed to engage every person's interest, earn their trust, and strive to learn about their social world.

Nested Questions

Interviewing offers varied opportunities to learn how social contexts are linked to individual lives. It can map consequential life events, explore how social arrangements shape personal experiences, investigate how people derive meaning from these experiences and arrive at decisions in response to them, and clarify how people craft life strategies in the short and long runs. The challenge is to construct an interview guide that explores all of these possibilities. A good way to do so is to compose a series of nested questions that tap the various dimensions of experience, perception, and reaction in an orderly fashion: first by asking about what happened, and then by following up with questions that dig deeper into the significance, meaning, and consequences of these events.[22] Another way to think about this process is that clustering questions to move from the most concrete (or, if you prefer, objective) to the increasingly abstract (or subjective) is an effective strategy for eliciting information that is both factually accurate and theoretically significant.

Here is an example of a nested series of questions we have used to gather information about people's job histories and experiences.[23] The questions begin by asking people to describe each of their jobs, including relevant details, and follow up with questions that probe their reactions to these experiences and the consequences for their future choices:

- Can you describe this job? (PROBE: What was your job title? What did you do in that job? About how many hours a week did you work on average? What was your schedule?)

- When did you begin this job? (PROBE: How old were you then?)
- What were your main reasons for taking this job?
- How long did you work at this job? (PROBE: Did your position or your tasks change over time?)
- How did you feel about this job during the time you were employed in it? (PROBE: What were the best aspects? The worst aspects? Did your feelings change from the beginning until the time you left?)
- Why did you leave this job? (PROBE: Was it your choice to leave, or was it someone else's decision? Did you have plans about what you wanted to do next, and if so, what were these plans? Did you consider your future plans at that time a step up, a step down, or a lateral move?)
- How would you say this job experience affected you at the time? (PROBE: Did it change your outlook on yourself or your plans for the future? On what you wanted from a job or the rest of your life? If so, how?)
- Looking back from today, how would you say this job experience influenced you? (PROBE: Does this view differ from the view you had at the time? If so, why?)

While these questions focus on work experiences and career trajectories, you can use the same format for any substantive topic that investigates people's life chances, identities, options, choices, and/or worldviews. The questions move from the most concrete—in this example, asking people about *what* jobs they have held and *when* they held them—to questions seeking progressively more interpretative responses, such as *why* someone left a job, *how* the experience felt to them and affected them, and *what consequences* it held going forward. There is no guarantee that factual details, such as job titles and tasks, will be entirely accurate, and for an unknown number of participants, they probably won't be. Total precision, however, is not the goal. Understanding the overall shape and consequences of an important experience does not depend on the unqualified accuracy or complete description of any one piece of information. Rather, when interviewees give details about past and present experiences, those details serve as an anchor for recalling consequential events and a trigger for taking a closer look at what the events meant to them when they occurred and what longer-term meaning they have today.

You can nest questions for any substantive topic, from highly private ones such as intimate relationships to very public ones such as civic involvement. Doing so for a variety of life arenas can highlight the interactions among them by charting how events in one reverberate in others (such as when a marital breakup affects decisions about work or when a job loss affects the quality of an intimate partnership). Asking how important life events unfold tells you about the events themselves and also gives people the chance to consider how these experiences influenced the shape of their trajectories in other life arenas.[24]

Crafting an Interview Structure

After developing questions for your topic areas, it is time to pull everything together. The challenge is to transform a long list of questions and question clusters into a coherent arc that makes sense to the participants, alerts them to what you want to know, and leads them to ponder matters to which they may not have given much—or any—thought.

From "Variables" to Narratives

People (including researchers) do not experience life as a set of interacting variables or even as part of a broad social trend. Instead, we think about our lives as a sequence of events that unfold over time.[25] This basic insight about human consciousness provides a useful point of departure for constructing an interview guide: chronological ordering is a good organizing principle for structuring depth interviews.

While a temporal arc may not be the right frame for every interview, it offers a worthwhile approach for organizing most. Life history interviews—a structure that asks people to discuss important events and experiences as they have taken place over a temporal arc from the past to the present—are useful for both methodological and analytic reasons. A chronological organization helps participants recall details of both fact and feeling while also providing a framework for analyzing the relationships among events and a person's reactions to them (an analytic strategy we discuss in Chapter 6). In addition to offering a format for studying individual lives, this approach is useful for studying institutional processes, such as tracing how a government agency or business organization creates, implements, and maintains or changes a social policy, or how a major social event unfolds from the situation prior to its occurrence to the factors contributing to it to the various facets of the event itself and then to the myriad consequences in its aftermath.

An interview structure that begins with a baseline and then asks questions that move forward in time gives interviewees an intuitively sensible format that encourages them to retrieve information that might otherwise go unmentioned—including the contextual details surrounding noteworthy experiences and how they reacted to them. It also minimizes the danger that discussing a person's current situation will "contaminate" recollections of the past by producing a false consistency that ignores or downplays life changes.[26]

Consider an example of what can happen when you ask questions temporally rather than in variable clusters. The research on work and family outcomes highlights the importance of work options, marital circumstances, fertility behavior, and internalized beliefs, attitudes, and habits. Yet creating separate sections for each of these areas would not offer much insight into how they interact with each other. To unravel such links, it is better to intersperse questions tapping each cluster topic in time-ordered sections, starting with baselines and then inquiring about ensuing events as they form a chain going forward until ultimately arriving at the present, when you can ask about current circumstances and also visions of the future. Such a format helps interviewees recall each event as it occurred and then probes for the range of contextual factors surrounding it. This structure produces an integrated discussion of the circumstances contributing to an event and the reactions it generated. And because the sequence of open-ended probes is grounded in time, space, and specific circumstances, it helps interviewees unearth relevant details and avoid the clichéd, overly general answers that more abstract questions invite.

At the Start

Since every interviewer needs to build trust, your initial questions should be as welcoming as possible. It's best to begin with simple questions that are easy to answer and demonstrate your genuine interest in the person you're talking with, even if they are not directly pertinent to your larger goals. Such questions can provide useful information and also serve to break the ice. Collecting uncontroversial demographic information such as a list of everyone in a person's household offers participants a chance to talk about their lives in a way that is both straightforward and personal.[27] Here are the questions we generally use to begin the formal interview after completing the initial greetings and introductions:

First, I'd like to just get some basic information or make sure the information I have is correct.
- Your first name is _____, is that right?
- How old were you on your last birthday?
- What is your marital status—are you never married, married, separated, divorced, or widowed? Do you have a live-in relationship?
- How about your work situation—are you are currently employed full-time, employed part-time, not employed, going to school, or something else?
  IF EMPLOYED:
  - What kind of work do you do? About how many hours a week is that?
  IF NOT EMPLOYED:
  - Are you looking for work or on a leave or a layoff from a job?

Now, I'd like to get an idea about who else lives in your household.
- What are the first names of all the other adults who live here?
- Now, how about children? Are there any living with you? What are their first names in order, beginning with the oldest? (Are there any others who don't live with you?)
- Is there anyone else who usually lives here or lives here temporarily, like a roommate, boarder, or relative?

FOR EACH PERSON LISTED, ASK AS NECESSARY (AND RECORD IN TABLE):
- How is _____ related to you?
- What is _____'s gender identity?
- How old was _____ on (his/her/their) last birthday?
IF OVER 16:
- Is _____ married, widowed, divorced, separated, or has (he/she/they) never been married?
- Is _____ employed full-time or part-time? What kind of work does (he/she/they) do?
IF NOT EMPLOYED:
- Is _____ looking for work, on layoff from a job, or going to school?

Establishing Baselines

After completing the introductory section, your next order of business is to gather information that will establish a baseline for pursuing a chronological trajectory on each topic area the interview will explore. We ask interviewees to describe their early outlooks and "habits" (to use the language of Pierre Bourdieu) by thinking back as far as they can remember. Since people differ greatly in terms of how far back their recall extends, these questions need to give everyone the leeway to articulate when and how their baseline orientations emerged. This openness encourages interviewees to consider matters they may never have given much conscious thought to.

Follow-ups and probes help participants clarify the meaning of reflections that may have just come to the surface. Though the differences between follow-ups and probes are subtle, they are worth noting. A follow-up question seeks information that logically flows from the previous question, while a list of probes seeks information that the participant may not have already offered spontaneously. Accordingly, both type of questions are integral to the interview process, but probes are more discretionary. Each helps people move from generalized accounts to concrete details and examples, especially when a response is overly vague or clichéd. As Robert Weiss recommends, techniques such as asking an interviewee to "walk me through that experience" or "give an example of what you mean by that" can gently help people move beyond generalizations to arrive at more fundamental insights.[28]

Here are questions that ascertain baseline views on work and family life, although you can revise them to apply to any substantive area. Notice that the format begins with the most general questions and then moves to more focused ones, striving to phrase each in a neutral way that allows for any response. Equally crucial, each beginning question includes a series of follow-ups and probes.

- Thinking back as far as you can remember, did you have any expectations or hopes for what your life would be like when you grew up? (PROBE: What did you think you would be doing? Why do you think you expected that? How old were you then? How did your outlook compare with your parents' expectations or those of other important people in your life? Were your hopes the same as or different from your expectations? Why?)

FOLLOW UP AS NEEDED:
- What about work? (PROBE: Did you expect to have a paid job or not? Did you have any particular job or occupation in mind? Did you want to work? Did you think you would have to work? Did you think it would be okay to work or not to work? Why?)
- What about intimate relationships? (PROBE: Did you have any expectations or hopes about getting married, cohabiting, or living alone? Did you expect or want to get married or stay single? Did you think it would be okay to stay single, cohabit, or get married? Did you think about a good age for cohabiting or getting married? Any thoughts about what you wanted an intimate partner to be like? Why?)
- Did you have any expectations or hopes about having children? (PROBE: Did you expect or want to have children or not? Did you think it would be okay to have children or to not have them? Did you think about a good age for having children, or how many you would like to have? Why?)
- Did you have any thoughts about whether or not you would like to combine having children with working outside the home? Why?
  IF WOULD LIKE TO COMBINE:
  - Did you think about how you would combine the two?
- All in all, how did your expectations compare with your hopes for the future? (PROBE: Were they similar or different? Why is that?)

This example shows how you can combine, rather than separate, different substantive areas (in this case, work, intimate relationships, childbearing, and childrearing). One section integrates several baselines and focuses on the points of departure for each and the reasons for them. This kind of format turns the attention to how a baseline in one domain may be connected to baselines in others. It encourages people to think about how different aspects of their lives are connected. It provides a framework to learn when, how, and why their early outlooks emerged. It creates a point of departure for charting if, how, and why each interviewee stayed on the original path or changed direction with the passage of time. If your focus is on an institution or social movement, it does the same by charting how an institutional arrangement or social movement developed and/or changed. This format also encourages people to distinguish between their expectations and aspirations, thus fostering a conversation about whether early wishes and aspirations coincided with or diverged from early perceptions about what seemed possible. And, finally, it lays the groundwork for asking later questions about the gap (or lack of a gap) between early aspirations and expectations and people's current circumstances and outlooks on the future.

The numerous follow-ups and probes can be adapted to the unique rhythms of each interview. Some of your interviews may proceed from one question to the next in the prearranged order, while others may require changing, reordering, adding, or even skipping some questions. No two depth interviews are ever exactly alike, and the interview guide needs to be flexible enough to respond to the contingencies of each interaction.

Charting Trajectories

Baseline questions set the stage for you to gather narrative histories for each substantive area.[29] These histories can chart almost any area of experience, including obvious ones such as job, marital, and fertility histories, along with those not commonly considered "events," such as histories of intimate relationships, friendship networks, religious commitments, political activities and orientations, and many more. Outlining a chain of events in one realm also invites the interviewee to explore their connections to other realms. A job history can prompt a discussion of how opportunities and barriers at work influenced personal decisions such as getting married, having a child, or seeking more education, while relationship and fertility histories can elicit insights about how personal circumstances opened or foreclosed job and career options.

Whatever the area of inquiry, applying the principle of sequential ordering will help you gather information about the various dimensions at play—the social opportunities and constraints that contributed to consequential events, the cognitive and emotional reactions these events evoked, and the behavioral responses people devised. To tap these diverse dimensions and explore their connections, the interview guide needs to include a nested set of questions for every topic that matters. These nested clusters build on the chronological format by asking people to describe what happened, the context in which it occurred, how it affected them, and what they did in response. This organization not only helps you gather information about one point in time but also helps you map the processes and mechanisms that link the events both to the social contexts that produce them and to their consequences. An event at one point (for example, losing a job or having a child) emerges from a set of prior conditions and has consequences for an outcome at a future time (deciding to become a parent or to quit a job), and these decisions, in turn, have consequences for future events and actions. These chains of events and actions—linked in a clear time ordering— highlight the connections between structure and agency by focusing on how social contexts shape experiences that then prompt responses that, while agentic, are not necessarily consciously developed or intended.[30]

One useful strategy for helping people recount time-ordered trajectories is to ask about possible points of change. It is easier to recall past moments when life did not proceed as planned. In contrast to ordinary, business-as-usual experiences, such turning points are likely to remain vivid, and you can use these "memory hooks" to help people recount details. As psychiatrist Richard Friedman notes, "Neuroscience research tells us that memories formed under the influence of intense emotion are indelible in the way that memories of a routine day are not."[31] In her study about rearing transgender children, for example, Tey Meadow found that many parents recalled an "epiphany" moment when they suddenly realized that their child might be transgender.[32] These moments brought a host of prior events into focus and helped to explain behavior whose meaning had seemed puzzling.

By asking questions about trajectories and turning points, your interview guide can uncover significant events and place them in the context of seemingly ordinary ones. Kathleen structured the following questions to help her participants describe their family histories and locate any changes in their family arrangements as they grew to adulthood:[33]

- Now, can you describe all the arrangements you lived in growing up and any important changes that occurred up to the time you left home? (IF NEEDED: By "different arrangements," I mean such things as changes in the people living with you, in your parents' relationship, in where you lived, in your parents' work situation, in who was taking care of you, or any other changes you consider important.)
  FOR EACH ARRANGEMENT, ASK:
  - Who lived in the household with you? (PROBE: Does that include everyone?)
  - What were the sources of family income during that time? (PROBE: Who was the main earner or earners? Were there any other income sources, such as another parent, other relatives, the government, or something else?)

- Who was or were responsible for taking care of you? (PROBE: Who did you consider to be your main caretaker or caretakers? What about others, such as another parent, a relative, or a paid caretaker?)
- How old were you when this arrangement started, and how long did it last?
- Compared to other families you knew, did this arrangement seem fairly typical, unusual, or somewhere in-between? (PROBE: Why? How did you feel about that?)
- There are advantages and drawbacks to any family arrangement. Compared to other situations, were there any special drawbacks or advantages to this arrangement? (PROBE: Were there any ways you wished the situation had been different? If so, why? How?)
- In general, did this situation make things better or worse than before or did things stay about the same?
- Did this situation teach you anything about how you wanted to live when you grew up? (PROBE: What did it teach you? How did it affect you or prepare you for the future? Did you want to live the same way or differently? In what ways?)
- Why did it end? What happened next?

GO TO NEXT ARRANGEMENT, AND REPEAT.

This question cluster is flexible enough to make sense to everyone. Whether they grew up in numerous different household arrangements or just one, interviewees can describe their experiences and discuss the consequences. The wording makes no presumptions about the composition of a person's household or whether it changed or remained the same. Nor does it convey any judgment about the worthiness of one arrangement compared to another. The format also facilitates comparisons on a variety of dimensions, from differences in types of family forms to differences in whether a family underwent change.

The distinction between stable and changing trajectories also helps clarify why some people have more to report than others. Without disregarding differences in interactional styles, interviewees who have undergone significant changes are more likely to offer extensive details than are their peers who did not. When nothing has happened to shake up early assumptions and worldviews, people are more likely to "just assume" their life trajectories are "natural" and were predetermined.[34] The relative silence of such "non-changers" may seem frustrating during the course of the interview. These interviews nevertheless assume greater analytic meaning at a later stage, when you are able to compare them with the accounts offered by those who experienced notable change. In the context of the more detailed assessments offered by "changers," these apparently thinner interviews help you decipher the underpinnings of a stable life path or institutional form.

Thinking (and Talking) About the Present

It may seem counterintuitive, but questions about the present can be more difficult to ask and answer than questions about the past. The common assumption is that retrospective reports require a degree of cautious skepticism, whereas discussions about current matters are less problematic.[35] Yet we find that even though people may describe the specifics of their current circumstances with ease, they often have more difficulty speaking with confidence about the *meaning* of present (in contrast to past) events. While they can place the past in perspective, they may have a harder time assessing the significance of actions and circumstances taking place right now—especially if these circumstances involve stressful predicaments, such as a dissatisfying work situation, financial uncertainty, a rocky relationship, or an intractable organizational conflict, to name only a few. Yet these questions likely address your study's most central concerns and are essential to include.

These complications underscore the wisdom of preparing the ground before you delve thoroughly into the present moment. Postponing questions about the present also minimizes any temptation an interviewee might have to "sanitize" the past. If the interview begins by asking about current circumstances and outlooks, the responses may influence subsequent recollections about the past, especially if they are discordant. Even if people are aware of inconsistencies between past and present, they may still wish to avoid appearing inconsistent. In either case, starting with questions as far back as possible and then moving forward—while also taking care to inquire about any twists and turns along the way—will encourage people to tell their story as it happened, without adjusting past events and actions to better align with current circumstances.

With a wide-ranging discussion about the past completed, it should feel relatively seamless to transition to the relevant details about a person's current life circumstances. In this context, posing questions that bring the previously discussed issues into the present and raise new issues that now seem relevant becomes straightforward rather than surprising or discomfiting. Answers to prior questions may also prompt you to adjust the phrasing of current ones. If your questions focus on work, they need to take account of earlier answers about the interviewee's employment history. If the questions are about current relationships, they need to flow from the responses about past ones. Depending on a person's current situation in any life domain, the questions should be comparable, though not necessarily identical, across the interviewees. Kathleen thus routinely sifted people into different categories based on their current work status and then asked comparable questions of each group:

- Okay, so now that we've talked about your past experiences, let's talk about what things are like in your life today, both at work and in your personal life. You said you were (employed full-time/employed part-time/not employed) at the moment, right?
  IF NOT CURRENTLY EMPLOYED FULL-TIME, SKIP TO "NOT EMPLOYED FULL-TIME" SECTION BELOW.
  IF EMPLOYED FULL-TIME:
- What kind of work do you do? (IF NECESSARY: What is your job title or position? What are some of your main duties? What kind of organization do you work for?)
- How long have you been (working at that job/in that line of work)? (SPECIFY YEARS OR MONTHS)
- What are the main reasons you chose that line of work? (IF NECESSARY: Why that job in particular? Did you consider doing something else? Did you consider not working?)
- About how many hours do you usually work in an average week?
- Do you work on a regular schedule, or is it different?
  FOLLOW UPS:
  Is this the schedule you prefer, or would you prefer a different one? What would be your ideal schedule? How much control do you have in deciding when, where, and how much to work?
- If you could arrange things just the way you wanted, what would you prefer to be doing—working at your current job, working at another job, or not working at all? (PROBE: Why do you say that?)
  IF PREFERS DIFFERENT SITUATION:
  - What would you like to be doing instead?
  IF PREFERS CURRENT JOB:
  - What do you like best? Anything you dislike?

- How would you say working affects you—especially your morale and outlook on yourself? (PROBE: Has working affected your feelings about yourself in any way?)
- Different people want different things from paid work. What would you like to get from work? (PROBE FOR IMPORTANCE OF: material rewards [advancement prospects, future security, pay] and intrinsic rewards [self-image, autonomy, social integration, balance with private life].)
- Considering what you thought an ideal situation would be growing up, how does that compare today? What brought about the change? What would an ideal situation look like now?

IF NOT CURRENTLY EMPLOYED OR IF EMPLOYED PART-TIME:
- What are the main reasons you are not working (full-time) right now?
- What do you spend most of your time doing (when you are not on the job)? (PROBE: going to school, looking for work, looking after the [children/house], doing something else)
- On the whole, do you prefer not working (full-time), or would you prefer to be working at a paid job (full-time)? (PROBE: Why do you say that? What are the advantages and drawbacks? What would be your ideal situation? Why?)
- How would your life be different if you had a (full-time) job? (PROBE: Would it change your relationships or affect your morale or feelings about yourself?)
- If you had a paid job, what would you look for? (PROBE FOR IMPORTANCE OF: material rewards [advancement, financial security, pay] and intrinsic rewards [self-image, autonomy, social integration, balance with private life].)
- Is not working important for how you see yourself, or not? (PROBE: How? Why?)
- Compared to what you thought an ideal situation would be growing up, how does that compare today? (PROBE: What brought about the change? What would an ideal situation look like now?)

Having completed questions tailored to each subset of the sample, you can now return to the general questions that apply to everyone. Again, you can use nested questions to tap the multiple dimensions of each participant's current life, inviting all of them to follow up on their concrete descriptions by asking how they feel or think about these situations.[36] Here are examples of questions that everyone can answer, regardless of their work, marital, or parental status. They ask how a range of life domains fit together and whether this fit is satisfying or problematic:

Now, some general questions about how you feel about work, family, leisure, and how they all fit together.
- Thinking about yourself, if you could have things just the way you wanted, what would be your ideal balance? (PROBE FOR BALANCE OF PAID WORK, CAREGIVING, AND PERSONAL PURSUITS: Would you like to make anything a first priority, or would you prefer an equal balance, or is there some other arrangement you would prefer?)
- How does your current situation compare with this ideal balance?
  IF NOT CURRENTLY IDEAL:
  - What do you think are the chances that you will be able to achieve this balance? (PROBE: Why do you say that? What are the obstacles?)
- Now, thinking about yourself and others, how have you arranged things with a partner or with other people? (PROBE: Who [has/will/would] be primarily responsible for earning income, caregiving, or other things?)
- How would you ideally like to arrange things with a partner or with other people? (PROBE: Would it be primarily you as breadwinner and partner as caregiver, primarily you as caregiver and partner as breadwinner, share breadwinning and caregiving, you do it all, or another arrangement?)
- Why (will/do) you divide up the responsibilities this way? (PROBE: Do you see any difficulties or drawbacks to this arrangement? What are they?)
- How does this arrangement compare with the way you were raised or the way other people you know manage things? (PROBE: How do you feel about that?)
- Do you ever feel a conflict between obligations to earn a living and obligations to care for others, whether that is a child, a parent, a friend, or anyone else you feel responsible for?
  IF YES:
  - What are these circumstances? How often does this happen? What do you do? How does that compare with what you feel you should do? With what you would prefer to do?
  IF NO:
  - Why do you think that is? How do you feel about that?

Asking About the Future

A good way to finish the section on current circumstances is to ask about the future, thus beginning your transition to the final and most speculative phases of the interview. Delving into future expectations, hopes, and plans may seem like a separate area of inquiry, but thinking about the future is an integral part of everyday human consciousness. Indeed, the ability to conceive and plan for the future makes human agency possible. As Anthony Giddens argues, the complex, ambiguous, and rapidly changing social contexts of modern life leave people with little option but to engage in some form of purposive thinking, or what he calls "discursive consciousness."[37]

People's views of their future may be speculative, but they are also highly consequential. To the extent they reveal people's aspirations—as well as their beliefs about whether or not these desires are achievable—such views represent important outcomes in themselves. They are also an aspect of what Iddo Tavory calls the "promissory structure of talk," whereby the act of considering future options and actions and then speaking about them becomes a preliminary feature in a process that can involve committing to acts that have yet to occur.[38] For all these reasons, asking about the future is integral to finding out about the present.

Here is an example of a set of questions designed to tap people's outlooks on the future:[39]

- In thinking about the future, what do you think your life *will* be like five or ten years from now? (PROBE: Why do you say that? Have you ever thought about how you would like to be living or to be doing? Can you describe that?)
- How do these expectations compare with what you would *like* your life to be like—is it the same or different from what you *expect* it to be like? (PROBE: What are the differences and/or similarities between your ideals and expectations? Can you think of some examples?)
  FOLLOW UP:
  - What is your best-case scenario? Your worst-case scenario? The most likely scenario?
  - What do you think are the chances of achieving your ideals—high, low, or somewhere in between? (PROBE: Why do you say that? What are the things that might prevent you? Do you see any of these ideals in conflict? Are you taking any steps to achieve any of them?)

- In thinking about your goals for the future, have they changed since you were a child? (PROBE: If yes, how? Why? If not, why not? Why do you think your goals have changed/remained the same?)

Coming to a Close

As your discussion of interviewees' current circumstances and outlooks nears its conclusion, it is time for you to gather any information that may have slipped through the cracks. Although an informal conversation can continue after the formal interview ends, this is a key moment (when the recorder is still turned on) to clarify earlier answers that remain puzzling and give your participants a chance to weigh in on any relevant matters they may not have mentioned. Throughout the interview, but especially when moving from specific to general sections of the interview guide, remember to ask for examples that help to ground and clarify more abstract views. Here are some catchall questions designed to elicit missing information and reconsiderations of earlier comments, along with a set of probes that help people add specificity to what might otherwise remain a vague response:[40]

- Before we finish, I'd like to make sure we've covered all the experiences or people that have been important influences in your life—especially when it comes to (THE TOPIC OF THE STUDY). Is there an experience or person you haven't already mentioned that has had an important influence on your past decisions, current situation, or plans for the future? (PROBE: What kind of influence did this experience/person have? Was it positive, negative, or some combination of both? Can you think of some examples?)
  FOLLOW UP, IF NECESSARY:
  - What about any traumatic or especially good events? (PROBE: Can you think of some examples? How do you think that affected you?)
  - What about people in your life that made a big difference? That you would like to emulate or avoid being like? (PROBE: Can you think of some examples? Who is that? Why do you say that?)

After eliciting your interviewee's general reflections on matters said and unsaid, the coast is finally clear to ask about matters deemed too sensitive, risky, or prejudicial to initiate in a previous section, or to follow up on this information if someone has volunteered or hinted at it without any prompting at an earlier point in the interview process. These areas might include questions about opinions, especially on topics that are highly controversial (such as abortion, divorce, LBGTQ rights, economic redistribution, racial inequality, immigration, and the like) or too implicated in the study's purpose to broach sooner (such as the moral status of other people's life choices).

Next—and last—it is time for you to collect any remaining demographic and related information needed to place the interviews in the context of the overall sample, including details that might be either too sensitive or too off-topic to discuss sooner. These questions might include asking about a participant's ethnic ancestry, religious affiliation, political loyalties, and the like. Since research shows that many people find it even harder to talk about money than about sexual activities, this is the place to ask questions about income, including personal and total family earnings. To avoid creating discomfort by asking for specific numeric amounts, you can provide a card with letters that designate different income categories and ask people to mention or circle the letter that applies (making sure to include many categories at the lower end so people will have sufficient options above the bottom).

Like a cool-down at the end of a workout, this final section should be simple and brief. You can then bring the formal portion of the interview to a conclusion by offering thanks and inviting participants to ask any questions that come to mind. Most will want to know more about the purpose of your study and how you plan to use the interviews. Since your comments can no longer influence the course of the formal interview, it is fine to disclose any personal information you deem appropriate. It is also wise to keep the voice recorder running (as we discuss in Chapter 5), since most participants will continue with a post-interview conversation that often reveals even more details and insights. A post-interview conversation also strengthens your bond and helps keep the lines of communication open should either of you wish to check back in at a later time.

Trade-offs in Interview Design

A good interview design provides a structure for collecting comparable information while also being flexible enough to adapt to the unique flow of each interview. This "structured flexibility" lets you conduct each interview confidently while also remaining attentive to the aha moments when unanticipated discoveries suggest new directions to incorporate into the guide. It allows you to balance questions about the past, the present, and even the future. And it enables you to collect the full range of information you need to answer your core questions, while avoiding a too-lengthy interview that tires the interviewee or cannot be completed within a reasonable period of time. In other words, constructing a good interview guide requires making careful trade-offs between structure and flexibility, comprehensiveness and brevity, and background and foreground. While these goals may seem conflicting, there are a number of ways to tackle them and surmount the apparent limitations.

Structure and Flexibility

Structured flexibility fosters a process that includes asking, listening, probing, following up, and adjusting accordingly. It calls on you to be open to significant findings that are unanticipated and to make changes if they arise. It also means you do not need to know everything that may turn out to be consequential before you enter the field. Indeed, a key asset of interviewing, especially compared to large-scale sample surveys, is your ability to incorporate new questions into the interview when needed as your research proceeds. This nevertheless creates a challenge: how can you achieve comparability among interviews when the questions are not identical? Fortunately, there are several ways to reconcile the need for structure with the need for flexibility.

First, it is important for your early interviews to explore new avenues. The sooner surprising findings emerge, the sooner you can incorporate these insights. Prior interviews may also contain comparable information, even if you did not explicitly ask for it. And, if necessary, you can get back in touch with people who participated in earlier interviews if a topic that emerges later becomes important. Just as comparability does not require asking exactly the same question in exactly the same way, it also does not require collecting exactly the same information from everyone. Interviewing is an exploratory technique, and comparability ultimately depends on reaching the point of saturation, when no new surprises of significance emerge. Your interview guide is a prelude to gathering sufficiently comparable information among a sufficiently large group so that you can later develop core concepts, identify shared patterns, make key comparisons, and muster sufficient evidence to support your conclusions.

Comprehensiveness and Length

An interview guide that covers the full range of potentially consequential factors, processes, and outcomes is likely to be long and complicated. For those who prefer a short list of questions, it can seem daunting and unappealing to construct and use a multi-page document with questions clusters, follow-ups, and probes. This format runs the risk of creating a time-consuming interview that asks so many questions that it tests the patience of your interviewees. Yet you can manage the length of an interview even with a comprehensive guide.

The first challenge is to distinguish between essential questions and optional ones, which you can place at the end of the interview or the end of the appropriate section (with the option to skip them if necessary). It also helps to remember that an interview is a conversation and the purpose of your guide is to facilitate that conversation, not dictate it. In practice, your participants are likely to volunteer much relevant information even before you ask about it. Some will speak so quickly that the time flies by, and others will say a lot with few words. As you grow familiar with your guide—for example, by practicing with volunteers before entering the field—you can transform its complexity and length into an asset rather than a drawback. Ultimately, you are in charge of the guide, rather than it being in charge of you. It is there to remind you of what information you wish to collect, but you can decide how to manage the scope and pace of the interview as you proceed to collect it.

All things considered, the benefits of being comprehensive far outweigh the disadvantages, especially when you consider how much you will miss if you opt for brevity. It takes more time and effort to recruit a participant and set up a meeting than to actually conduct the interview. In our experience, even the most skeptical participants find they enjoy the experience once the interview begins. The length of an interview is elastic; if needed, it can be extended or completed in a follow-up meeting. In the long run, breadth matters more than speed. Since the rationale for interviewing is to delve deeply and range broadly, it would be a lost opportunity if you resist doing so.

Background and Foreground

A comprehensive interview guide includes asking questions about each person's personal background. A temporal ordering clearly helps to identify trajectories that develop over time, but it is valuable even when individual life histories are not the focus of your research. If the purpose is to interview an informant to learn about an organization, you still need to learn enough about each informant's personal history to gauge how and why they arrived at their current perspective on the organization so that you can place their views in this context. Of course, the balance between collecting background information and current views is a matter of judgment. Each interview project is unique, and the guide should be tailored to reflect its distinct goals.

Into the Field

A thoughtful interview guide provides an efficient and effective framework for conducting interviews. In addition to making sure you collect the appropriate information, it also helps you to build trust, create collaborative interactions, and foster a worthwhile experience for both interviewer and interviewee. Notwithstanding all the forethought, the guide is not a fixed set of commands that dictate how each interview will proceed. No matter how much time you spend constructing the initial design, the interview guide will remain a work in progress during the early period of interviewing. As you begin to conduct interviews, you will continue to develop its shape and content. No matter how carefully developed, an interview guide remains a flexible instrument that can continue to take shape as you move from one interview to the next and adapt to the specific conditions of each interview. The silver lining is that, once developed, a good guide sets the stage for coming upon the fruitful surprises that lie ahead once the interviewing begins.

5

Conducting Interviews

Seeking Discoveries That Matter

Now it's time to conduct the interviews, when the challenge of melding structure with flexibility—science with art—takes center stage. No two interviews are identical. Each will have its own rhythm and contain revelations that will require on-the-spot judgments about when (and how) to probe and when to move on. The beginning interviews are especially demanding not only because they launch your fieldwork but also because they will likely yield unanticipated findings that will shape what you do in following interviews.

The need to incorporate surprises into your design as you conduct interviews can be unsettling. Yet you can take some identifiable steps to bring clarity to the process. These include making preparations before entering the field; honing your skills and adjusting your interview schedule in response to what you learn during the early interviews; gathering momentum and establishing a rhythm as you move forward with interviewing; and deciding when you have learned enough and can shift from interviewing to focusing on analyzing and writing about what you have found.

Each interview also requires you to take a series of steps, including creating rapport at the beginning; making sure you use active questioning, attentive listening, and careful probing in the middle stages; and preparing for closure as you near the end. Numerous practical and ethical challenges can arise at any point within each interview and along the path from the first interview to the last. While there is no magic formula for tackling these challenges, you can use certain techniques to manage the uncertainty, bring order to a necessarily unpredictable process, and maintain high ethical standards at every point along the way.

Preparing for the Field

Before entering the field "officially," it is important to pre-test your interview guide and devise a system for recruiting interviewees. Pre-testing enables

The Science and Art of Interviewing. Kathleen Gerson and Sarah Damaske, Oxford University Press (2021). © Oxford University Press. DOI: 10.1093/oso/9780199324286.001.0001

you to troubleshoot before engaging with your study participants and to become more comfortable with conducting interviews. Formulating an effective strategy for contacting potential participants is equally important. While it goes without saying that you need to find willing interviewees, it takes a well-designed procedure to secure a high rate of participation.

Pre-Testing, Practicing, and Troubleshooting

Pre-testing provides you with a chance to try out the interview guide—locating and adjusting any trouble spots and becoming familiar with how your sequence of questions unfolds in practice. By finding any questions or even whole sections that may fall flat, seem confusing, feel awkward, or generally miss the mark, pre-testing will alert you to how the targeted sample groups are likely to respond to the wording of your questions and the flow of the sections in the guide. This is your last—and best—opportunity to revise, reorganize, and generally fine-tune the guide before moving on to the more important terrain of talking with strangers.

Pre-testing also lets you learn about and hone your interviewing style. This less formal context makes it easier to pay attention to your own reactions. The more you learn about when awkward moments may arise and how to manage your emotions, the easier it will be for you to create a safe and inviting atmosphere for participants, especially when you are discussing sensitive issues. By familiarizing you with the questions, practicing will also help you become a more attentive, supportive, and neutral listener.[1]

Since receiving feedback is the goal, it is fine to use your personal contacts to find pre-test volunteers—although it is best to reach beyond your own network. It is also best to seek volunteers who can serve as stand-ins for the various subgroups you plan to target in the sample. Including a representative for each theorized "ideal type" makes it possible to assess how well the interview guide works for each group.[2] Conducting the pre-tests in conditions that mimic a formal interview as much as possible also helps you prepare for the interviews to come.

Although the pre-test is not an official interview, you should try to replicate the formal setting and format as closely as possible. You can start by explaining the research topic (in a general way that does not imply your personal opinion or telegraph too many details about what is to come), the reasons you are soliciting the participant's help, and the hope that they will find the experience worthwhile. Then proceed as if the interview were official. This includes asking for permission to record the conversation, requesting a signature on a consent form if needed, and turning on the recorder (more on this later). Not only does this serve as a dry run for mastering the technical aspects of the process, but it also provides an audio record to review when you complete the interview. Like athletes who learn from game tapes, listening to recorded pre-tests can help you learn about and improve your interviewing skills.

Another benefit of pre-testing is that institutional review boards often do not require advance approval for these "practice" interviews.[3] There is thus no need to hit the pause button while waiting for official approval or to re-submit a previously approved interview guide after using the pre-tests to fine-tune it. If this is your first experience, you might also want to seek feedback by sharing the recordings with a more experienced researcher who can listen and make suggestions about how to sharpen your skills.

In addition to pre-testing, it can be helpful for novice interviewers to gain experience by joining an ongoing interviewing project with a more experienced partner. Sarah often asks graduate students to join one of her interviews (after obtaining permission from the institutional review board and the participant), which gives them a sense of the interview process before embarking on their own research. After conducting several of their own pre-tests, each student first observes an interview that Sarah conducts and then conducts an interview that Sarah observes (again, with appropriate clearance).[4] Participants typically enjoy the prospect of helping a student and may even offer useful additional feedback. Finally, after transcribing the interview, the student reviews the interview with Sarah, and they debrief together. Combining pre-testing with in-the-field collaborative interviews helps newcomers develop skills and confidence, and if the newcomer is part of a research team, the joint interviews build camaraderie and a shared understanding of the research goals.[5] Barbara Risman, for example, describes a similar process in which faculty reviewed at least one transcript completed by a student, providing feedback to ensure greater consistency for a project that included graduate students, undergraduates, and faculty as members of a large research team. The team held "ongoing interview training and weekly meetings to talk about interviews completed."[6]

There are thus various ways to gain experience before beginning a solo project. What's most important is to feel confident that you know your interview guide thoroughly and can focus squarely on each participant rather than struggling to remember the questions you need to ask.

Making Contact

The first task in launching the "official" stage of interviewing is to contact potential interviewees and ask for their participation. This process can be intimidating. Few of us feel comfortable asking people we do not know for a favor. Even the most outgoing person may find it unnerving to reach out to strangers and ask them to share their personal experiences and valuable time, especially when the purpose may seem obscure and even murky. In this era, when most people feel overwhelmed and stretched for time, it has become especially difficult to ask strangers to agree to what is likely to seem an odd request. While the rise of cellphones, email, and social media has lowered the barriers to contacting people, it has paradoxically made it more difficult to get them to respond. We are so inundated with appeals—including many that appear to be scams—that we now suspect requests we might once have met with curiosity and enthusiasm. Simply getting people to answer a call or respond to an email from an unknown source poses a hurdle.[7]

For all these reasons, it takes concerted effort—and a bit of chutzpah—to reach out to potential subjects. Even if the prospect of asking strangers to take the time to meet and discuss personal matters with you may not seem appealing, you can take steps to meet this challenge and succeed. First, get prepared. How you prepare will depend on what you know about potential interviewees and how you plan to contact them. And since the sampling procedure shapes the kind of information you will possess about potential interviewees, it influences the strategy for contacting them. If you have a home or email address you can use, the ideal strategy is to send a personalized, hand-addressed letter or electronic message that introduces and describes the study and lets your potential interviewees know how you chose their name. The letter or message should alert recipients to expect a follow-up phone call or email to answer any questions they have and, if they agree, to set up a time and place to meet. If you lack a usable mailing or email address, social media provide other options for getting in touch and following up.

Appendix A presents introductory letters and other materials that can be used to make initial contact with the people you hope to recruit. A letter of introduction such as one of these can achieve a number of objectives. It can introduces you to the people you hope to interview, establishes your professional credentials, and clarifies the reasons you wish to speak with them. In addition to describing (in very general terms) the purpose of the study and the procedure by which each potential participant's name was chosen, an introductory letter can point to the range of benefits participation offers, including the opportunity to learn about oneself, contribute to a worthwhile project, have an enjoyable experience, and receive a small payment or other reward (if available). Such a letter seeks to provide assurance about your project and to lower understandable skepticism. It also provides an alert to expect a follow-up phone call or message so that people will not be surprised when you reach out to them.

Because this moment marks the beginning of the recruitment process, it is also important to keep a record of every letter sent and every effort made to contact a potential interviewee. It is helpful to use a form (such as those presented in Appendix A) to create a written record of the information needed to track the outcome of each attempt to make contact. This record will guide your recruitment efforts as one proceeds through to the point where it concludes with either a completed interview or a recognition that an interview will not be possible. (Appendix A, endnote 1, presents an example of how to prepare a verbal statement and set of guidelines for introducing yourself and the research when it is not possible to send a letter or email message in advance of meeting a potential interviewee in person.)

Once you have paved the way with an introductory letter, the next step is to reach out directly, ideally through a phone call or email (depending on the available information). Your success rate is likely to be substantially lower than was possible before cellphones, since spam phone calls, caller ID, and the internet have inundated people with intrusive requests and improved our ability to screen calls and ignore the ones from unfamiliar sources. Despite these obstacles, if you approach this task with sufficient enthusiasm and determination, many people will be interested and/or curious enough to answer your call or respond to your email or text. Some may respond to your first effort, while others may require numerous attempts, but sooner or later your persistence will pay off. Even better, those you *do* contact are also more likely to agree to participate.

However you make these initial contacts, you want to be ready to make a compelling case for joining the study. Kathleen keeps this script available to guide these first conversations:

- Hi. May I speak with (NAME), please? (IF INTERVIEWEE IS NOT AVAILABLE, ASK FOR A GOOD TIME TO CALL BACK. IF NECESSARY, EXPLAIN WHO YOU ARE AND WHY YOU'RE CALLING.)
- TO INTERVIEWEE (AND OTHER RELEVANT PARTIES): My name is (NAME) and I'm a (GIVE TITLE AND INSTITUTIONAL AFFILIATION). I'm calling to follow up on a letter I recently sent about participating in a study I am conducting on (TOPIC).
- Did you receive the letter? You may recall that the letter asks for your help by participating in an interview that will give you a chance to talk in depth about your experiences and views on (TOPIC) and other issues that matter to you.

EXPLAIN AS NECESSARY:

- Your name was chosen randomly by a careful scientific procedure, and it's important that we talk with everyone so that we can get an accurate view of all the various outlooks people hold. Others report that they find the interview both fun and interesting, and I'm confident you'll find it worthwhile.
- In addition, I am happy to provide a cash gift of (AMOUNT) as an expression of appreciation for your help. I'm also happy to treat you to a snack or drink at a place of your choosing.
- The interview can take place at any time and place that is most convenient and comfortable for you, whether that is your home, your office, or a restaurant or coffee shop.
- It usually takes about two hours, but the length is hard to predict and is up to you.
- Most of all, everything is completely voluntary and confidential.

AFTER ANSWERING ALL QUESTIONS ABOUT THE STUDY AND THE INTERVIEW:

- Can we set up a convenient time and place for an interview?

IF NOT AVAILABLE IN NEAR FUTURE:

- Since there is no hurry, I am happy to call you back when your schedule looks better. What would be a good time to get back to you?
- If it will help, do you have an email address (and/or cellphone number, if this is a landline) to reach you?

There is no need to follow this script verbatim or even to ask the same questions. The specifics of each conversation will vary and should shape your approach. The key is to convey sincerity, enthusiasm, genuine interest in the person you are contacting, a clear explanation for why their participation is important, and the belief that they will find it worthwhile. Communicating concern for the practical realities of each person's circumstances and making every effort to address these concerns is the best route to dispelling doubt and creating a desire to meet in person.

When Sarah recruited participants for her study of women's paths to work, she found it helpful to say, "I'm doing a study of women's experiences at work and at home and how they feel about working or not working." This phrasing highlights an important aspect of women's lives, but it does not convey a "right" or "wrong" position on the topic. Both the words and tone of your first call (or message) should convey your support and commitment: why you are excited about the research, why it matters to others, why it will be a worthwhile experience, and why everyone has something valuable to contribute.

After introducing yourself and describing the purpose of your research, be prepared to answer a wide range of questions. It helps to put yourself in the "role of the other" and think about how you would react if a stranger approached you with a similar request.[8] Like you, potential participants will want to know what the interview will ask about and why they should agree to take part. Here are some ways to frame your answers to common questions and concerns:

Q: *What will the interview be like, and how long will it last?*
Here the key is to stress the open, free-flowing, and flexible nature of the interview. Without misleading anyone, you can explain that the length depends on how much each person has to say and that they will be in control and can skip any question or stop the interview at any time. You can add that many are surprised to find the interview so enjoyable that they extend it well beyond the time originally planned.

Q: *Since I'm too busy (or unusual in some way), why do you need to interview me?*
If someone reports being too busy, explain that an accurate picture depends on speaking with busy people as well as those who are not. Express your sympathy and understanding, but stress why you wish to hear their story. Without the participation of busy people, it will not be possible to get an accurate picture of how people in a similar situation feel about and cope with

the pressures. It is thus important to learn everyone's story, and especially the stories of those who might not be represented.

We typically say: "I know you're very busy, but if I only speak with people who aren't busy, then I won't understand what everyone's life is like these days or what can be done to help people facing your pressures." This approach lets people know you understand and sympathize with their constraints, while also stressing their importance for the study. By emphasizing each person's unique contribution, you provide a reason for taking the time to meet and let all participants know they are valued.

Q: Why should I do this, and what's in it for me?
You can describe both the personal and social benefits of participating. In addition to providing information that can inform others, the interview is an opportunity to share one's thoughts, learn about oneself, and have one's voice heard. You can point out to skeptics that most people *do* find the interview enjoyable, worthwhile, and fun. If funds are available, you can offer a small gift or monetary incentive (but make sure to check with your IRB about allowable types and amounts of such gifts). Although some worry that providing a payment might be inappropriate, most committees charged with protecting human subjects allow modest amounts that minimize the danger of bribery or coercion. A small payment provides a tangible way to express appreciation and compensate participants for sharing their valuable time—a gesture that is especially appropriate for those who are economically disadvantaged and might otherwise not be well represented.[9]

Q: Is it possible to conduct the interview long distance via a video meeting technology or over the phone?
You can explain that the interview is typically more enjoyable and works better if you meet in person. Offer to meet at a time and place that is most convenient and comfortable for them, whether at home, at a workplace, or in a public place such as a restaurant, diner, or coffeehouse. If funds are available, you can also offer a meal or snack (in addition to any gift mentioned in the letter). When meeting in person is not possible for any reason, an acceptable option is to offer to talk via a computer-assisted video program (such as Zoom, Skype, or Facetime), or if that is not possible, via a phone conversation. It is important to keep in mind, however, that access to technology may differ within your sample; accordingly, do whatever you can to limit how such differences in access shape your sample and findings.

Yet a virtual online meeting or phone conversation is far preferable to for-going an interview altogether, even if it may not duplicate the intimacy of an in-person interaction.

Q: Will the interview be private and confidential?
To assuage any concerns about privacy, you can assure people that every-thing they say will be kept in strictest confidence. This means reporting any findings either in the form of confidential quotes and stories or as part of statistical summaries. Explain that pseudonyms will be used to report any quoted material and, in line with the regulations governing social research, any identifying information will remain confidential. (Later in the chapter, we discuss the importance of maintaining confidentiality and steps you can take to allow research transparency without sacrificing it.)

How you recruit participants depends on what you know about them before making contact, how you feel about the process, and how much skepticism you anticipate encountering. Whatever the difficulties, persistence—along with a bit of creativity—is the key to reaching out.[10] It may take numerous phone calls, made at different times of the day and on both weekdays and weekends, to reach most people. Yet repeated efforts greatly increase your chances of success. Putting in the effort to get in touch not only leads to contacting more people but also demonstrates your commitment, which in turn encourages those who are contacted to agree to participate.[11]

Amid the rapid pace, activity overload, and unwanted media intrusions of twenty-first-century life, even pollsters offering generous monetary incentives find it difficult to achieve the high response rates that were once common. Since depth interviewers have a strong stake in getting people to participate, we can personalize the recruitment effort by stressing our enthusiasm for the topic, conveying a desire to learn about each person's life, and presenting our-selves in personal as well as professional ways. We can also offer maximum flexibility when it comes to scheduling a good time and place to meet, even if that means postponing well into the future. The depth interview offers a chance—for many, a unique one—for people to share their experiences confi-dentially with an interested, sympathetic listener. Considering the constraints and pressures participants are likely to face in their daily lives, perhaps the most heartening takeaway is how many of them agree to participate eagerly and enthusiastically—and, we would add, how many express gratitude for the opportunity when the interview comes to an end.

The Interview Process

Interviews, like lives, follow an identifiable trajectory. From gaining trust to discussing the core issues to reaching a close, each stage poses distinct challenges. The beginning goal is to make a personal connection and establish trust so that the rest of the interview can flow comfortably, effectively, and even enjoyably. The heart of the interview—and the lengthiest stage— is when you ask the core substantive questions and follow where they lead. The final stage requires bringing the interview to a close, taking care to make certain that each interviewee feels satisfied with the experience and ready to finish.

All these different stages require close attention, not just to *what* participants are saying but also to *how* they are saying it. Active listening is integral to building a collaborative process that takes you where each person's responses lead. Creating and maintaining an atmosphere of acceptance, respect, and reciprocity contributes to open, full, and thoughtful disclosure. It is also the right thing to do. Participants are offering you their time and their most personal thoughts. Just as we depend on their generosity, we owe them our appreciation and empathy. From the initial efforts to gain consent to the follow-ups after you complete the interview, carefully building a collaborative process is essential to safeguarding the integrity of the interviewee as well as the interview. It improves the quality of the experience and the outcome, increasing the chances that both of you will feel the effort was worthwhile. It will also leave you looking forward to conducting the next one.

In the Beginning: Building a Collaborative Relationship

Since your goal is to create a conversation between an interested listener and a thoughtful speaker, the first order of business is to establish a sense of comfort and trust so that the collaboration you seek can grow and flourish. Participants, too, will have goals, and those goals may not coincide with yours. Some may have agreed to participate enthusiastically because they want to tell you their story, hear what you have to say, get something off their chest, or receive validation and respect. Others may have agreed begrudgingly or only for free coffee or a gift. Unless they volunteer their reasons, you will not know why participants consent or what they expect to happen. It is possible, nonetheless, to foster an atmosphere that even the most skeptical person learns to enjoy and find valuable.

A number of verbal and nonverbal techniques, some obvious and others subtle, can help set the right mood. How you present yourself—from tone of voice to demeanor to dress—sends powerful signals. Upon arrival, you can start with an upbeat introduction, express thanks to the participant for taking the time to meet with you, and restate the purpose and format of the interview. If the meeting occurs in a public place, make sure the interviewee knows how to recognize you, and arrive early enough to find a sufficiently private spot to converse openly. (More on practical matters, such as what to wear and where to conduct the interview, later in the chapter.) You might also restate your professional status. Since many people are not familiar with categories such as researcher, graduate student, or faculty member, this explanation helps clarify your interests and reasons for the interview—including assurance that you have no ulterior motive, such as a financial incentive or tell-all exposé.

At this point, some participants may ask personal questions, such as your age, family circumstances, or personal views. Since offering such information may influence a person's responses, you will need to balance the need to provide a neutral picture that creates an atmosphere of acceptance with the need to humanize yourself to some degree. As the therapist and author Lori Gottlieb points out, "Not one person I know—well, maybe the very narcissistic—wants to talk to a therapist without a deep inner life, the human equivalent of a brick wall."[12] While interviewers are not therapists, they, too, ask people to participate in a process of intimate sharing and owe participants the courtesy of some self-disclosure. With this in mind, at the interview's start you can offer limited details that do not compromise your credibility or ability to encourage openness, while also explaining you will be happy to answer more questions about yourself at length after the interview is completed.[13]

After the introductions, you can ask for written consent if needed. Unless the research has received an exemption, institutional review boards typically require you to get written consent from all research subjects. Rather than being onerous or inconvenient, however, gaining written consent provides a good opportunity to explain how the interview will proceed and allay any concerns a participant may harbor, particularly regarding confidentiality. Since people have different levels of familiarity with research protocols, this is one more chance to emphasize the voluntary nature of the process, clarify each participant's rights, and demonstrate that you will be a sympathetic and supportive listener. This is also a good time to ask for permission to record the interview. Fortunately, this request rarely prompts a refusal. Very few are likely to express concern, although it is crucial to reassure those who do that they retain the option to turn off the recorder at any time during the interview or to ask that the recording be deleted at a later time.[14] (Later in the chapter, we consider the steps to take when it is not possible to record or the recording equipment fails.)

The First Formal Questions: Building Rapport

You can now begin the interview, starting with the set of easy-to-answer, noncontroversial questions (such as details about people's living and work arrangements) that you selected for your interview guide. Even if you already possess this information, it is useful to confirm its accuracy and ask for any clarifications. From this point forward, you can remain alert to discrepancies between what you wish to know and what your participant shares. If an interviewee appears to misunderstand an early question or provides a vague or incomplete answer, it is fine to clarify or rephrase the question. If, however, someone appears reluctant to pursue a given subject, make a mental note to try again later and move on for the moment. You will have ample time to explore sensitive topics at a later point, and you may short-circuit the interaction by forcing a question too soon.

Building collaboration requires remaining flexible about the timing of questions and their phrasing. As you steer the conversation toward the core questions, you may find that some people refuse to answer a question or focus on only one aspect of it. Keep in mind that part of your job is to learn from what participants do *not* say as well as what they do. These silences may be frustrating, but they can be informative. Such nonresponses tell you what an interviewee either cannot or does not want to discuss. We have found it to be rare that participants completely refuse to discuss a topic— usually they begin with more abstract ideas that require us to follow up with questions that ask for more specific examples and details.[15] Remember also that others will provide answers to the same questions, and the significance of nonresponses will become more apparent when you have conducted enough interviews to compare those who are either unable or unwilling to discuss certain topics with those who offer in-depth responses. (In Chapter 6, we discuss how this kind of analysis can lead to important theoretical insights.)

Building and sustaining a collaborative interaction begins by conveying a supportive, curious, and nonjudgmental tone at the start and maintaining it throughout. Since at least some of your participants may describe actions and views you find upsetting, you may need to make it clear to everyone (including yourself) that your goal is to learn, not to evaluate. We have heard interviewees report all manner of unsavory views and behaviors, including spousal abuse, misogyny, racism, drug dealing, and more. (We consider how to handle the issue of illegal behavior later.) Conveying acceptance and neutrality at the outset sets the standard for the trickier questions to come. It signals that, no matter how sensitive the topic, participants can share information with you that others might consider less than praiseworthy. Your willingness to discuss controversial behavior and views is, accordingly, a sign that you are looking for honest disclosure and there is no need to feel resistant or defensive.

The Heart of the Interview: Asking, Listening, and Following Up

Ideally, interviewing becomes a smoothly flowing conversation that prompts insights for all involved. The degree of insight will vary, of course, with some offering richer and more apparently useful information than others. Yet there is no such thing as either a perfect interview or a wasted one. Your job is to help every participant to offer as much as she or he or they can and then combine them to get a wider view than any single interview can provide. Even interviews that may not seem especially informative will become more meaningful in a comparative context. It is thus important to treat each interview as an integral part of the whole, even if its individual significance is not yet clear.

Judging whether a question hits its mark requires knowing what information you are seeking and listening carefully to decide if your question elicited it. Missing the mark can happen for many reasons and in many ways. Participants may begin to answer and then go off topic. They may not understand the question. They may find the question uncomfortable and prefer to take it in a different direction. Or they may offer a response that surprises you. Each scenario requires a slightly different response.

When people veer off topic, it is best to refrain from interrupting until they finish and you can redirect the discussion back to the original question, perhaps by framing it in a slightly different way while taking care to elicit similar information. If you feel a participant has misinterpreted the question, you can rephrase it and provide more detail. If someone resists answering a question or does so in a way that suggests it is too personal or off-putting, it may not be helpful to pursue it at that time. Insisting on an answer to every question can undermine trust and disrupt the entire interview. Everyone has a right to refuse to disclose information—or, as is more often the case, duck answering a question—and your respect for their position will sow goodwill and leave the door open to return to a similar line of questioning at a later time. Signaling that you do not accept an answer—or wish to interpret it in a different way than intended—is counterproductive on numerous levels. Hearing only what you expect or want to hear conveys disrespect and subverts your goal of making discoveries, thus undermining both the interview process and the quality of the information it provides. Fortunately, the temptation to put words in someone's mouth is more likely to provoke a strong rejection of your words and a stronger declaration of their own. It is your responsibility to treat what people have to say—and how they say it— with respect. There will be ample opportunity at a later time to weigh the theoretical significance of everyone's words.

Interviewees may also offer information before you have posed the relevant question, or they may provide a response that addresses more than the question intended. Because both of us study the connections between public and private life, we frequently confront such situations. When Kathleen begins her interviews by asking people to describe what they do for a living, they frequently launch into a long discussion about job-related matters that the interview guide has placed much later in the interview. Providing relevant information before you ask the question demonstrates that the interviewee is comfortable and has a lot to say. Yet it can also create confusion. The challenge is to decide whether to encourage the conversation when it occurs, even if it is premature, or to suggest a brief postponement until you reach the relevant part of the interview.

There are no hard-and-fast rules about how to respond when people offer information out of order or provide more information than the question asks. Just as an unanticipated traffic jam might prompt a driver to reconsider the best route, you can trust your own judgment at these moments. Your familiarity with the interview guide will give you a clear sense of when a participant is veering off course and inform your reaction. You can decide to steer the interview back on the intended course or, alternatively, "strike when the iron is hot." This need for flexibility and quick thinking is another reason to both pre-test repeatedly and listen carefully.

Probe, Probe, Probe

Depth interviewing is unique precisely because it allows you to go deep. Every question comes with an invitation to delve further, and any answer invites further exploration. Formal questions mark a starting point, but they can and often do lead in unanticipated directions. Probes are thus the heart of the interview process and essential to its success, not departures from your formal questions. The key is to train yourself to recognize and take advantage of them. Effective probing depends on choosing the right follow-up questions and asking them at the right moment. This requires a mix of advance preparation, active listening, and thoughtful reacting.

Although it isn't possible to know in advance exactly when and how to probe, you can prepare. As we discussed in Chapter 4, the interview guide likely already contains sets of nested questions that involve a string of follow-ups. These question sets should move from the most concrete to the increasingly interpretive, from the details of an experience to a description of the social context in which it occurred to its perceived consequences in the short and longer runs. Just as the structure of the interview encourages people to tell their stories from the beginning forward, each question set should also take a sequential form—in this case from the details of a specific event or experience (which anchor memory and provide a point of departure for exploring its significance) to the contexts surrounding the experience (which point to possible explanatory factors) to the reactions these experiences elicited (which tap the meaning attached to each experience and the actions it prompted as a consequence).[16] This structure encourages people to tell their stories in an organized yet open-ended way so that descriptions of events and insights about their meaning flow smoothly.

The prompts listed in your interview guide help anticipate the probes to pursue and also serve as reminders to ask about any important information that does not emerge spontaneously. While relying on listed follow-ups is highly effective, it is only the tip of a much bigger iceberg. These predictable follow-ups also suggest a logic for adding probes on the fly, but the key, as always, is to pay close attention to what the interviewee is saying and use a deft touch when you think asking a follow-up question will elicit valuable information.[17] Such moments can be among the most significant in the interview, for they may raise new questions and challenge prior assumptions. Such surprises call on you to dig deeper for findings that may reorient your analysis. Failing to listen carefully, resisting hearing what you do not wish to know, or moving on without probing at a key point may all cost you the opportunity to develop a game-changing insight.

So how do you listen actively? Of course, you need to prepare sufficiently to recognize when an important or surprising moment arises. And you need to stay alert for them. As James Poniewozik, a *New York Times* reviewer, observed about Matt Lauer's failed attempt to interview Donald Trump during the 2016 presidential race, "There's a difference between an interviewer who has questions and one who has knowledge, and Mr. Lauer illustrated it. He seemed to be plowing through a checklist, not listening in the moment in a way that led to productive follow-ups."[18] A thoughtful interview guide will help you avoid this trap, but you must also be ready to improvise in order to follow up on something important that the guide did not anticipate.

Active listening also calls on us to recognize overly vague, clichéd, or seemingly offhand answers. Open-ended questions can invite what Poniewozik calls "word clouds." Probes that ask for examples and specific details are the only way you can bring these word clouds down to earth. Some questions help people add specificity to their responses: Can you think of an example? Could you walk me through that experience? What was going on in your life when that happened? Can you tell me what you mean by that? What happened next? The goal is to find the question or questions that help each participant get to the heart of the matter.

In his guide to interviewing, Robert Weiss points out that participants tend to be less than fully aware of their emotions and their motivations. Yet this does not mean you should disregard their self-reports. Instead, it is more helpful to treat these statements as likely incomplete.[19] Following Marvin Scott and Stanford Lyman's notion of "accounts," Sarah has found participants create such personal accounts in order to tell the stories of their lives in a way that aligns favorably with their own preferred self-image as well as predominant cultural schemas.[20] Allison Pugh has similarly argued that belief statements are how some participants endeavor to display themselves in an "honorable" light.[21] These accounts offer important information as long as we take care to recognize them and place them in their proper situational context. Careful probing that delves well beyond the surface can unearth the process of constructing personal accounts as well as many other kinds of information that reveal the multiple meanings participants attach to their behaviors. When faced with a word cloud, probing for specific examples and then pursuing their significance encourages precision and also exposes the ways any specific experience can be seen from different angles and used for different purposes.

Staying alert to and following up on incomplete, unexpected, or vague answers gives an interview depth. Probes that explore the meaning of initial answers help people think more deeply and consciously about their experiences. They also help interviewers distinguish between the accounts people give for their actions and beliefs and the more fundamental if less obvious reasons that may explain them. When you ask participants to more thoroughly discuss matters that they have taken for granted, the two of you can work together to uncover nuances that are consequential but have been residing just beneath the surface of consciousness.[22] As Weiss points out, even though people cannot be expected to have a full understanding of their motivations, your careful probing can illuminate them. (And by making comparisons among participants, as we discuss in Chapter 6, it becomes possible to discover patterns that individual interviewees cannot see.) Probes are thus central to making discoveries that not only lead to more powerful arguments but also make the interview a more compelling experience for everyone.

Coming to a Close

Ending an interview can be as challenging as beginning one. More often than not, you have converted a stranger into someone you know well in the space of just a few hours. It can be difficult to say good-bye to this sense of camaraderie. Indeed, the best interviews can be the hardest to finish. People have shared personal confidences, including some they may never have shared with anyone else, and both of you are likely to feel a sense of connection. This may be especially so for difficult interviews that have revealed sensitive matters. It is thus important to anticipate the end and prepare to disengage. This is the last chance for you to gather any missing information, to follow up on important issues that emerged unexpectedly or remain unclear, and to provide reassurance to your interview partner.

If a number of questions remain with time running out, you should alert the interviewee and discuss possible remedies—such as extending the interview a bit longer or scheduling a follow-up meeting at a convenient time. In our experience, very few refuse this request. Most eagerly agree to continue or meet again. On the rare occasion when neither an extension nor another meeting is possible, another option is to arrange a phone or computer-assisted conversation (or another one, if the interview is already taking place long-distance).

Assuming there is enough time to complete the interview, the closing section is a good place to ask if you have missed anything important or if something needs clarification. Once you have no more questions, it is time to invite participants to ask any questions they may have, including questions about the interview, the study, and you. We prefer to ask *what* questions participants have rather than *if* they have questions, which invites them to take the lead in adding any important insights. At a minimum, it creates a space to relax, share further details about the research goals, and receive feedback on the interview experience. If a substantive conversation ensues, it is advisable—and usually fine—to continue recording. Like the proverbial therapy session where a patient offers a crucial bit of information while getting up to leave, it is not unusual for some of your most important findings to emerge after the formal portion of the interview is complete and your interviewee is reflecting on all that has been said.

Bringing the interview to a close can seem like saying farewell to a friend whom you are unlikely to meet again. It is thus important to express your appreciation and (barring concerns) provide contact information in case anyone wishes to get back in touch. Indeed, it is good to encourage a follow-up to report any new thoughts or important life changes. If you have IRB approval to contact participants again, this is also the time to ask if a follow-up would be welcome (and to prepare participants for such a possibility).

After the Interview

After completing the interview, it's good to send a thank-you note, most often via email, to express appreciation, invite updates, and offer to send the results when they are available. Whether or not an interview has been recorded, this is a good time to write up a brief summary, including your impressions of the participant, the setting, the conversation, and any other details that may aid recall when you begin your formal analysis. This written record can include any details that stand out about the person and the locale, any especially important experiences expressed in the interview, and any new substantive or theoretical insights the interview sparked, reinforced, or undermined. We compose such a memo for each interview. (Later in the chapter, we consider how to take detailed notes during the interview in the event you cannot record or the recorder malfunctions.) Writing such memos in the early stages also helps you to think through changes and additions to your interview guide, as well as when to conclude the fieldwork later in the research process.

From One Interview to the Next

Unlike surveys, which can be administered simultaneously, the interviewing process unfolds one interview at a time over an extended period. While ethnographers are likely to hit roadblocks at the beginning when they seek access to a site, that problem typically recedes after they enter the field. Quantitative analysts may also contend with obstacles in the search for appropriate data, but their access problems fade after they find the relevant data. For interviewers, however, each new participant requires another recruitment effort. In this recurrent process, finding the last interviewee can feel as challenging as finding the first. Roadblocks and slowdowns can happen at any point along the way, and it may not be possible to know when or where they will arise.

Each new interview may present a challenge, but it also provides an opportunity to hone your skills and become more comfortable with and confident about the interviewing process. You can create a rhythm by continuing to recruit new participants while conducting interviews with those who have already agreed. Each successfully completed interview produces momentum for the next, even when you encounter detours and delays. At these moments, taking heart in your forward progress and staying focused on reaching your destination will provide the mental boost needed to get there.

Getting Started and Adjusting to Surprises

The early interviews will reveal that some of your questions work better than others and will point you toward making adjustments in the interview guide. You may need to revise some questions and add others. When Sarah began interviewing people about their unemployment experiences, some women reported losing financial control in their households—a finding that prompted her to expand the questions about the management of household finances.

Unanticipated findings can also produce aha moments that reorient theoretical thinking. For Kathleen's research on growing up amid the family and gender revolution, a young man reported living in a stable breadwinner-homemaker household in a prescreening phone interview, but the face-to-face conversation revealed a far more complicated family history when he explained that his home had actually shifted from a traditional structure to a single-parent home to a dual-earner arrangement as his parents separated and then reunited over the course of his childhood. This early—and, at the time, unanticipated—finding not only led Kathleen to add a "family history" section early in the interview but also prompted her to reformulate her core questions and possible range of outcomes. Since prevailing conceptions of families as categorical "types" did not capture the dynamic experiences that most participants were reporting, her research shifted toward conceiving of families as unfolding, potentially nonlinear, pathways that could and often did change as children grew to adulthood. This shift provided her with a new and more analytically powerful way to make sense of her earlier interviews and to refocus her future ones. It also eased the process of moving forward after all the interviews were conducted and the time arrived to systematically compare and analyze them.[23]

These examples have a simple lesson: interviewing requires both deductive and inductive reasoning. You must prepare deductively to enter the field—by framing the questions, considering the range of relevant theoretical approaches, developing a research design, selecting a sample, and constructing an interview guide. Once you begin conducting interviews, however, you need to shift to an inductive approach. This phase invites you to reassess earlier presumptions by moving back and forth between theory and findings, reshaping the line of questioning and the analytic frame in tandem.[24]

Gathering Momentum

Whether or not early findings confirm or undermine your prior assumptions, it is too soon to know if they point to a trend or merely reflect the experiences of your first interviewees. Each finding is provisional until sufficient information is available to distinguish an anecdotal story from a consistent pattern. While early interviews provide fertile ground for finding counterfactuals and making pertinent adjustments, your middle interviews allow for a concentrated focus on the search for patterns.

The key is to create a rhythm and gather momentum. Interweaving contacting potential participants, scheduling meetings, and conducting interviews creates a steadily flowing pipeline. The speed of the flow is less important than creating a tempo that works for you. Moving too quickly can produce physical and emotional burnout. Moving too slowly can be demoralizing and result in missed opportunities to recruit participants who might be eager to talk or introduce you to their networks. We find that doing three to four interviews per week creates a steady tempo with enough time to rest and reflect between interviews. But definitions of "fast" and "slow" are matters of personal taste. The right pace is the one that helps you stay on course without feeling either stalled or burned out.

The middle and later interviews can also produce aha moments where the accumulation of unexpected findings leads you to breakthroughs in orienting questions and theoretical approaches. You can savor these moments if they occur, but do not despair if they do not. Breakthroughs can happen quickly, but they can also take time. They can occur during the process of conducting interviews, but they can also occur after you have completed the interviews and can now see where each fits within the whole. Whether a breakthrough strikes early or involves a gradual rise to consciousness depends as much on when in the research process critical information emerges as it does your cognitive style. In any case, it can be hard to relinquish preconceptions and let the significance of unanticipated findings sink in, but the power of cumulative findings—along with a measure of mental flexibility—will help bring them to awareness eventually.

Deciding When Enough Is Enough

Knowing when and how to make the transition out of the field is a challenging task, especially because there is no strict rule to guide the decision.

Glaser and Strauss (as noted in Chapter 3) recommend leaving the field when you have reached "theoretical saturation," which they define as the point when surprising findings are no longer emerging.[25] In interviewing, this would mean leaving the field when each successive interview yields no new answers. While collecting enough interviews to recognize such patterns is certainly a necessary criterion for leaving the field, it may not be a sufficient one.

It takes time to arrive at saturation, and it's important to resist the temptation to conclude too soon you've arrived at that point. Deciding what constitutes a sufficient number of interviews also rests on factors other than reaching saturation. Even if each new interview fails to offer a new theoretical avenue, it adds support for the findings provided by earlier ones and adds weight to your conclusions. It is thus necessary to interview enough people not only to develop a theoretical argument but also to support it with sufficient evidence.

You will, for example, need enough interviewees in each conceptual category to conduct a convincing analysis. In Kathleen's research on the new economy, some emerging categories (such as "egalitarian couples") may not be as prevalent in the wider population as others (such as "hyper-traditional households").[26] Because it may take longer to gain saturation for a less prevalent group, it is better to continue conducting interviews than to stop before obtaining enough people in every category that appears to be consequential.

Since reaching saturation is an ambiguous goal, it is safer to conduct more interviews than the minimum number that may be needed hypothetically. When each new interview tends to confirm what you have found in the previous ones *and* you have enough cases in each important category to establish patterns convincingly, then it is time to consider leaving the field. To make that decision, you can review your memos and notes from previous interviews and take stock of the overall picture you have captured. If you possess enough information to answer the questions you now wish to pose and convincingly demonstrate their validity, then it is time to move on to a systematic analysis of all the material you have collected.

Ethical Challenges and Conundrums

For interviewers no less than physicians, the first responsibility is to "do no harm."[27] This means interviewers confront some special challenges. How do you reassure skeptical participants that they can trust you, especially if they

are members of groups with good reason to be suspicious? When you interview someone with whom you strongly disagree, how do you manage your
own biases? When an upsetting conversation occurs within an interview,
how do you navigate the sensitive emotional terrain you have entered? How
do you gauge sincerity and truthfulness, especially if a participant seems resistant or disengaged? How do you safeguard their privacy and confidentiality? At least one of these challenges is likely to arise at some point, and
you may encounter far more. Since you can't know in advance when, how, or
how often they will arise, the best preparation is to consider the options for
handling them.

Responding to Skepticism and Social Distance

It is no surprise that people of all stripes are more likely than ever to greet an
interviewer's request with skepticism and resistance. Members of marginalized groups, who are more likely—and rightly so—to perceive a wide social
distance separating them from any researcher, may harbor especially strong
suspicions; worse, such concerns are not unwarranted. It is a challenge under
any circumstances to demonstrate that your research is in the best interest
of the participants, but it is even more difficult when research subjects are
exposed to potential harm. Some of the most notable past cases of harmful
exposure have involved psychological or biological harm—such as the
Stanford prison experiments, when some participants were allowed to bully
and even brutalize others, or the Tuskegee syphilis experiment, when African
American men with syphilis went untreated.[28] Yet qualitative interviewing is
not immune to such dangers. In one infamous study of same-sex encounters
among men who identified as straight, for example, Laud Humphreys used
deceptive practices, first by covertly observing public restrooms to find men
who engaged in these behaviors and then by tracking them down through
their license plates and asking them to participate in an interview without
explaining its purpose.[29]

   For interviewers, not only are deceptive practices of this kind deeply un-
ethical; they are also, in most instances, counterproductive. Only by fully
and honestly explaining your selection process and research purposes (albeit
in generalized terms that do not signal any "right" or "wrong" stances) can
you overcome skepticism *and* safeguard each participant's well-being. This
is why gaining informed consent is a bedrock principle, and even the most

promising study cannot justify the use of deceit. By embracing informed consent (rather than viewing it as a bureaucratic roadblock) and carefully going over the nuances of the written document at the start of each interview, you can lay the first building blocks for establishing trust. This is why we conceive of interviewees not just as respondents, but as *participants* who are willing and fully informed partners in the research process. While few will be familiar with the specific details of deceptive studies, many will wonder about any researcher's motives and methods.

Although it is both an ethical requirement and an effective practice to explain your research goals and commit to an open, respectful interaction, it is equally important to recognize that, by its nature, the structure of the interview process involves a power imbalance. The goal may be to establish a reciprocal relationship, but it is not a symmetrical one. The interviewer controls the flow of the interaction, decides what information to gather, and asks participants to disclose far more information than they receive. Through later analysis and writing, the interviewer also controls how this information is interpreted and shared. Social differences—of race, class, gender, education, and/or ethnicity, to name only a few of the countless ways interviewers and participants may experience social distance—magnify the imbalance inherent in any interview.

In these instances, well-founded concerns about cultural appropriation, stereotyping, and patronizing interactions may make it difficult to recruit interviewees or to conduct a collaborative interview if a potential recruit agrees to participate. An interviewer may also enter the field with preconceptions about the group of interest, especially if this group is subject to marginalization or ill-treatment. Such preconceptions may influence both the questions an interviewer feels comfortable asking and the answers a participant feels comfortable providing. Since any suspicions and biases that interviewers and interviewees bring to their interactions are likely rooted in broad social inequalities and stereotypes it may not be possible to completely overcome them. Yet you can strive to recognize and respond to these challenges in an appropriate manner. Without downplaying the legitimacy of a participant's concerns, you can explain why and how the interview will be a worthwhile experience that respects their autonomy and enables them to explore matters they care about. To do this, of course, you need to have confidence that your project is important in itself and that you will listen openly and carefully to your participants in order to learn from and respectfully portray their voices.

The next challenge is to recognize and grant legitimacy to any skepticism a participant expresses. Instead of ignoring a source of tension or distance, recognizing these moments offers an opportunity to explore their implications and learn important lessons about the social worlds and worldviews of your interviewees. Acknowledging each person's concerns creates an opening to delve further and uncover the concerns people harbor as well as the reasons they harbor them. Rather than viewing skepticism as a roadblock, the key is to follow skepticism where it may lead. In the end, everyone has the right to opt in or opt out, just as everyone who opts in retains the right to decide what they wish to disclose or withhold. Whether you wish to convince a skeptic to participate or dampen suspicion once an interview begins, your belief in the importance of the research and commitment to hearing the story each person has to tell are your most effective tools for addressing any skepticism on the part of your participants as well as for demonstrating respect and safeguarding well-being.

Managing Your Biases

Interviewers need to take particular care to minimize the influence of their own biases—a considerable challenge for most of us. After all, we are likely to harbor strong opinions about the topics we choose to study. It is thus understandably tempting to impose our values on the actions and beliefs expressed by others or to see them the way we expect or would like them to be. While passion has its place—it helps sustain motivation and gives purpose to research—the interview setting is not the place to express it. The interview needs to empower participants to express *their* passion, and this cannot happen if they are exposed to and grappling with our beliefs and stereotypes. While it is not possible to rid ourselves of bias (which would require ridding ourselves of opinions altogether), we can endeavor to become fully conscious of our biases and strive to put them aside, at least temporarily, in order to listen openly, respectfully, and nonjudgmentally to each participant's story, especially when that story conflicts with our own beliefs or values.

Kathleen Blee's study of women who are members of organized racist hate groups and Kristen Luker's research on abortion activists illustrate the analytical payoff for remaining ideologically neutral, even when your interviewees harbor views that clash dramatically with your own.[30] Luker interviewed women on opposing sides of the abortion debate and found that their ideological differences reflected differing family and work commitments. Employed women were more likely to stress the right of women to exercise personal control over their reproductive lives, while domestically oriented mothers tended to believe that motherhood, even when unplanned and unwanted, should take precedence over all other life commitments. Had Luker let her own political views intrude on the interview process, she would not have discovered the reasons for this deep divide among women or so compellingly illuminated why some work actively to rescind an option that others are equally dedicated to preserving. Remaining neutral in the context of the interview provided the only route to learning how and why women with different life experiences came to perceive women's interests in such disparate ways.

In a parallel way, researchers oriented toward social justice concerns may be tempted to avoid seeking disclosures that might portray members of a disadvantaged group in an unfavorable light. Yet avoiding such inconvenient findings runs the risk of gathering a set of highly circumscribed stories that rob interviewees of their agency. In Katherine Newman's study of downwardly mobile workers, *Falling from Grace*, the reader's empathy for the unemployed men she interviewed is not inhibited by the unflattering finding that some took their misery out on their families.[31] Portraying the full range of experiences among these unemployed middle-class men revealed their humanity, including their less-than-edifying reactions to a painful set of events. Seeking purely idealized depictions of those with whom we identify or sympathize, like failing to grant the humanity of those with whom we disagree, relinquishes one of interviewing's greatest strengths—the ability to uncover the dynamic, multi-dimensional links between social structural arrangements and the agentic responses people develop in response to them.

How, then, is it possible to manage our own biases and prevent them from undermining the interview process? We have already discussed some ways to resist bias, such as phrasing questions that offer a full range of acceptable responses, seeking "surprises" that do not support your preconceived ideas, standing back to view each participant's responses in a larger context, and making comparisons to distinguish idiosyncratic findings from general trends. It also helps to keep in mind that you will have the opportunity to take a moral stand at a later stage, after you've had a chance to make your case by placing each interview in the context of the whole and analyzing the patterns across participants' lives. The interview setting, in contrast, is the place to focus on hearing each person's perspective and seeking their reasons for holding it.

In Kathleen's interviews with young adult men for *No Man's Land* (1993), she would hear accounts of actions and opinions that almost anyone would find distasteful. One man explained he could easily replace his girlfriend with another one, just as he could easily replace his car with a newer model. He expressed a view about women and relationships that, although not unusual among some social groups, might not have been stated so candidly had he anticipated disapproval.

You can also take some active steps to reassure participants (and remind yourself) that you are not evaluating them or their statements. Simple follow-up phrases—such as "I understand" or "That's interesting" or "What I hear you saying is . . ."—convey curiosity rather than judgment and give interviewees a chance to explain what they mean. Neutral follow-up questions—such as "Can you say more about that?" or "How do you feel about that?"—invite interviewees to think more deeply about what they believe and why. If the topic is especially sensitive, you can even offer support by making affirmative statements such as "Anything you say is fine." These techniques yield information without passing judgment and help maintain rapport even when tackling highly charged issues and confidences. They also offer the added benefit of giving people a chance to clarify what they are saying.

Conveying acceptance through words, tone, and body language helps foster a satisfying interview experience for everyone. Indeed, interviews with those who hold views that diverge from our own are often the most enlightening. By putting aside personal opinions and giving participants permission to discuss why they act and believe as they do, you do more than grant respect to the interviewee; you also increase the chances of making an important discovery.

Shedding light rather than heat on controversial subjects requires a leap of empathy. This process may be unproblematic when an interviewee shares your concerns or worldviews, but it becomes more complicated when an interviewee describes actions or beliefs you find distasteful. In these instances, it is helpful to make a mental distinction between approval and empathy. You need not endorse an action or belief in order to understand its sources and consequences, but you will likely need to climb over what Arlie Hochschild calls "the empathy wall."[32] In the absence of an empathic stance, the risk increases that you will skew your findings by projecting your own experiences, views, and judgments onto your participants.

Sensitive Questions and Upsetting Conversations

Broaching potentially upsetting and disconcerting issues is common, often unavoidable, and frequently integral to a study's goals. If the research focuses on a clearly sensitive topic, such as Sarah's study of job loss and unemployment, participants will know to be prepared for potentially painful questions. In other instances, apparently less sensitive questions may unexpectedly prompt emotional reactions and revelations, surprising you and perhaps the participant as well. When asking about job or marital histories, we cannot know in advance whether the history people recount is one they see as uplifting or one they find distressing. The participants, in turn, cannot anticipate the questions or know how they will respond. Some may approach the interview as an opportunity to discuss an upsetting experience for the first time. As one of Sarah's interviews neared its close, her interviewee shared what the woman considered to be an exceptionally private secret—that she had recently learned her husband had engaged in numerous affairs and only informed her because he'd contracted HIV and feared she was at risk. Unwilling to disclose her fears and anger to friends or family, she saw the interview as an opportunity to share this information in a confidential setting and relieve some of the burden she had been carrying alone.

Since even the blandest topics can raise sensitive issues, it is not possible to anticipate which questions will evoke the need for special care. Whether such conversations are integral to the topic or tangential, you are called on to convey support, acceptance, sympathy, and respect and to take all possible measures to limit harm. The good news is that it will be easier to delve into sensitive matters—and often more welcome—if you have already established trust and rapport. Being an attentive guide and neutral listener sends the message that the interview is a safe space and prepares the ground for navigating any emotionally charged disclosures that may come, even when they arrive unexpectedly.

It is also important to avoid signaling that one response is more appropriate than another. Rather than presuming to know how participants processed each experience, let them describe their reactions. As we discussed in Chapter 4, each of your questions should offer a full range of options or contain a neutral follow-up. Rather than saying, "That sounds tough," it is better to ask, "How did you feel about that situation?" or "Was that tough or not so much?" If you decide that offering a personal anecdote would be appropriate and helpful to demonstrate understanding, do so with a vague allusion to a similar experience and be careful to withhold details until the interview is completed. Not only does the focus need to remain on the interviewee, but telling your own story runs the risk of implying there is a "correct" way to respond or feel. In the end, every participant has the right to decline discussing painful or embarrassing experiences. While you strive to create a setting that invites full and open disclosure, everyone needs the leeway to decide how much or how little they wish to disclose. This requires striking a delicate balance between probing deeply and respecting each person's boundaries.[33]

In this setting, most will appreciate having a chance to tell their story as they see it. Yet it is never appropriate to exert undue pressure on a participant to divulge information, or to question a person's sincerity. In contrast to empathetic probing, expressing explicit skepticism is more likely to spark defensiveness than elicit useful information. Rather than dismissing an account that seems dubious to you, you can take the opportunity to explore the meaning of and reasons for inconsistencies or omissions. Probing of this kind encourages people to dig for more insight. We have listened as participants discussed drug use, participation in illegal activities, extramarital affairs, domestic abuse (as both perpetrators and victims), alcoholism, abandonment of children, and racist and misogynistic beliefs, to name only a few of the many sensitive issues participants may divulge.[34] Some may disclose these stories in a self-justifying way, but most find a measure of relief in delving more deeply. In either case, the significance of these accounts depends not on their "objective" truth but rather on their role in each person's "construction of [their] reality."[35]

Despite your best efforts, some interviewees will not wish to answer some questions or will try to say what they think you want to hear. Yet this dynamic does not invalidate the information they provide. In the end, every interview has something to offer, and even those who strongly resist full disclosure provide useful material for analysis. You will be able to assess the significance of each person's responses—as well as their nonresponses—at a later time, when they can take their place among the responses of everyone in your sample. The interviewing stage is a time to focus on the answers you receive, not the ones you do not. There will be abundant opportunity going forward to assess the meaning of all the answers and of the silences as well.

Privacy, Confidentiality, and Post-Interview Contact

Privacy and confidentiality are core principles in interview-based research. Respecting these principles serves to protect research subjects, encourage participation, and create a safe environment for open communication. Yet while these precepts may seem obvious, they are not uncontroversial. Colin Jerolmack and Alexandra Murphy argue, for example, that social researchers should opt for transparency rather than privacy. Identifying research participants—or, as they put it, "unmasking"—is crucial to assessing the validity of a researcher's findings and to pursuing replication or disconfirmation of the results.[36] They argue further that some subjects may want to be identified and that even if they do not, masking gives them a false sense of security. Yet there are good reasons to conclude that this argument underestimates the benefits of nondisclosure as well as the risks of disclosure. Some studies involve interviewing people—for example, undocumented immigrants, or minorities who fear policing in a racially polarized setting—who are navigating highly charged and even dangerous social or political environments. Fraught contexts like these call on us to conceal the identity of participants not just to protect their safety but also to create an environment in which they feel safe enough to discuss the issues you wish to understand.

Regulations requiring confidentiality were developed to address the dangers posed by research practices that fail to shield human subjects from the potentially harmful consequences, anticipated and unanticipated, of not protecting their privacy and confidentiality.[37] As for the purported benefits of unmasking, Michael Pratt and his colleagues point out that "transparency advocates conflate replication with trustworthiness."[38] We would add that there are safer and more effective ways to enable replicability. The key is not to provide identifying information about each participant but rather to make clear arguments and present your results so that others can test them with different samples in other research settings.

On matters of privacy and confidentiality, it is also useful to distinguish between interviewing and ethnography. Ethnographers—especially those who observe legally or ethically dubious as well as manifestly dangerous activities—can and often do grapple with complicated choices about what activities to participate in and whether they need to disclose actions that might endanger their subjects or others. Since interviewers do not observe or participate in the activities they investigate, however, there may be less reason for concern about the possibility we could be asked to provide our memos, notes, or transcripts. Yet interviewers can take further steps to maintain confidentiality by creating secure records, using pseudonyms or ID numbers, and disguising potentially identifying personal details. These practices provide protection and enhance the interview process without sacrificing the information needed to build and test your arguments. These practices create a safe space where participants can discuss a range of matters, however dubious or traumatic, without putting themselves or others (including you) at risk.

Even when we agree that confidentiality is a necessary ethical and practical principle, some circumstances may test your ability to maintain it. If the interviews take place in a large city, where the chances of meeting unexpectedly are low, preserving confidentiality may be straightforward. If the locale is a rural or suburban area in which you both reside, however, you may want to ask participants how they would like to handle a future chance meeting that might include others. Do they wish to acknowledge a prior relationship? And if they are comfortable saying hello, would they prefer to describe the relationship in ways that do or do not include the interview?

A contrasting challenge can arise if an interviewee wishes to continue the relationship after the interview. The interview experience can be moving, and some may wish to extend involvement by staying in touch. Meeting again for a brief follow-up can be helpful, and it is certainly good to encourage people to get back in touch if they have new information to share. If the request suggests an explicit or implicit desire for tangible help, however, it is advisable to set clear boundaries. Researchers are neither trained nor qualified to perform therapeutic services. Instead, you can respond supportively by suggesting alternative options, such as a counseling center or other appropriate service provider that can better meet a person's needs.[39]

Where to Interview

The ideal interview location offers privacy, comfort (including a sense of safety), and the chance to talk for as long as necessary. It is difficult to maximize all of these criteria simultaneously. An interviewee's home is likely to offer comfort, but its degree of privacy depends on whether others are present. Public places like a restaurant or coffeehouse are neutral territory, but they may not offer a private spot for lengthy conversation. An office may be convenient, but it, too, may invite interruptions from co-workers and others. If it is your own office, the location may reinforce status differences that you wish to downplay. While it can be more challenging to foster an open, free-flowing, and intimate atmosphere using online video technology or the telephone, circumstances may make these the only options. Since every setting involves trade-offs, let's consider the options.

Meeting In Person

Whether the setting is private or public, meeting in person is the gold standard of interviewing.[40] Home is the most convenient and comfortable setting for many, although a substantial group will prefer their office or a local coffeehouse or restaurant. Meeting in a person's home has the added advantage of offering a glimpse into domestic details that can inform the interview, but it can also create challenges. Curious partners, parents, children, and friends may hover nearby, inhibiting full disclosure and interrupting to answer questions or comment on the original answers. Scheduling a time when others are less likely to be present or require attention helps minimize these disadvantages but may not always be possible. If the presence of others proves unavoidable, ask to settle in a space that is as private as possible and then focus on the interviewee and politely redirect questions if anyone else wishes to join. In any case, it is often a good strategy to pause briefly so that the participant can attend to a child or other household member, greet an unexpected guest, or take a break of any kind. Even when complete privacy is not possible, you can glean additional information by observing the interactions that take place with those who are nearby.

Another option is to meet at a workplace. Like home, a participant's office may provide a private space and an opportunity to observe details (in this case, about the work environment), but here, too, it can be difficult to establish privacy and create a relaxed atmosphere. Nearby co-workers or bosses may constrain what participants feel they can say as well as how much time they feel comfortable spending with you. In these instances, it helps to clarify the interview structure in advance and arrange to meet when and where work activity is likely to be at a minimum, such as at the end of the workday or in a room that affords separation. Conducting interviews in your own office, if it is private, offers more control (although it is wise to remove any objects—such as political posters or personal photos—that might undermine a neutral presentation of self).

An increasingly popular alternative is a local restaurant or coffeehouse. Whether working on a laptop or hanging out with friends, many routinely spend long hours in these public spaces and feel more comfortable conversing there than at home or in the office. Public spaces of this sort can also nurture a sense of meeting a "stranger on a train," where conversation can seem outside the bounds of "normal" life. The key in these settings is to find a spot that affords sufficient privacy, is not too noisy to converse or record, and invites settling in for as long as needed.

Trade-offs aside, the best location for one interviewee may be the worst for another. Letting each of your participants choose the time and place to meet is integral to offering a sense of control and setting the stage for a collaborative partnership. We routinely conduct in-person interviews in the full range of these settings. Since there is no one-size-fits-all choice that works for everyone, the best location for an interview is the one each participant prefers.

Beyond In-Person: Online and Phone Interviews

The rise of sophisticated web-based online technologies for conducting meetings and other interactions as well as the explosion of cellphone capacities has greatly expanded the options and potential geographic range for depth interviewers, making it possible (in theory) to interview anyone anywhere and under a wide range of circumstances. Although in-person meetings remain the first choice for conducting interviews, a long-distance format is preferable to no meeting at all, especially when conditions make it unfeasible or impossible to conduct an interview in any other way. The rise of remote work arrangements, as well as the 2020 pandemic-triggered stay-in-place orders that left people confined to their homes, has highlighted the ways that video-enabled and, to a lesser extent, phone interviews can stand in for in-person meetings. The increasing use of virtual technologies in both ordinary and extraordinary times has thus greatly enhanced the comfort level that researchers and many participants bring to a technology-enabled, long-distance interview.

Of course, online and phone interviews, even at their best, can only approximate the intimacy that in-person meetings make possible. Virtual meetings, where we see faces on a screen, cannot convey the subtleties of eye contact and body language that are important elements in the process of conveying emotion and building trust. The verbal interactions that take place on virtual platforms also take on a somewhat different dynamic. Cross-talk can become more problematic, even when it involves brief reactions intended to convey support. The silences that encourage deep reflection may also become more difficult to sustain without the comfort that comes with occupying the same physical space. Even aspects of in-person interviews that we often take for granted, such as taking breaks or relaxing with a cup of coffee or tea, are greatly attenuated in a long-distance setting. Phone conversations, moreover, lack any of the body cues and facial expressions that a video arrangement as well as an in-person interview may allow.

Relying on computer-aided technologies also raises concerns about how to maintain privacy and confidentiality. It is important to consult your institutional review board and IT professionals to confirm that the use of any chosen online technology abides by all human subject confidentiality requirements. The process of setting up an online or phone interview may require some additional steps, such as sharing consent documents in advance and receiving a signed version electronically or via snail mail prior to the start of the interview.

Reviewing the conditions of consent with your participants, whether you do so when they first receive and sign the document or when you "meet" virtually to conduct the interview, remains crucial. These interviews—like the ones you conduct in person—should always begin by asking for permission to record and explaining how the recording and subsequent transcription will be protected. Additionally, make sure to familiarize yourself with the relevant legal obligations that pertain for recording video or phone conversations (since state and local jurisdictions differ in their laws governing such recordings).

Despite these contingencies, there are a number of ways to address the challenges posed by online and phone interactions and to approximate the conditions of an in-person meeting. The key is to maximize privacy and comfort and to allow for sufficient time, especially because it may take longer to establish rapport and complete the interview at a reasonable pace. Before the start of these interviews, alert participants in general terms about the nature of what's to come and suggest they find a place to talk that is as private as possible. You may also want to ask participants if they have head-phones with a microphone, since this may enhance the audio quality of the recording, the ease of hearing your questions, and even the sense of pri-vacy. At the start, after stressing that participation is voluntary and that each person may decline to answer any question and may choose to halt the in-terview at any time, the next step is to move at a pace that feels right, taking time to make a personal connection despite the distance between you. As you move forward with the interview, you may want to check in at regular intervals to ask if they would like to take a break. These pauses might occur naturally during the course of an in-person interview, but it is likely to be more difficult to gauge a participant's energy level or need for a pause via long-distance interaction.

If you offer in-person interviewees a modest compensation for partic-ipating, you will also want to do this for video or phone interviews, even though it will involve taking additional steps such as confirming the best mailing address and (especially if required by your institution) alerting them that along with the compensation they will receive a form acknowledging its receipt to return in a preaddressed stamped envelope.

Finally, if a majority or large portion of your interviews take place long-distance, it's important to ask if and how this strategy may have influenced the shape of your sample. Technology expands the options interviewers possess, but it also runs the risk of systematically excluding participation for members of groups who lack access, as we saw happen during the 2020 pandemic when students from low-SES backgrounds were particularly disadvantaged in their access to web-based home schooling when classes moved online.[41] By remaining alert and vigilantly searching for this possibility, it becomes easier to locate inadvertent sam-pling biases that may have undermined your intended sampling frame and thus influenced the range of variation you sought to study. If this occurs, the next step is to develop creative solutions for incorporating those who may have been left out. Video interviews may offer the best reach for some of your sample, but phone calls may work better for those who lack a reliable internet connection or the necessary supporting tech-nology. Yet some phone plans may limit the number of "free" minutes, posing another type of constraint.

Fortunately, virtual interviewing offers some noteworthy benefits along with these challenges. Computer-assisted conversations often take place in domestic spaces, such as a bedroom or home office, that offer a window into private worlds that in-person interviews (even when they take place in living rooms and kitchens) do not provide. Video and phone interviews can also reinforce the sense of safety that fosters a "strangers on a train" atmosphere, which encourages disclosing thoughts, feelings, and experiences that might never be shared with friends and intimates. Long-distance interviews can be easier to schedule since there is no need for you to find and travel to an appropriate location or to ask the interviewee to host you at home or the office. And because the logistics involved in getting together are substantially reduced, relying on a virtual meeting also makes it easier to conduct a follow-up interview if needed. For those who cannot or do not wish to make time in their schedules to meet in person, options that enable people to meet in other ways also make it easier and, for some, possible to participate.

Online options also include other forms of virtual data gathering, such as audio diaries. Paper diaries, which ask participants to keep a log of their daily activities, have long been a research tool.[42] Web-based technologies now make it possible to invite participants to complete an audio diary of their daily, weekly, or even monthly experiences. While this technique is still used sparingly, it adds a new means for collecting information that some researchers have found "encouraged a more personal disclosure of private emotions and feelings."[43] Such diaries also make it easier to continue gathering findings after a formal interview concludes, thus expanding the reach of the research to tap responses and insights that may occur after the "official" interview has concluded.[44]

The most obvious—and most important—advantage to long-distance interviewing is that the virtual world reduces the barriers to traversing space. It allows you to interview members of groups who would otherwise be difficult or impossible to include, whether because they are spread across a large geographic area or they are simply unable to meet in person. When the goal is to study a widely dispersed group, as well as during times when meeting in person is just not practical, online and phone interviewing becomes a lifeline that makes your research possible. When they are necessary, these interviews, like their in-person counterparts, can create an atmosphere that allows participants to share their stories, explore the significance of their life experiences, and consider the events and social contexts that surround these experiences. In this way, long-distance interviewing provides another option that makes interviewing possible when circumstances put meeting in person out of reach.

Delegating to Others

For those with the resources, delegating some of the interviewing to an assistant becomes an additional option. Delegating can enhance a study by expanding the sample size, providing novel insights, and serving as a check on any biases you may be unconsciously imposing on the material. The key is to do so in moderation and only after you have conducted enough interviews to feel confident about its structure and content. Many of the key insights that inform your analysis (which we consider in depth in Chapter 6) emerge during your time in the field. Before any assistant joins in that search, then, that person will need thorough training that helps them develop a good understanding of what you are looking for and why. Additionally, they will need regular debriefing sessions that allow you to learn about their findings and insights as the interviews proceed.

Although some researchers rely on a team of assistants to conduct all their interviews, we do not favor this strategy. As a general rule of thumb, we recommend personally conducting at least half to two-thirds of the interviews.[45] Since the heart (and enjoyment) of interviewing is the exploration and discovery that encountering other people's social worlds makes possible, there is no substitute for direct engagement with the people you seek to understand. Conducting the interviews is the primary way—in some instances, the only way—to discover and pursue analytic surprises. Although letting others conduct your interviews may seem efficient, this strategy will likely consume far more time and effort in the longer run as you struggle to make sense of interview material that you did not collect and you wish for the additional information you might have pursued had you personally conducted more of them.

Personal Safety

Safety is another important consideration in deciding where to interview, and this is just as important for you as it is for the participant. Fortunately, the structure of the interview process—including the fact that you select the participants, approach them in a professional manner, and set the terms of the interview—makes it unlikely that any harm will result. Indeed, we have never experienced or heard of an interview that proved to be dangerous, including one-on-one meetings that take place at night or in secluded, high-crime, or other potentially risky areas.

Feeling safe is nevertheless as important as *being* safe. To cope with safety fears, it helps to start by considering why you or the interviewees may have these concerns and deciding how best to respond. In most cases, you can identify any safety concerns prior to the interview and take steps to avoid them. First, insist on meeting at a time and place that lessen your own concerns. If you are uneasy about the prospect of meeting at a particular location or time of day, ask to schedule the meeting at a time and place that lowers discomfort, and add an incentive (such as a meal or snack) for meeting there and then. Even though it is usually best to let participants choose, you need to feel safe in order to create a comfortable atmosphere for both of you.

A more problematic situation arises when a safety concern emerges unexpectedly. These instances call for exercising judgment in the specific context. Some rare contexts may call for stopping the interview, although this has never happened to us or anyone else we know. Far more often, the challenge is to find sources of assurance and convey the professional nature of the encounter through words and actions. Sarah was initially concerned when she arrived at a home with guns on display, but she quickly realized that to the interviewee they symbolized safety rather than danger. One young man met Kathleen at the door of his apartment wearing only a pair of denim shorts, and another met her at his private social club with two drinks waiting and no other members in sight. Yet she soon concluded that neither situation posed a threat, even if these men were eager to impress her. These examples illustrate how social and cultural differences can elicit concern on the part of an interviewer as well as on the part of an interviewee. And just as interviewers have a responsibility to help interviewees feel at ease, they also have a responsibility to transcend their own cultural presuppositions—whether they involve a distrustful view of guns or skepticism about displays of masculine pride.

While it is not unusual to encounter unexpected difficulties, on rare occasions personal jeopardy may be involved. Upon arriving to interview a young woman, Sarah was greeted by a partially dressed man who appeared high on drugs. When her interviewee did not arrive after a period of waiting, she decided to leave and reschedule the interview. Moments like these illustrate the importance of trusting your judgment. When a context appears manifestly unsafe, leaving is not only appropriate but also necessary.

Wherever and whenever an interview is scheduled to take place, take steps to secure not just your safety but your sense of safety. Routine practices such as leaving the details of each interview location with a friend, partner, or research assistant are easy and straightforward, and they provide a safety net if an emergency arises. More fundamentally, if a safety concern emerges either before or during the interview, you can always bring the interview to a close and leave. Your most important resource is confidence in your judgment and your ability to exercise it.

Practical Matters

It is easy to overlook a number of practical matters because they fall into a category that can be considered "just details." How to dress? What materials to use? How to handle mishaps? While these matters may seem mundane, they can make the difference between an exemplary interview and a barely useful one.

Dressing for Success

Since appearance creates a first and lasting impression, clothing matters. It is best to aim for an image of professionalism and respect for the occasion, while also conveying accessibility rather than intimidation. Dressing in a professional manner means conveying neutrality rather than eccentricity by avoiding clothes that are too trendy, overstated, or ostentatious in favor of simple, understated styles. There is plenty of room within those limits to choose what feels comfortable and tailored to the specific setting. If the interview takes place at someone's home or a local diner, you can expect the interviewee to dress informally and to feel more comfortable if you do so as well. If the site is an office, it is wise to dress more formally unless the work setting is informal. Regardless of the locale, appearance, like demeanor, should signal that you take the occasion seriously but also wish to create a relaxed atmosphere that lends itself to an enjoyable experience.[46]

Materials for the Field

It is useful to create a written or mental checklist of everything you will need for the field. Sarah routinely prepares a "field kit" that holds the materials in an accordion folder. In addition to a blank copy of the interview guide, with sufficient room between questions to take notes, these materials include any screening information that has already been collected, two copies of the consent form (one for the participant to sign and return and another for them to keep), any cash payment or gift card (in an envelope), two digital recorders (one as a backup if the first fails to operate properly), and backup batteries.

Recording the interviews, as we mentioned earlier, provides a complete and accurate transcript of the conversation and frees you to focus on conducting the interview. Although it is possible to jot down some information (usually brief details) as the interview takes place, it is quite difficult to take detailed notes, much less a verbatim record of the long, complicated answers that will become the basis for developing and supporting nuanced arguments. There will be time after the interview to record your general impressions and recollections—including descriptions of the setting, the participant's physical and verbal style, and other observations that might help jog your memory later. The interview is a time to pose questions, listen closely to answers, and follow up with new questions that you had not (and could not have) planned. This process requires alertness, eye contact, and attention to verbal and nonverbal cues—all of which suffer if the focus is on recalling and writing down exact quotes or even general summaries. Fortunately, digital recorders are so plentiful (and, with cellphones, almost ubiquitous) that most participants feel comfortable with them, and many will quickly forget one is present and running.

Recorders are also user friendly and create digital files that you can easily upload to a computer and store until they are transcribed. Although some find it valuable to transcribe all their interviews themselves in order to hear and review the exchanges, we find that if you have the financial resources to employ a transcriber or transcription service, doing it yourself is too time-consuming to be worth the payoff. (Voice recognition technology is also improving rapidly, providing a far less costly and increasingly accurate means for creating interview transcriptions.) Since it takes far longer to transcribe an interview than to conduct one, the money spent saves valuable time that you can use to conduct more interviews or analyze the ones you have collected. If the funds are not available—and transcriptions are likely to be the most expensive item in your research budget—the silver lining is that transcribing even a subset of the interviews is an excellent way to listen carefully for findings that have gone unnoticed and use them to develop new ideas. For those whose budgets allow transcription, however, careful reading of the transcripts can accomplish the same end, revealing content that might not have made a strong impression during the interview but becomes central later on. In either case, verbatim transcripts are central to analysis and well worth the effort and investment of either time or money.

When Recording Isn't an Option

There are circumstances when audio recording is not an option. In Lynne Haney's study of incarcerated fathers, the prison forbade the recording of the interviews.[47] In another study, Mark Anner found that recording interviews with leaders of Vietnamese workers' rights movements could put them in danger of arrest.[48] And Lauren Rivera could not record the deliberations of recruitment committees at two top-tier universities as they made decisions about whether to interview married women applicants.[49] While the inability to record poses a challenge, it need not derail the process. Instead, it requires more extensive and careful note-taking, both during the interview and immediately thereafter.

Since ethnographers like Haney and Rivera routinely confront the challenge of taking field notes, you can learn from their strategies for note-taking. Robert Emerson and his colleagues suggest jotting down brief notes rather than trying to capture responses verbatim.[50] This allows you to remain focused on listening and probing so that conversation can continue to flow. These jottings can then serve as prompts to recall details after the interview, when you have time to write a more thorough memo. Even though direct quotes will not be available for later use, good notes provide material to paraphrase and include in the overall analysis. Discussing ethnographic note-taking, Jessica Calarco suggests keeping a brief nightly log of the day's events and then detailing the three most relevant events, including those that do not support your hypotheses or the patterns you expected to find.[51] Next, she advises, write a "story with clear context, characters, action, motivation, and resolution." Applying this strategy to interviewing would mean creating a memo that contains as much detail about the interview as comes to mind and then identifying the most vivid aspects of the conversation, particularly those instances that stood out as surprising. Whether or not this specific approach to note-taking seems apt, constructing an interview narrative is an effective way to create a written record when a verbatim transcript is not possible.

Mishaps in the Field

Mishaps are not inevitable, but they can and often do happen. The recorder may malfunction, or the batteries may run out, or you may forget to turn on the recorder for some or all of an interview. We have experienced all of these mishaps and more—from forgetting to turn on the recorder for the first several minutes of an interview to discovering that the recorder has failed to record large portions of the ensuing interaction.

Fortunately, no single mishap is fatal, even if it is a big one. No study depends on every interview or every verbatim stretch of information within it. In the end, most studies collect far more information than will be used, and it will hardly matter that some cases are less than fully precise or complete. Yet taking steps to avoid mishaps and, when they do occur, to recognize them in time to rectify the situation reduces anxiety and saves time. It is easy to bring backup batteries or even a backup recorder in case an equipment breakdown occurs. It is equally straightforward to make certain the recorder is working properly at the beginning and perhaps at intervals throughout the interview.

If a mishap occurs, you can take a number of measures, including those used when recording is not possible, to lessen its significance. General notes taken during the interview will help jog your memory should it be necessary to recreate a conversation. Systematically going through the interview guide after the interview and filling in as much detail as you can recall helps to recreate a general summary of the interview's flow and content. Even if you have lost specific quotes, the interview can still contribute to the overall analysis. Finally, if you cannot recover crucial details, you can usually contact the participant and fill in the missing information. The larger message is not to panic. As long as you have learned enough to classify each case in the overall analysis, the interview will be not only useful but worthwhile.

Learning in the Field and Beyond

Conducting interviews can be an exhilarating experience for all involved. The key is to take an open, collaborative approach that respects the knowledge everyone offers while probing to discover the deeper meaning of that knowledge. As an "outsider," an interviewer provides participants with a chance to be heard and, in the process, reach insights that they may find new and surprising. There will be plenty of time after all the interviews are completed to step back and develop a broader perspective. In the interview context, your job is to listen carefully, respect what each person has to say, and search for the meaning beneath the words. You will not be disappointed if you tackle each interview with respect for the participant and genuine curiosity about the surprises that may be waiting. At the best moments, the interview becomes a space where learning takes place for both of you. As unlikely as it may seem, this process has the power to create a shared bond between two people who just met. As one participant concluded after an interview with Kathleen, "There's something about telling your story to a complete stranger that makes it almost easier to talk about it."

6

Analyzing Interviews

Making Sense of Complex Material

Whether you conceive of analysis as a process of discovery or creation, analyzing interviews involves a search for the patterns concealed within the complex material transcripts contain. Amid the apparent disorder, the challenge is to find the hidden structure. The nuance and richness that make depth interviews worthwhile also make the transition from collecting interviews to focusing single-mindedly on making sense of them seem intimidating.

The prospect of seeking order amid the apparent disorder of your interview material may seem overwhelming at the outset. Confronted with such complexity, you may be tempted to focus on describing—that is, summarizing—your findings. Yet even if rich description were sufficient (and we prefer to see it as an essential prelude to developing an explanation), you must still decide what is worthy of attention and why. Now it is time to return to your core empirical and theoretical questions and, based on what your interviews have taught you so far, decide what information is foreground, what information is background, and what does not belong in the picture at all.

This stage once more invokes the question of rigor in qualitative research. Yet, as Mario Small points out, we cannot and should not use the same yardsticks as quantitative researchers to achieve rigor and demonstrate the scientific validity of our approach.[1] Interviewers need to have their own distinct analytic techniques to discover and confirm the patterns, connections, and "deep truths" that faithfully capture our participants' lives.

Here we offer a systematic yet flexible approach to transforming rich, wide-ranging interview material into a set of focused findings and theoretical arguments. Nicole Deterding and Mary Waters describe a similar process when they discuss peeling back the layers of each interview via the use of memos, the application of finer-grained codes, and the connection of theory to data.[2] Interviewers begin the journey to discovering patterns and explaining them by developing a systematic process for coding and analysis (as Deterding and Waters also note).

The Science and Art of Interviewing. Kathleen Gerson and Sarah Damaske, Oxford University Press (2021). © Oxford University Press. DOI: 10.1093/oso/9780199324286.001.0001

We recommend beginning your analysis by immersing yourself deeply in the interview material and ending with the construction of an explanatory framework. In between, we consider how you can use coding and categorizing to make analytic sense of your material. This involves constructing overviews with memos and matrices; conceptualizing various outcomes; distinguishing between accounts and explanations; and charting and explaining trajectories, with particular attention to transitions and turning points. By breaking the analytic process down into concrete steps, you can make analysis more manageable, less intimidating, and even more fun. These steps will increase your ability to develop robust, thoughtful, and significant arguments and to demonstrate their significance in a clear and convincing way.

Attributing Meaning to Interview Material

What meaning can we impart to interview material? Answering this question is fundamental to making sense of all types of research-generated information, but it is especially pertinent to findings based on self-reports. Even though your interviews have sought to gather honest reflection and full disclosure, your narrators are necessarily unreliable to some extent. This does not mean that participants have deliberately deceived you or failed to disclose important truths. Rather, as we and others have emphasized, participants are socially situated actors who are rarely positioned to know the full array of institutional arrangements, cultural forces, and deeper motivations that influence their actions and worldviews. The only way to discover how such unseen forces shape perception and action is to distinguish among the different *kinds* of information that participants provide and to search for patterns across the entire sample.

People are prone to describe and interpret the same events differently.[3] The challenge is not to decide whether to believe what your interviewees say or whom among them to believe, but instead to discover why they all say what they do and *what* they mean by it. This would matter even if interviews only measured perceptions. Perceptions do not fall from the sky or emerge from a disembodied mind; people form them in response to specific experiences in specific contexts. These contexts have effects.[4] The goal of your analysis is to find out how and why such perceptions emerge and what consequences they have for people's lives.[5]

Good interviews measure far more than "mere" perceptions. If you have constructed your interview guide carefully and your interviews have tapped the multiple dimensions of experience, including triggering events and the personal responses they elicit, you can analyze how real-world experiences interact with mental constructions to shape worldviews and life trajectories. While interviewing (like any method) elicits information with varying degrees of accuracy, it can provide an overview of the arc of a life and the timing or duration of a set of experiences. And since memories tend to crystallize around experiences that mark transitions (as we discussed in Chapter 5), the transcripts can provide ready access to the details that mark important events. Participants may wish to tell narratives in ways that shape the tenor of these accounts, but your careful probing for specific examples should have obtained additional evidence about these experiences. You can now systematically examine each individual answer in the context of the entire interview and examine each individual interview in comparison to all the others.[6]

Making sense of interview material requires you to take participants' views seriously *and* to place them in a larger empirical and theoretical context. While you do not want to simply take interview responses at face value, you also need to avoid reducing them to "false consciousness." The problem of distinguishing between "true" and "false" consciousness is closely connected to the challenge of analyzing the worldviews of participants rather than imposing one's values on them.[7] The goal of analysis is not to reduce people's views of their own experiences to "true" or "false," but rather to understand how and why people develop their particular views and take the actions they do. This approach stresses explanation—that is, a search for the factors and mechanisms that explain why and how the patterns you find in your interviews take the form they do.

While socially embedded actors may remain unaware of how social arrangements shape their lives, the job of analysis is to find these hidden structures. By reviewing the full range of responses and placing them in a comparative framework, your analysis can reveal patterns of similarity and difference and then draw conclusions about what is driving them and how they unfold. Armed with the practical and conceptual tools to discover relationships amid the apparent uniqueness of diverse experiences, a thoughtful analytic strategy can distinguish between interviewee accounts and the social factors and processes that explain them. A systematic analytic approach also helps you address the issue of positionality by clarifying your own analytic stance toward the interviews and their meaning. Consciously used, a carefully developed analytic framework helps you step back from your personal perspectives and place in the social world to focus on the experiences of the participants as seen through *their* eyes.

This explanatory approach seeks to avoid either an "abstracted empiricism" that is disconnected from theoretical concerns or a purely interpretive argument that confirms prior assumptions without addressing potentially disconfirming findings.[8] Instead, it searches for the sources and significance of people's efforts to create meaning. Drawing on the traditions of both Max Weber and Emile Durkheim, it seeks to discover "social facts" that extend beyond apparently "objective" measures (for example, birth rates or election results) to include subjective dimensions of human experience that cannot be directly observed or easily measured. In an era when power holders use terms such as "alternative facts" and "fake news" to undermine the notion of verifiable findings, building your argument through careful analysis will make it clear that your conclusions are not just one person's interpretation.

Initial Immersion

It may seem obvious to start your analysis by reading the interview transcripts carefully and thoroughly, but the immersion process is not just an extension of the process of conducting interviews. Even if you personally conducted all the interviews and already possess a general sense of what they have yielded, the magnitude and complexity of the entire set of data raise a different set of challenges. Each interview may contain its own insights, but it is a challenge of a different order to transform these insights into a coherent set of analytic arguments. Yet just as eyesight gradually adjusts to darkness, your thinking will gradually coalesce as you acquaint or reacquaint yourself with the details of the collected material.

The first step is to select a qualitative software program that will help you organize, conceptualize, and detect the patterns that are waiting to be found in the interviews. Once you have chosen a program, the next step is to become familiar with its format, upload the transcripts, attach any related notes taken during the interviewing stage, and begin to code the interviews. Organizing the research material this way gives you a framework for reading the transcripts, summarizing the findings, creating memos for each case, and maintaining notes that track, record, and make use of insights as they occur during the analytic process.[9] It also facilitates the steps to come, including developing and applying codes and concepts, deciding how to group and categorize participants, and discovering patterns and relationships.

Once the interview transcripts are ready to analyze, you can begin to read them closely and carefully and take notes along the way, whether in the margins of each transcript, in a separate file, or both.[10] This is a good time to begin a preliminary list of coding categories and, if you wish, begin coding blocks of text—as long as you are prepared to return when your list of codes is more fully developed.[11] Take care to distinguish different categories of notes, including those focusing on each person's life, those pointing to possible trends, and those documenting any emerging theoretical ideas. Sarah divides a thin notebook into three parts: one-third for initial notes on each participant, one-third for coding ideas, and the final third for emerging themes that could become chapters and/or arguments. Kathleen creates a memo for each participant, with one section for an overview (with subsections on specific topic areas along with any especially telling text that points to important findings or insights) and another section for any general ideas, arguments, or analytic approaches that the interview inspires or supports. There is no one right way to do this. Especially in this early period of analysis, it is good to choose whatever system feels most comfortable, whether that means simple jottings, a list of bullet points, or more detailed summaries.

With categories like these to organize your work and the full array of interviews to consider, you can read each transcript with some basic questions in mind:

- What does this transcript tell me that is surprising and/or appears important?
- Why does this finding or idea surprise me or seem consequential? Because it conflicts with or adds to my expectations? Because it conflicts with or adds to conventional wisdom? Because it conflicts with or adds to others' descriptions of empirical trends? Because it conflicts with or adds to dominant theories?
- What information seems central and what peripheral to summarizing this interview or making a theoretical point?
- Does the interview clarify or change the way to depict an outcome or outcomes? Does it expand, clarify, or challenge the factors and/or processes that contribute to the outcomes?

While reading through the interviews, you can also begin to consider the potential relationships among them:

- How does each interview appear to fit within the larger picture emerging for the whole group?
- Are similarities and differences emerging among the interviews that point toward groupings within the sample?
- If groupings are emerging, where does each interview fit? Do some fit more clearly in a category, while others are more difficult to categorize? What makes some cases clear? What makes others ambiguous? Do these ambiguous cases point to new categories or to a new way to combine and/or distinguish among all the categories?
- If groupings are not emerging, why not? What are you missing that would help you group some people together or distinguish them from other groups? How does this regrouping change the way to think about the problem?

It is too early to have definitive answers to these questions, but it is never too soon to ask them. This is the time to write down any thoughts that come to mind, however far-fetched they may seem. You will have other opportunities to refine or drop preliminary ideas later, but if you do not record them, you will lose the opportunity to consider whether they are worthwhile. Yet you also need to resist the temptation to treat early ideas as conclusions. Have patience. Your immersion in the interview data will enhance your familiarity with and feeling for the material. It provides a chance to see each interview anew and place it in the context of the others. It encourages thinking expansively and entertaining a wide range of ideas, whether or not they ultimately prove to be valid. Initial immersion can whet your appetite for digging deeper and in a more organized way, but it cannot take the place of systematic analysis, which is the only way to find out whether an interesting finding is merely an anecdote or a telling example of a consistent pattern of empirical and theoretical importance.

Developing Concepts by Coding and Categorizing

When you feel sufficiently familiar with the content of the interviews, the next step is to begin to impose a clearer order on the material. The challenge is to transform the array of individual stories into a set of abstract codes and categories. If conducting interviews is like collecting a wealth of film footage, then analyzing them is like studying each frame and developing a guide for editing them.[12]

Abstraction requires simplification, which inevitably means losing some original richness and detail. Considering how much effort it took to collect these details, the prospect of disregarding much of it may not seem appealing to you. Yet it is a necessary price to pay for the gain in analytic power. Analysis is not possible without creating conceptual categories, understanding how to apply them to the information you have gathered, specifying the variation within each category, and exploring where each belongs in your analytic framework. Just as a photographer must decide what elements belong in a photo, where they belong, and by extension what to eliminate, building an argument requires making choices about what is integral to the argument and what may be interesting but ultimately is not relevant.

Developing conceptual categories is an interactive and iterative process that involves moving back and forth between the interview transcripts and an evolving list of substantive and theoretical categories. It requires you to work both deductively and inductively, shifting back and forth between assigning codes to segments of transcripts and developing codes to apply to them, repeating the process for as long as it takes to frame an argument and gain confidence in its validity.

Everyone needs to start somewhere. Rather than starting with a blank slate, a good place to start is by generating a list of codes that reflect the concepts you have already deemed important. This preliminary list can and should include the current state of theoretical thinking along with any new concepts that have emerged in the process of conducting the interviews and reading through the transcripts. At the least, it can reflect the sections and subsections of your interview guide, since they reflect your original approach. Deterding and Waters refer to this as an "index" that serves as the starting point for creating more fine-grained codes moving forward.[13] These early codes may be quite general, but they provide a baseline for further refinement.[14]

Equipped with a list of preliminary codes, you can begin assigning codes to the relevant interview material and simultaneously assess how well—or poorly—they capture the content, and then refine them accordingly. To take an example, you might explore the role of parents in shaping a person's early aspirations or ultimate destination with a general category called "parental influence." As your coding proceeds, you can develop more nuanced ideas about parental actions and messages that a general code cannot capture. Parents can support some aspirations but not others, can offer verbal messages that conflict with their behavior, and can disagree with each other, to name only a few of the many ways parental influences can be multidimensional and contradictory. It may also become clear that children's evaluations of their parents' messages do not always reflect their parents' intentions. Accounting for these complexities calls for separating the general category into a number of subcategories. You can retain the larger conceptual category and also generate subcodes within it.

Transforming vague or overly general categories into more distinct groupings clarifies their meanings and enables you to explore the relationships among the emergent dimensions. Instead of assuming parental influence is a coherent concept that can explain child outcomes, for example, you can refine your coding to examine the relationship between parental messages and actions as well as children's reactions to them as they grow. As you develop new codes and refine initial categories, you will attain increasing clarity and theoretical inspiration. Though typically slow and painstaking, this process will reward you with new concepts that more closely reflect what the interviews reveal and point toward promising theoretical breakthroughs. Such efforts can lead to aha moments when you are able to see your material in a new way. Though these moments are among the most exhilarating aspects of the analytic process, much work nevertheless remains to verify such insights and investigate their implications.

The procedure for developing analytic codes is a two-way street. Rather than inductively developing "grounded theory," as Barney Glaser and Anselm Strauss advocate, the process involves a dialogue between the interview findings and the range of theories purporting to explain them.[15] This dialogue sets the stage for theoretical and empirical discoveries. As you incorporate new insights into past coding, the process may require you to let go of prior operating assumptions. Though it may feel as if you are moving backward rather than making progress, this is how breakthroughs happen. Fortunately, the recoding process will likely involve a small number of interviews and only require adding subcategories to already existing codes rather than adding new general ones. In any case, the analytic payoffs of these efforts make the time and effort well worth it.

Here, for example, is a list of the general categories and subcategories Kathleen generated as she moved between early theoretical concepts and interview findings to analyze her interviews about the work and caretaking strategies emerging in the new economy:

CHILDHOOD AND EARLY EXPERIENCES
    Baseline: Caretaker/Breadwinner
    Baseline: Class Trajectory
    Baseline: Education Trajectory
    Baseline: Family Trajectory
    Baseline: Father as Parent/Worker
    Baseline: General
    Baseline: Mother as Parent/Worker
    Baseline: Parental Aspirations/Support
    Baseline: Parents' Relationship
    Baseline: Work-Care Aspirations/Expectations/Views
CURRENT FAMILY CIRCUMSTANCES
    Family: Current Situation
    Family: Fictive/Extended Kin
    Family: Giving/Receiving Support/Conflict
    Family: Kids and Dependents Situation
    Family: Partner Situation
GENERAL CATEGORIES
    General: Agency/Strategies
    General: Comments/Interviewer
    General: Comments/Post-Interview
    General: Comments/Pre-Interview
    General: Community Integration/Isolation
    General: Demographics
    General: Enumeration
    General: Future
    General: Future Certain/Uncertain
    General: Good Quote
    General: Identity/Models/Influences/Contexts
    General: Looking Back/Road Not Taken
    General: Money/Income/Housing Trajectory
    General: Personal Trajectory
    General: Turning Points/Change/Non-Change
    General: Unintended/Intended Consequences

CHILDREN
  Kids: Childcare Division of Labor/Arrangements
  Kids: Child-Rearing Culture/Institutions
  Kids: Fertility Trajectory
  Kids: Ideals/Aspirations/Fears
  Kids: Parenting Identity/Morale/Trajectory
  Kids: Plans/Expectations
  Kids: Trade-offs
OPINIONS
  Opinions: Causal Accounts
  Opinions: Childrearing/Parenting/Ideal Parent
  Opinions: Employers/Unions
  Opinions: Gender/Breadwinning-Caretaking Identity/Ideology
  Opinions: General
  Opinions: Government/Policy/Politics
  Opinions: Marriage/Cohabitation/Family
  Opinions: Other Models
  Opinions: Work-Care Division of Labor
  Opinions: Work/Economy/Ideal Worker
CURRENT PARTNER SITUATION
  Partner: Current Job
  Partner: Ideals/Aspirations/Fears/Background
  Partner: Plans/Expectations
  Partner: Relationship Trajectory
  Partner: Status
  Partner: Support/Conflict
  Partner: Work Schedule
  Partner: Work Stable/Unstable/Trajectory
  Partner: Work Status
CURRENT RELATIONSHIP SITUATION
  Relationship: Current Status
  Relationships: General
  Relationships: Ideals/Aspirations/Fears
  Relationships: Marriage Culture
  Relationships: Plans/Expectations
  Relationships: Stable/Unstable
  Relationships: Trade-offs
  Relationships: Trajectory

WORK-CARE LINKS
  Work-Care: Breadwinner/Caretaker
  Work-Care: Current
  Work-Care: General Balance
  Work-Care: Ideals/Aspirations/Fears
  Work-Care: Identity/Morale
  Work-Care: Plans/Expectations
  Work-Care: Self vs. Other
  Work-Care: Sharing/Division of Labor
  Work-Care: Spillover/Conflicts/Supports/Trade-offs/Dilemmas/
    Contradictions
  Work-Care: Trajectory
WORK
  Work: Current
  Work: General
  Work: Ideals/Aspirations/Fears
  Work: Identity/Morale
  Work: Plans/Expectations
  Work: Schedule/Structure/Culture
  Work: Stable/Unstable
  Work: Status/Money/Mobility
  Work: Trade-offs
  Work: Trajectory

This example contains many subcodes within the general categories, but there is no prescribed "right" or "wrong" length for your list of codes. Each person's approach to coding is a matter of discretion, the needs of the project, and analytic taste. In Kathleen's list, the general categories (which are noted by the first term assigned in each code) give order to the coding scheme by lumping related areas into the same general conceptual group. The subcategories (which are described after the first term and separated by a colon) provide nuance and specificity to the general areas, allowing a finer-grained analysis when the time arrives to explore the links among conceptual categories and develop an explanation about how and why they are linked.

Although the general categories and some of the subcategories are obvious well before formal coding begins, many subcategories emerge during the early stages of coding. Regardless of when a code is created, it is better to err on the side of making more rather than fewer categories and subcategories.

Once coded, sub-categories can always be combined into a more inclusive one, but overly general categories cannot so easily be disassembled into a series of more refined ones. With most qualitative computer programs, combining several codes to make a more general grouping is a straightforward matter, while disaggregating a general code into more precise groupings is not possible.

The coding list also contains different types of categories, including codes we would term *substantive, theoretical,* and *methodological*. A substantive code refers to the specific details an interviewee provides that are relevant to the analysis. Most of the codes in Kathleen's list are substantive in nature, whether they refer to past events, current situations, future plans, or views of oneself and others. These codes refer both to actually occurring events, such as marriages, births, jobs, and so on, and to the subjective reactions and interpretations attached to them.

Another set of codes flags the importance or theoretical significance of any substantive selection of text. Codes such as "causal accounts," "turning points," or "unintended consequences" are abstract categories that you can apply to any substantive area to point to the role they may play in the analysis. Kathleen uses the code labeled "causal account" to flag any quote that represents an interviewee's explanation for why an event occurred (e.g., "luck" or "hard work" or "bias") or why they behaved in a certain way (e.g., "that's how I was raised"). When combined with substantive codes, these codes make it possible to analyze the theoretical status of substantive information—in this case, by distinguishing an interviewee's account of why, how, and with what consequences an event occurred from the explanation you will develop by placing these interpretations in an analytic context.

Some codes can also refer to the methodological status of a piece of text. You can use a generic code, like "good quote," to designate any important or especially vivid statement that illustrates a concept or emerging pattern. Many selected quotes—especially if they stand out for their richness—may apply to more than one substantive category and are also likely to warrant a theoretical or methodological code as well. Since substantive, theoretical, and methodological codes are distinct, any section of text can (and often will) have multiple codes. Adding theoretical and methodological codes to substantive quotes signals their meaning in the interpretive framework. These codes also make it easier to retrieve the best examples when the time arrives to present and provide evidence for the argument. Most important, these codes form the early scaffolding—the conceptual framework—that allows you to move from description to analysis. They are the filters that allow you to sift through the material, focus on what is pertinent, and decide why and how it matters.

Constructing Overviews with Memos and Matrices

As your coding proceeds, it helps to construct a condensed description of each interview, a technique that casts light on how each individual fits within the sample as a whole. We recommend two strategies for compiling this overview: writing summary memos and constructing a data matrix. Most software packages have tools for writing and attaching a memo to each coded interview file (and if the chosen package does not have this option, you can always create separate text files). Creating a summary memo of each case as you code it adds another layer to the organization of complicated qualitative material. These memos summarize each case in a way that helps you zero in on the most enlightening aspects of each interview, compare them with each other, and discover patterns among them.

To build on the coding example given earlier, each memo can contain sections on similar variable clusters—for the case of Kathleen's categories, these include clusters such as childhood, work history, family history, current circumstances, and future plans. Within each variable cluster, memos can also delineate subheadings that distinguish among different levels of analysis, including a summary of important events (that is, *what* happened) along with a consideration of the prior circumstances and surrounding social contexts (*how* and *why* they happened) and the consequences of these experiences (the views and actions that followed these events as the interviewees developed short- and long-run responses). The memos create a textual summary of all the elements you think might contribute to developing your argument. By noting the social contexts that shape each interviewee's options as well as how the interviewee perceives and reacts to these circumstances, your summary memos provide a format for detecting sequential interactions between structure and agency. They transform each person's narrative into an organized set of analytic categories, which can then form the framework for developing a theoretical argument. In contrast to the memos constructed immediately after the interview, which were important for noting interview details and emerging ideas, these new memos are a definitive part of the analytic process.

It is equally useful to construct a data matrix that summarizes the crucial information for each interview and facilitates the discovery of overall patterns within the entire sample. The matrix need not be complicated. A simple spreadsheet that designates how you have coded each case on core measures and concepts makes it possible to sort the data by code and thus discover patterns and relationships that may not become evident from the textual coding alone.[16] Once the matrix has been constructed, it is simple to add more categories as they emerge—including ones that are created by combining original codes. You can, for example, build a code that designates a trajectory by combining a baseline measure with a current measure of the same phenomenon to create a code that designates whether or not it has changed and, if so, how.

Memos and matrices help guide the analytic process from beginning to end. They impose order by providing avenues for charting the contours of the interview material, the emerging key categories, and the textual materials that provide especially good examples of those categories. Put differently, they make it easier to find relationships to pursue in greater depth qualitatively. The key is to begin with a preliminary list and add to the list as textual coding progresses. Here is the list of matrix categories Kathleen developed to analyze her interviews on strategies of work and care in the new economy:

PARTICIPANT IDENTIFICATION
   ID Number
   Name/Pseudonym
DEMOGRAPHICS
   Gender Identity
   Racial Identity
   Ethnic Identity
   Sexual Identity
   Age
   Residential Location
FAMILY STATUS
   Partner
   Number of Children
   Other Dependents
   Age of Youngest Dependent
   Ages of All Dependents

FAMILY AND EDUCATIONAL BACKGROUND
    Educational Attainment
    Parents' Occupation, Class
    Parents' Breadwinning-Caretaking Division
    Where Grew Up
    Religion Raised In
WORK
    Work Status
    Occupation
    Occupational Sector
    New/Old Economy Job
    Secure/Insecure Work
    Work Hours
PARTNER
    Partner Status
    Partner Work Status
    Partner Occupation
    Partner Occupational Sector
    Partner New/Old Economy
    Partner Secure/Insecure Job
    Partner Work Hours
WORK-FAMILY ARRANGEMENTS
    Work-Family Situation
    Primary Breadwinner (All That Apply)
    Primary Caretaker (All That Apply)
    Work-Family Plan
    Work-Family Ideal
    Work-Family Expectations
ECONOMIC SITUATION
    Personal Income
    Total Household Income
LIFE TRAJECTORIES
    Baseline (Starting Work-Family Aspirations)
    Work Path
    Caregiving Path
    Work-Caregiving Path
MISCELLANEOUS
    Religious Affiliation, Identity

Political Affiliation, Identity
Work-Family-Gender Opinions
Relevant Details (Not Already Specified)

These categories overlap with and may (but need not) be identical to the codes in the text analysis. You can divide each broad substantive area into more specific categories that are (or are emerging as) theoretically important, just as they are in the textual coding. A matrix of this kind provides another technique for creating overviews of each case, searching for patterns, and deciding how each case fits within the whole. As the textual coding proceeds and new conceptual insights emerge, it is possible to add new categories to the matrix along with adding new codes to the qualitative analysis.

Combining textual coding, summary memos, and variable-oriented matrices permits you to summarize and organize your findings and find the dominant trends and individual subtleties across all the cases. As you begin to see each subsequent case in relation to the whole, the differences among your main subgroups come more clearly into focus, and you can discover what binds some participants together and distinguishes them from others. Given the complexity of each individual case, creating analytic groups is bound to be difficult and fraught. An intersectional perspective reminds us that each interviewee possesses a bundle of identities, including some that they choose and some that are socially imposed. Since it is not possible to analyze the sources, shape, and consequences of inequality without first identifying the relevant social groups, how they do or do not overlap, and who belongs to each, the challenge is to recognize and incorporate these intersectional complexities without reducing each interview to a unique case.

This process, which Eviatar Zerubavel calls "lumping and splitting," requires some sacrifice in nuance in the service of identifying larger social patterns.[17] Categories of race and gender, for example, cannot capture the full complexity of identities and experiences among members of these groups. Yet avoiding decisions about which categories to foreground and who belongs in each forfeits the chance to recognize or measure differences and similarities that you deem important, much less explain their roots or trace their consequences. Fortunately, the qualitative coding process makes it possible to attach multiple codes to the same block of text. While the distinctions you decide to focus on will be deeply rooted in the data itself, you retain multiple options about how to lump and split the interview material as the analysis moves forward. The key is to let the core questions and findings guide decisions about which distinctions are integral to the analysis as well as how and when to make them.

These strategies for organizing and coding interview material set the stage for constructing new theoretical concepts. This "second-order" coding grows out of a later round of coding in which new concepts emerge from the first round. This process can involve developing a more refined conceptualization of an original code or, alternatively, creating a more complex code by combining two or more original ones. To take an example of how to refine a code by breaking it into subcategories, Kathleen can sort the category of "accounts" to focus on a range of life circumstances, including accounts of inequality, insecurity, parenting norms, gender norms, and the like. Similarly, the category of "strategies" can include strategies for accommodating a dissatisfying situation, resisting unequal arrangements, and other behavioral and mental ways of managing problematic life circumstances.

In the case of combining codes to create a new concept, Kathleen routinely merges measures of past and current circumstances to create a set of "trajectories" that trace how a person's life path develops over time. The categories under the general heading of "life trajectories" (that is, work, caregiving, and work-caregiving paths) were built by combining measures of baseline aspirations with measures of current circumstances.

You can create these trajectories for a variety of substantive areas and tailor them to almost any research topic. Although our work tends to focus on work and family trajectories, you can conceive of virtually any life area or institutional cluster as a social form that develops through time, whether by reproducing prior arrangements or by changing in some significant way. Michael Ramirez uses this frame to illumine the pathways of men and women who pursue informal music careers as they move into adulthood.[18] This "life course" approach, which sees social life as a dynamic process, thus offers an analytic method as well as a theoretical perspective. Similarly, institution and social policies—like individuals—have a trajectory that begins with an initial organizational form or set of rules and then unfolds over time. A number of interview studies have shown how some follow a path set in place at the outset (what social policy analysts refer to as "path dependency") and others diverge from these beginnings as a constellation of socially embedded actors with a variety of interests contribute to unintended consequences as they enact abstract rules on the ground.[19]

These analytic techniques can also help you uncover consequential but overlooked theoretical distinctions. Some economists tend to presume they can use choices as a measure of preferences, while sociologists are more attuned to the differences between what people desire and what constrains their options for achieving it. Rather than conflating "preferences" with "choices," a more nuanced approach to coding can distinguish between concepts such as "preferences" and "aspirations," on the one hand, and concepts such as "choices" and "expectations," on the other, making it possible to systematically analyze the relationships between them.[20] Coding transcripts with an eye to these conceptual differences fosters a closer look at how and when different mental states are in harmony or in conflict, which then leads to a closer look at how those who do not expect to achieve their aspirations cope with such blocked opportunities. Though this is just one example, it illustrates how careful coding that avoids conflating important conceptual distinctions opens new analytic possibilities.

Whether your analysis captures a pathway across points in time, a current position that includes multiple life spheres (such as occupational and domestic spheres), a complex orientation toward the future (such as ideal aspirations and practical strategies), or countless other conceptual possibilities, these techniques serve as analytic points of departure that can and likely will lead to additional insights. A multi-layered database that includes textual coding, condensed case summaries, and matrices of key measures and concepts lays the groundwork for creating innovative concepts and categories, conducting a comparative analysis within and across the interviews, and making theoretical breakthroughs. As your analysis moves forward, these strategies will help you organize your material (including earlier notes composed during the interviewing and immersion stages) and continue your search for empirical patterns and the framework that will explain how and why they fit together.

Conceiving Outcomes

Now that the first round of coding is complete and your interview material no longer resembles a bewildering expanse of undifferentiated transcripts, you can put your core goals—description, discovery, and explanation—front and center. Describing your findings depends on first deciding what information among all that you have gathered is relevant to frame and then answering the questions you now wish to pose. Explanation involves your search for the nature of the relationships among all the phenomena you have selected to describe. Discovery—the quest for new ways of seeing and conceiving the foci of your research—is at the heart of both description and explanation.

While remaining alert to anomalies and puzzles is important at all stages of the research, now is the time to actively search for them. If none are evident, this is a good indication you are on the right track. More likely, however, your findings will not fit neatly into any preconceived framework. Since these moments signal the need to think more deeply and creatively about your analysis, they can be disconcerting. Yet they provide an opportunity to make theoretical contributions by refining and reconceptualizing accepted arguments (and your own preconceptions) that are missing something important. Unanticipated findings and puzzling results thus deserve especially close attention.

If even a small number of interviews show patterns that do not fit with the overall trends, you should note these exceptions, not ignore them. Unlike quantitative analyses, which tend to smooth over outliers, qualitative analyses can acknowledge and closely examine these nonconforming examples in a search for their meaning and implications. Rather than force these cases into a larger frame where they do not fit, you can use them as grist to think more deeply about any weak links in the current frame and the kind of adjustment (whether a tweak or a larger shift) that would provide an appropriate place for them into the overall analysis.

One place to start is to return once more to a focus on the outcomes. You need to describe an outcome before you can explain it, but this can be surprisingly difficult with qualitative material. This is because such complex and rich material makes it hard to decide which outcomes will become the focus and, by implication, which will take a backseat or be set aside altogether. In addition, you must confront the possibility that the findings do not support your original conception of the outcomes, thus requiring you to rethink them. Though the task of selecting and defining your outcomes can seem intimidating, it becomes much easier when you break it into a series of steps.

First, it is helpful to ask how best to *conceptualize* the study's outcomes. Has your coding suggested a preliminary set of categories? If not, can you define them now? If so, do they resemble or differ from the ones you initially expected? What about those that currently structure the frameworks used by others? How well or poorly do these categories account for the findings now that the coding has produced a more precise overview? If the fit is poor, what conceptual frame or frames would do a better job, especially considering the outliers that do not fit the current one?

As these questions suggest, you can develop an overview of the core outcomes by ascertaining how well or poorly prevailing approaches describe the similarities and differences among them. Is it possible to assign each case to a category without losing important information? Since conceptual categories necessarily represent ideal types (which some real-world cases will resemble more closely than others), it will be easier to categorize some cases than others. If a noticeable number of cases do not fit clearly into these categories, however, then the framework is likely to be inadequate. While there is no rigid rule for deciding when the number of ambiguous cases is high enough to trigger a reassessment of the categories, it is better to err on the side of fewer than more. Since the option always remains to return to the original frame, there is little harm in considering alternatives. Ignoring outliers and ambiguous cases, however, is likely to lead you in unpromising directions and make it more difficult to develop a convincing explanation. Equally important, it represents a lost opportunity to break new theoretical ground.

Once you have located ambiguous, difficult-to-categorize cases, the next step is to ask how and why they complicate the original categories. Such moments provide you with the opportunity to reconceive the fundamentals of your initial conceptual framework and construct a more theoretically powerful approach to slicing the pie. Take Sarah's research on the experiences of and reactions to unemployment.[21] Prior studies largely argued that men and women experienced job loss in similar ways, with most qualitative research focused on middle-class workers who treat job searches as if they were also a job (what Sarah terms a "deliberate" search pattern) and fewer researchers emphasizing the lack of focus and immediacy of searches among those in the working class (what Sarah terms an "urgent" search pattern). Sarah's interviews on the process of searching for work found that this binary distinction did not capture the full range of search strategies, which also included temporarily suspending the search (an approach used primarily by a group of middle-class men who expressed a wish to "take time" off before rejoining the workforce) and withdrawing from the job search entirely to focus on family responsibilities and financial strains (an approach adopted most frequently by working-class women who were "diverted" from seeking paid work). Adding these patterns to the overall analysis expanded and reframed the range of options available to people in the wake of job loss and revealed a more complex picture of how gender and class shape reactions to this experience.

As this example suggests, the challenge is to find a frame that most thoroughly and accurately captures your interview findings, speaks to your central questions, and addresses the outcomes that have become your focus. Doing so requires a comparative assessment of how well or poorly original categories capture the full range of information in the interviews. If they cannot do so fully and faithfully, you can use this disconnect to develop a better frame for conceiving of what you wish to explain. Clarifying your outcomes will likely require an iterative procedure that moves back and forth between preliminary concepts and the interview material—all the while seeing how well or poorly alternative ways to lump and split work for describing your cases— until the overwhelming majority of your cases clearly belong in one category or another and each category has enough cases to allow you to analyze the mechanisms that account for how they arrived there. Postponing this conceptual work will not make the problem go away nor make it easier to address at a later time. The process may be painstaking and time-consuming, but it will save time and frustration in the long run.

Since settling on how to conceive of the outcomes involves deciding how to draw distinctions among participants and conceptualize the range of variation among them, it will have major implications for your future analysis, including some that are value-laden. When the variation captures widely accepted values, such as equality of opportunity in education, earnings, or occupational options, it is largely uncontroversial to claim that some outcomes are better than others (although scholars of inequality might debate the adequacy of measures of educational attainment, income categories, or job opportunities). Qualitative coding, however, often generates conceptual categories that are complicated and ambiguous, including perceptions, choices, and worldviews that are highly controversial. In these instances, just as during the interview process, it is important to refrain from imposing personal views, no matter how strongly felt, in favor of conceptualizing how interviewees perceive the moral, ethical, or value implications of their own and others' actions and outlooks.

In Sarah's study of unemployment, many participants made strong statements about the "deserving poor" versus the "undeserving poor," and some made explicitly racist statements. Rather than simply condemning these statements, she analyzed their content and found gender and class differences in how women and men framed their views. Had Sarah not taken this closer look, she would not have discovered the range of variation among these outlooks or how different social groups deployed them in different ways. A major strength of depth interviewing is its ability to find the broader cultural meanings embedded in controversial and profoundly distasteful views so that we can better understand their roots and uses. The payoff for this effort will come later, when you complete your analysis and use your findings to make your conclusions clear. As we discuss in Chapter 7, once you've done the work of careful interviewing and analysis, you have earned the authority to take an open and forceful stand in the service of your findings.

Explaining Outcomes

Whether the act of conceiving outcomes involves a more nuanced description of the original categories or a significant conceptual revision, it represents a first step in a longer process, for now the challenge is to explain how and why each outcome occurs and, if you wish, their consequences. What explains the range and variation of outcomes? Or, to pose the question specifically for interview material, by what *process* do outcomes develop, and what *factors* and *mechanisms* influence their emergence?

While a skeptic might argue that qualitative analysis cannot address issues of causation, we believe it is neither possible nor desirable to avoid asking explanatory questions. This debate depends partly on what is meant by "causal," a term whose definition remains controversial even among those who work exclusively with quantitative data. Qualitative researchers make no claim to a level of statistical specificity that measures the degree to which a particular factor (assuming others are controlled for) has a distinct effect. Interview material lends itself, instead, to the search for patterns and relationships that are difficult—and often impossible—to discern through either statistical analysis or direct observation.

Given the relatively small number of cases at hand, you cannot precisely decipher the relative weight of each discrete factor the interviews reveal, but the richness and depth of the material powerfully illuminate the variety of social forces at work in people's lives and the various ways these forces interact in multiple social contexts and through time. Any form of analysis (regardless of the type of data) is likely to contain an argument about causal connections, intentionally or not, and it is better to make that argument explicit. If it is left implicit, the implications will remain unstated and thus unexamined.

Distinguishing Between Accounts and Explanations

The first step in developing an explanatory framework is to distinguish between "accounts" and explanations.[22] Accounts, as we have stated, are the cultural scripts and mental categories on which people draw to make sense of their lives and the world around them. They can be found in the stories people tell—to themselves as well as to others, including interviewers—about how they arrived where they are and why they hold the views they do. These accounts are not causes but results. That is, they are subject to the same social and psychological forces that shape behavior. The analytic task is to chart how and why people develop specific accounts and to discover how these accounts compare with the less obvious forces that contribute to shaping life trajectories and worldviews. By placing people's accounts in both a social context and an analytic one, you can explore the reasons they occur, the processes that propel them and give them force, and their consequences for other outcomes of interest.[23]

To distinguish people's perceptions from the less visible factors that influence them, you can begin by determining which accounts do *not* explain the outcomes. This may seem counterintuitive, but it helps in the search for the more fundamental underpinnings of action, feeling, and belief. If everyone offers a similar explanation even though they have made different choices or hold different beliefs, there is good reason to conclude that this "explanation" is actually an account. When Sarah asked women why they had pursued a steady work career, pulled back from work, or followed an interrupted work path, almost everyone replied their choice was the best one "for the family."[24] This response is undoubtedly true in the sense that each woman placed great importance on her family's well-being. Though that is an important finding in itself, it does not solve the puzzle of *why* women constructed different work paths in their efforts to care for their families. However "true" as an expression of a cultural and personal mandate for women (and arguably for men, too, albeit in a different way) to put family first, it does not explain why these women followed different paths. Explaining such variation requires a closer look at the diverse circumstances each woman faced as she endeavored to enact a "family first" mandate.

It is not surprising that people often attribute their actions or outlooks to widespread values and social norms. These norms and values are real, and it is reasonable to see them as motivating behavior. Yet they do not drive behavior in the direct manner often depicted. People can possess similar values but enact them in different ways, and they can possess different values but act in similar ways. They can also hold a complex set of inconsistent values that make it problematic—even impossible—to use them as guides to action.[25] When participants invoke the same norms as the "cause" of different actions, this is a good sign that these perceived motives are more appropriately understood as accounts.

If the interviewees articulate motivations that do not explain outcomes (at least when taken alone), how do you discover what is missing? Fortunately, you possess substantive knowledge and methodological tools that participants do not. Drawing on information from all the interviews allows you to place each in the context of the whole. By asking what each woman did before asking her why she did it, Sarah was able to find the factors that some shared and others did not. Women who reported a lack of childcare, a difficult boss, disrespect at work, and little support at home chose to pull back from work, while those with good childcare, a promising job, and support at home were more likely to remain in the labor force, even though members of both groups attributed the decision to their families' needs. As this case exemplifies, distinguishing between contextual factors and personal accounts can be a powerful analytic tool for finding more fundamental (if not necessarily visible) forces that help explain both worldviews and "real world" practices, even if interviewees are unaware of them.

Attending to "Non-Relationships"

Another analytic strategy is to look for interview findings that do *not* confirm expected relationships. This may seem surprising given the prevalence of "publication bias"—the tendency to report in published works only statistically significant relationships and ignore or downplay nonsignificant ones. It is nevertheless quite useful to find out whether purported explanations actually help explain the conceptualized outcomes.[26] Despite the common assumption that financial need drives women's attachment to paid work, Sarah found that middle-class women were more likely to take a steady work path than were working-class and poorer interviewees. Similarly, Kathleen found that children whose parents stayed together were only slightly more satisfied with their upbringing than children whose parents separated. In both cases, the relationships hypothesized in the literature proved to be weak or even reversed. While the absence of an expected relationship is not grounds for rejecting a theoretical frame, it signals the need to analyze the links—in these cases, between class resources and women's work decisions or between parental breakups and children's views—in a more nuanced way that uncovers factors and processes not included in other explanations.

Unraveling the Puzzle of Contradictory Statements

Still another analytic strategy is to explore the reasons for contradictory responses. Material of this sort may signal that earlier analyses either miss something important or conflate several core ideas. When analyzing young adults' plans for the future, Kathleen found it difficult to classify them on a single continuum from "traditional" to "egalitarian." Instead, most interviewees expressed a desire for relationship and marital equality at some points in the interview while expressing equally strong reservations at others. Though conflicting statements of this kind may seem at first to undermine a participant's credibility, a more sustained analysis revealed that they masked two distinct dimensions. The vast majority were expressing egalitarian aspirations but also indicating skepticism about their ability to achieve equality amid the pervasive obstacles—suggesting a need to distinguish between aspirations and expectations (a point relevant to our earlier discussion about how to develop concepts). This insight solved the puzzle created by what originally appeared to be a discrepancy, and it led to the creation of a conceptual distinction between "ideals" and "fallback positions" should those ideals prove out of reach.

The takeaway is that you should never dismiss seemingly incompatible responses as unreliable or unimportant. Since neither human psychology nor social arrangements can be presumed to be internally consistent, you must accept the validity of inconsistent findings and seek the reasons for their presence. More often than not, inconsistency and ambivalence are neither misstatements nor attempts to deceive but instead are understandable reactions to incompatible options or ideals and ambiguous social circumstances.

Analyzing contradictory statements also offers an opportunity to address concerns that interviewees are prone to present themselves in a positive light. Rather than dismissing this as "bias," it is more useful to see it as evidence. Such statements tell us what people perceive to be socially desirable and thus normative. For example, even if some men express egalitarian aspirations because they believe such views are more socially acceptable, their answers provide important clues about how the social norms and cultural scripts they draw from have shifted. By taking all answers seriously, rather than rejecting some as insincere, it becomes possible to tease out the meaning of socially desirable answers and place them in the context of everything else that is known about the individual participant and the sample as a whole.

Charting Trajectories

You can take advantage of the time ordering at the heart of life history information to situate accounts within an explanatory chain. Whatever your substantive focus (which can be on almost any aspect of social life), you can construct a trajectory that compares each person's or institution's baseline with their or its position at the time of the interview. This provides a framework for examining the temporal ordering of a person's or group's exposure to life events and their personal or collective reactions to that exposure. Then the analysis can locate the external forces and internal processes—the interdependent influences of structure, agency, and interaction—that contribute to various destinations.

One useful approach is to distinguish between trajectories of stability and trajectories of change. When matters go "according to plan," interviewees are prone to see their current circumstances as a predetermined or "natural" outcome whose causes are self-evident and need no explanation. When interviewees report significant change, however, they are more likely to notice the events and experiences that pushed or pulled them "off course." These "changers" are then in a better position to notice the social forces that "nonchangers" are less likely to see. In the interviews for *Hard Choices*, Kathleen found that women who did not undergo significant change were less likely to notice the experiences that supported their early plans and aspirations. In contrast, women whose adult decisions did not reflect their early plans found it easier to identify the occasions that prompted change. The experience of change made it easier to locate "turning points" when unexpected obstacles foreclosed earlier expectations and unexpected opportunities opened new options. Whether they pursued an occupational career or turned toward domesticity, the trajectories of both groups were shaped by exposure to a set of unanticipated opportunities and constraints; yet members of the changing group were better positioned to notice the experiences that triggered change in life direction and personal outlook.[27]

If the focus is a social movement or institutional form rather than an individual trajectory, you can apply a similar approach. Organizations and groups, like individuals, must either reconstitute or change their shape and functioning over time. They, too, typically encounter occasions when circumstances compel a response of some kind. Interviewing the various participants involved in the relevant institutional field can reveal the contending forces and decision-making processes that, especially at critical moments, lead to either maintaining the status quo or following a new direction.[28]

Some may object that interviewees will reinterpret the past to fit their current circumstances and will thus omit information that does not support their most recent view. Many participants may indeed report a smooth line from the past to the present—that is, they may believe that "what happened had to happen." Yet, as an analyst, you possess counterfactual information from other cases as well as from their earlier statements that points to possible discrepancies and helps disentangle perceptions from unnoticed but nevertheless important factors.

Kathleen's interviews revealed that the vast majority of participants believed early childhood socialization, and especially a mother's "model," explained their adult decisions. Yet half of those with a stay-at-home mother had forged strong work commitments, while half of those with an employed mother had left the workplace to rear children. Constructing and comparing these different trajectories revealed that early experiences mattered, but not in the direct or determining way the interviewees (and many theorists) believe. Instead, the women interpreted and reinterpreted these early models as they grew, with some finding a mother's example less appealing or unrealistic in adulthood. They drew on "socialization" as a cultural script to explain their choices, even though their childhood experiences were subject to revision as they encountered obstacles to achieving early life goals or opportunities to pursue different ones. By comparing the experiences of those who describe turning points with those who do not, any lack of awareness among those who stay on course becomes analytically meaningful. These comparisons point not just toward the significance of events but to the significance of "non-events" as well.[29]

Explaining Trajectories

Comparative analysis of trajectories provides a technique to overcome the human inclination to perceive harmony between the past and present as well as to discover the "non-events" that matter in people's lives. After charting the variety of trajectories among interviews (including possible differences between stable and changing ones), you can turn your attention to analyzing why and how people and groups follow a particular path and arrive at a particular destination. This kind of dynamic analysis can reveal the factors that shape a variety of outcomes, including the social positions, actions, and beliefs of individuals or the developmental paths of organized groups. Everything has a life history, and it is as appropriate to analyze the chain of events that propel groups and institutions as it is to focus on the diverse paths of individuals.

Returning to the example of deciphering children's views on their family life, Kathleen first found that the usual suspects—such as a parent's marital status or a mother's work commitment—did not explain why some children viewed their families as supportive while others did not. In the search for another explanation, she discovered that a parent's or guardian's ability to respond in a gender-flexible way to an unexpected contingency (such as a parental job loss or breakup) enhanced a child's sense of support. When households confronted crises in their ability to provide income or care, families that adapted by developing more flexible strategies were able to develop more supportive family paths than families that were unable or unwilling to revise their arrangements by transgressing established gender boundaries.

Finding what cannot explain an outcome—or at least cannot do so alone—will prompt your search for alternative or additional explanations. In this example, the degree of gender flexibility, rather than the specific household form, did a better job of accounting for children's varied views about their upbringing. By mapping the sequential interaction between exposure to social changes (such as the rise of marital fragility or job insecurity) and individual reactions, the analysis uncovered a different way to conceive of family life and how it influences children's experiences.[30] It also linked the dynamics of widespread social and cultural shifts to the dynamics of individual lives and social groups. While this example focuses on families, you can use the same analytic strategy to theorize about almost any topic. In essence, it provides a concrete way to examine the interplay between structure and agency as diverse and possibly changing social contexts spark specific human responses, which then have social consequences going forward.

Finding the Figure in the Stone

Almost everyone agrees that qualitative material lends itself to telling vivid stories and describing the richness of social life. We would add that it also offers a unique and potent opportunity to build novel and convincing explanations of how, why, and with what consequences the stories people tell take the forms they do. To take a metaphor from a very different creative pursuit, one way to conceive of the analysis of qualitative interviews is that it is akin to Michelangelo's view of sculpting. Just as he proclaimed that every block of stone has a statue inside it, and it is the task of the sculptor to discover it, there is a hidden structure within the complex material that interviews provide and the job of analysis is to find it.

We have outlined a number of strategies to "find the figure" in interview data. These include immersion in the findings, organizing the material conceptually, attending to non-relationships and contradictory findings, and applying basic rules of logic such as conducting a comparative analysis and examining the time order of events. All of these steps provide ways to impose order on messy material, which then increases the chances of making theoretical as well as empirical discoveries.

While we have suggested a number of methodological strategies, methods are only tools. Each analyst must decide whether and how to use them. There is no surefire route to arriving at an "aha" moment, but systematically analyzing your findings is the route most likely to get you there. More often than not, inspirational breakthroughs sit atop groundwork that took time and care to build. These moments of inspiration result from careful design. If and when they occur, a figure that was once obscured becomes clear. As it becomes visible, you will be able to offer a picture that leaves others wondering why no one had seen it before.[31]

7

Pulling It All Together

Telling Your Story and Making Your Case

It's time to head for the finish line. This means clarifying the arguments you have worked hard to develop and working out a plan to present them clearly and effectively. Analytic principles need to guide your decisions at this stage, no less than at the previous ones, but the process of writing now joins them at center stage. Building and presenting an argument with interview material has much in common with other forms of social science and general non-fiction writing, but it also poses specific challenges. How do you navigate the tension between presenting an explanation of your findings and taking a stand about their ethical implications? How do you pull the disparate parts of your analysis together and select the appropriate evidence to support it? How do you present the material in an engaging, compelling way without sacrificing the logical principles that guide scientific inquiry? The process of finishing involves addressing these challenges.

Interviewing as Science and Art, Revisited

As you near the finish, this is a good time to reflect again on the tension between analysis and moral judgment. While physicists, chemists, and biologists need to ask themselves whether their methods are ethical and whether their findings will be put to beneficial uses (which is why scientific groups have codes of professional ethics), it makes little sense to attribute moral responsibility to a molecule or even to an animal of the nonhuman variety. In the social sciences, however, the moral dimension is inescapable. Since humans possess consciousness, live in social groups, and adopt moral codes, how we make sense of human activity inevitably raises questions with ethical and political implications. Are individuals responsible for their beliefs and actions, or do these represent the power of "external" forces? Are such beliefs and actions worthy of praise or opprobrium? Is it your professional

The Science and Art of Interviewing. Kathleen Gerson and Sarah Damaske, Oxford University Press (2021). © Oxford University Press. DOI: 10.1093/oso/9780199324286.001.0001 goal—and responsibility—to evaluate as well as to explain your findings? We cannot provide definitive answers to questions that neither philosophers nor scientists can resolve, but we offer some ways to think about and navigate the tensions they pose.

A good way to begin is to distinguish between the reasons that motivated your research and the analytic approach you used to find the answers. Your motivation—which likely involved an interest in matters with moral, political, or policy implications—provides the point of departure for setting up the research problem in the introduction to your article, book, or research report. It also sets the stage for returning to the moral or political implications of your findings in the conclusion. This leaves the space in between—whether in an article or in book chapters—to focus on presenting and analyzing (rather than judging) your interview findings—an analysis that should be driven by your desire to understand, whatever your value concerns may be. Here your goal is to present what you found, not what you wished to find.

The importance of distinguishing between analysis and evaluation is not the same as asserting that analysis needs to be "value free." All researchers hold values, and it is disingenuous to claim those values do not influence what we study and how. Instead, the challenge is to pay close attention to when, where, and how values enter your research and writing process. Just as setting your personal judgments aside helps you conduct effective interviews and learn about the worldviews of each interviewee, effectively presenting your findings depends on building an evidentiary case for the answers you propose to the core research questions. You have followed and demonstrated a rigorous methodological strategy in developing and conducting the interviews, and your manner of presentation is one more step in the process of building trust in the findings. As we've noted, qualitative data cannot be judged by the same criteria used to assess the validity of quantitative analysis. Yet methodological rigor matters in qualitative research, and a clear presentation of the evidence that supports your argument (as well as the acknowledgment of any that does not) is the best response to such scrutiny. By letting the findings tell the story, you clear the path to a concluding position that draws on and flows from them.

This is also a good time to remember that interviewing provides a window onto the social world that cannot be accessed in any other way. To the quick judgments gathered by surveys and the observations gathered by ethnographies, interviewing contributes knowledge about the role of meaning in human experience and the social processes that link it to social structures and human actions. These unique insights are not accidental by-products of ordinary conversation. They are the product of a specific set of analytic and practical techniques that together constitute a systematic and rigorous method.[1]

Writing It Up

By bringing people's personal reflections to life on the page, interview material can make for compelling reading. Yet first you need to decide what to present and how to present it. Although the ability to write well is invaluable, we will not focus here on the general issues that face all writers. Many others have offered detailed, helpful guides for preparing to write, carving out the space and time to write, identifying your audience, and developing the practices that help organize the writing process. For those seeking guidance about how to tackle social science writing, Howard Becker's *Writing for Social Scientists*, Kristen Luker's *Salsa Dancing into the Social Sciences*, and Eviatar Zerubavel's *The Clockwork Muse* are especially helpful.[2] For more general considerations about how to write well, there is no substitute for William Strunk and E. B. White's classic, *The Elements of Style*.[3] Anne Lamott's *Bird by Bird* also offers guidance and inspiration for writers of any kind.[4] Some mainstays for writing a nonfiction book are Susan Rabiner and Alfred Fortunato's *Thinking Like Your Editor* and William Germano's *Getting It Published*.[5] And those writing for journals will find Abbie Goldberg and Katherine Allen's "Communicating Qualitative Research" full of helpful advice.[6]

These sources offer various nuggets of wisdom about how to prepare for, begin, and sustain a writing project as well as how to write well regardless of the genre or audience. Here, we focus on the particular challenges facing depth interviewers as they build an argument, choose the evidence to present and how to present it, and tell a compelling and convincing story. The sheer volume and complexity of interview material make it especially challenging to present in written form. What writing strategies are most likely to help bring focus and order to it? What presentation style can most effectively draw on this data to make a strong case for your argument? And what format is likely to engage readers? From the introduction to the presentation of findings to the closing arguments, your goal is to use the interview material to tell a convincing and compelling story that builds a strong case about how to solve the empirical and theoretical puzzles you have posed.

Setting the Stage and Introducing the Question(s)

The introduction should present the empirical and theoretical question(s) or puzzles(s), explain why they are important and why your answers make a contribution, and sufficiently engage readers' interest so that they will continue reading. Although some authors prefer to wait to compose the introduction until after they have completed the rest of the writing, most find that writing a preliminary version of the introduction helps sharpen the argument, locates areas that remain fuzzy and need further clarification, and sets the stage for the pages to follow. You will have ample opportunity for revisions, but even a vague introduction provides a start and a provisional map for the rest of the writing journey.

Unlike a work of fiction or narrative nonfiction, social science writing should not leave the reader in suspense for long. Instead, as journalists say, "don't bury the lede."[7] Unlike a news report, the first few sentences need not contain a main data point, but neither should the reader have to search for the puzzle you plan to solve. First impressions count. For this reason, try to state the research focus and question concisely (and vividly) as soon as possible.

Interview material gives you several options for introducing the problem. One standard approach is to present one or more concrete examples, either from the interviews or another source, that illustrate the puzzle you wish to solve, adding a brief discussion of how the following pages will solve it. To begin her book on the far-reaching consequences that financial insecurity has on people's lives, Marianne Cooper starts with a news item about an unemployed man who, after a "fruitless three-year search" for a job, robbed a bank and then gave the money to the security guard and waited for the police to arrive, believing that jail would provide the security he'd failed to find in his search for a job.[8] Though an extreme example, this story colorfully depicts the terrain—experiences of economic insecurity—her book will explore.

Selecting one or more illustrative examples from the research can spark a reader's interest (and both of us have used this technique), but it needs to be an appropriate one. An especially colorful example is not necessarily a theoretically significant one. To carry the weight of introducing an argument, your opening example needs to represent a large pattern in your data and embody core elements of your argument. A colorful example may be attention-getting, but if it is unique or too unusual, it is not empirically apt or theoretically interesting. A good introductory example represents an "ideal type," to use the language of Max Weber (and Plato before him), that conveys both the essence of the empirical story and the theoretical argument you plan to flesh out in the analysis to come.

As a second option, you can begin with an empirical puzzle drawn from the current state of knowledge as it appears in relevant sources on your topic, such as scholarly studies, current analyses of historical trends, or even debates taking place in the popular press or other public arenas. In her discussion of employed youth in the United States, Yasemin Besen-Cassino juxtaposes the widely held view that the retail and service jobs commonly associated with teenage employment are "bad jobs" with evidence that the adolescent labor market is actually "dominated by more affluent youth."[9] She could then ask a question without an obvious answer: why are financially advantaged young people more likely to hold these poorly paid and generally unappealing jobs?

In addition to beginning with an illustrative example or an empirical puzzle, a third approach can focus on a theoretical debate the research addresses. Janice McCabe's study of friendship networks in college, for example, points to conflicting arguments about the role of friendship groups in enhancing academic performance, with some researchers arguing that such groups are an important source of support and others taking the position that they can undermine school success.[10]

No one approach to framing the question is inherently better than another, and your introduction can contain any or all of these elements. The shape an introduction takes is a matter of choice and often depends on your audience and venue. Journals are more likely to prefer an introduction that focuses on an empirical puzzle or theoretical debate that is firmly established in the literature, since this provides a condensed format that readers anticipate. Books, on the other hand, often begin with illustrative examples that can be presented in a lengthier and more vivid fashion.

The most important job of the introduction is to grab readers' attention and tell them why they should keep reading. Ask yourself now, as you did at the outset of your project: why would the reader care? Even though the answer to that question may seem obvious to you, it may be less obvious to others. You can bring readers on board in varied ways, and what works for some audiences may not be effective for others. Pointing out a study's theoretical or empirical significance will spark the interest of specialists, while referring to media stories does better at drawing in nonspecialists and a wider lay audience. Using an illustrative quote or story from your interviews may signal to specialists and nonspecialists alike that your topic is timely and important.

The introduction should also explain how and why the research adds to the existing state of knowledge. What does your study contribute? Lynne Haney, an accomplished ethnographer who integrates interviews into her research, suggests three main ways that qualitative research helps build theory: you can address a gap in the literature, merge multiple literatures, and/or change the level at which the problem is understood.[11] As we note in Chapter 3, posing empirical puzzles lets you address gaps in what we know. For example, if we tend to think X about a phenomenon but Y is also true, then how is our current understanding of X limited and what else do we need to know to fully understand it? In the social sciences as in the hard sciences, as Thomas Kuhn writes in *The Structure of Scientific Revolutions*, the accumulation of empirical developments that do not fit existing paradigms propels the search for new—and often higher-level—paradigms.[12]

Another way to frame your contribution is to explain how your research combines previously disparate and unconnected areas. In his discussion of the late nineteenth-century cholera epidemic, Owen Whooley synthesizes the study of social movements with the analysis of medical professionalization to provide a broader understanding of how the cholera epidemic marked a turning point in the development of American medicine by destabilizing the still nascent American Medical Association and upending the medical community.[13] Likewise, Grace Yukich combines the literature on social movements with the literature on religion to demonstrate the influence of liberal churches on the debate about immigration in contemporary politics.[14]

Still another way is to enlarge the scope of the problem or the evidence used to make sense of it. If a topic has been addressed primarily at the macro level through the analysis of large quantitative data sets, qualitative interviews can illuminate the micro processes that explain how and why these trends unfold. Ofer Sharone, for example, compares the experiences of unemployment in the United States and Israel to develop a theory about how contrasting cultural norms influence expectations about what unemployed job seekers must do and the extent to which they feel shamed and responsible for their situation.[15]

These three goals—introducing the questions, engaging readers' interest, and establishing significance—are intertwined.[16] Certainly, explaining the problem and its importance should engage people's interest, although how you do this depends on the audience. Journals attract readers who will want to know an article's contribution to theory and research, while books, which must also make a significant contribution to their fields, contain a wider range of styles and may wish to appeal to a general audience as well as specialists.

Addressing Theoretical and Empirical Debates

After introducing and setting up a problem, your next step typically is to consider the state of relevant knowledge about it. Though the more common label for this section is "literature review," we prefer to conceive of it as an analytic introduction—that is, its goal is to introduce prevailing theoretical paradigms. Instead of summarizing everything known about a topic, your analytic overview should consider the theoretical—and, for some, political—debates surrounding it and assess each theory's relevance for answering your research questions. What are the strengths and weaknesses of each contending theoretical approach and what evidence currently supports or casts doubt on them? This helps to clarify why and how your study—and the findings and arguments that flow from it—will contribute to these debates.

Although a critical assessment is central to this process, it is good to resist the temptation to create "straw figures" by oversimplifying the work of others. (More on this later in the chapter.) Scientific progress depends on subjecting existing paradigms to rigorous testing and critique, and no body of work can be considered the last word. Careful, thoughtful critique recognizes the significance of others' contributions and addresses the strongest version of their arguments. Done respectfully, incisive critique can be the highest form of flattery, for it signals you consider the work to be important and influential (or why would you be discussing it?). Above all, clarifying how your project builds on or challenges prior work provides a point of departure for presenting your theoretical approach and research design.[17]

Clarifying the Research Design

It is now time to connect the questions and theoretical overview to your research design by telling the reader why you relied on interviews, which groups you included, and why you chose to interview them and not others. This is the place to elaborate on how the interviews and their findings contribute to solving the research puzzles you have posed. The key is to concisely lay out your research design and why it is appropriate. Given how much thought you have put into developing and implementing the design, it should be relatively straightforward to present your rationale and procedures. The format and degree of detail will nevertheless vary depending on whether it will be part of an article or book. Books provide more space to present the methodology, even though it may be better to place many of the specifics in an appendix (or several) so that the body of the text can focus on your findings and analysis— that is, on telling the story rather than on explaining how the story came to be. The first or second chapter should nevertheless include a methodological overview so that readers know who was interviewed and why. Appendices can then present greater detail for interested readers, including a lengthier discussion of the methodological rationale and more details about how the sample was selected and whom it contains.

For a stand-alone article, a section on methods will likely follow the analytic overview and precede the presentation of findings. Wherever it appears, the presentation of methods must do some heavy lifting in a small space. It needs to clarify the rationale for conducting interviews, selecting participants, and collecting and analyzing the findings. It should describe the resulting sample and consider any implications for reaching conclusions about a larger population. Since readers who use other research methods may not understand the principles that guide depth interviewing, it helps to walk readers through the logic underpinning the methodological choices and demonstrate that you have taken a rigorous approach to collecting and analyzing your data. Journals often require detailed information about the process of data analysis and will expect a succinct description of the methodological approach in terms that are well accepted among the relevant audiences.[18]

Making Your Argument

Now on to the heart of the matter: presenting your argument and analyzing your findings. Whether the format is a lengthy book or a pithy article, this effort will take up the bulk of the allotted space. If presented accessibly, systematically, and vividly, interview material makes for interesting reading. Yet even at its most compelling, qualitative material does not speak for itself. It is not sufficient to simply list quotes and assume the reader understands their significance. The writing challenge is to present each piece of evidence in a context that makes its meaning clear and unambiguous.

If you feel hesitant to "impose" meaning on your material, remember that no one else knows it as intimately and thoroughly. You are the only person who has met the interviewees, pored over the transcripts of their interviews, and pondered the details of their lives. Long after the participants have forgotten—or at least become far removed from—the interview experience, you have continued to grapple with the information they have shared. Who else is better prepared to explain the meaning of their responses? After all the hard work, this is no time to shy away from making clear, confident, and even bold assertions that clarify how and why a selected quote demonstrates a concept, pattern, relationship, or argument.

While the analytic framework will guide the quotes, stories, and quantitative summaries you select, they can be presented in a variety of ways. Some studies divide the material into thematic areas, while others do so by distinguishing among sample groups. In her presentation of "the anxieties of affluence," Rachel Sherman does both.[19] The opening of her book describes how the very rich viewed themselves compared to others: did they see themselves as possessing relatively little (those she terms "upwardly oriented") or did they see themselves as possessing a lot (those termed "downwardly oriented")? The remaining chapters of the book then present her analytic categories, particularly those that delineate the "moral dimensions" of these orientations, with chapters on working, consumption, financial giving, household labor, and parenting. Still another option, which we often employ, is to trace and explain the paths that led to the various outcomes of focus as well as the factors that shaped the direction of each path; the next step analyzes the consequences of each outcome.[20]

Whatever form your presentation takes, it will likely include several analytic categories: the outcomes, the factors and mechanisms that contribute to these outcomes, how these factors interact with each other, and what consequences they have for identities, beliefs, and action strategies. There is also a likely order for this presentation. Since you cannot explain something until you define it, describing the outcomes you have conceptualized and how they vary comes first. In a study of those living in rural areas of deep poverty, for example, Jennifer Sherman first describes the distinct levels of "moral capital"—including higher, lower, and negative moral capital—her interviewees depicted before she explains how and why they developed these distinctions among themselves.[21]

The next step is to explain how and why the outcomes that are your focus take the form they do. What factors—as you have conceptualized them—contribute to explaining the variation in your outcomes, and what factors that you originally thought might contribute to the explanation actually do *not*? Sherman thus turns next to examining the connection between rural poverty and its potential sources. Contrary to the widespread focus on the central role of personal and family dysfunction, she shows that American politics, government policies, and the cultural stress on individual responsibility provide a more useful frame for understanding how the rural poor make sense of their economic disadvantage.

This section can also highlight the implications of your findings for prevailing theories, building on the discussion of the limitations of existing explanatory frames in the introduction. Here is where the payoff for your prior analytic work becomes most clear, for you can now demonstrate what does and does *not* contribute to explaining an outcome. In a prelude to a social structural analysis about why some MBA graduates continue to work in business while others do not, Sarah Patterson and her co-authors drew on their interview findings to show that perspectives stressing the role of "family devotion" did not adequately explain differences in the work outcomes of these women because they generally shared beliefs about the importance of family.[22] Similarly, Kathleen set the stage for arguing that children see their families as "a film rather than a snapshot" by first demonstrating how a focus on static family "types" could not account for their experiences growing up or their ultimate views about family life.[23]

Although it is useful to begin by demonstrating that some explanations do not suffice to explain the findings, it is never sufficient just to point out the limitations of another argument. Instead, such a critique can become a point of departure for building your own argument about what *does* matter. There are a variety of ways to do this. We prefer to first depict the various paths that lead to disparate outcomes, then present the reasons that account for these differences and the various factors—including critical events and turning points—that contribute to arriving at one destination or another, and, finally, analyze the consequences that ensue after arriving at each destination.

Jennifer Sherman's book, for example, establishes the relationship between poverty, morality, and lack of work in the lives of her interviewees and then turns to analyze the consequences for the participants' family life and especially for views on masculinity.[24] Sharone's study of unemployment in the United States and Israel first introduces the American system, including how job seekers search for work, and then discusses the Israeli search process, pointing to the differences in how these two systems are socially constructed (creating more deleterious consequences for American job seekers' sense of self).[25] And McCabe's study of college students first identifies "tight-knitters," "compartmentalizers," and "samplers" as the main groups of students categorized by the strategies each group used to create friendships. She then delineates the factors and processes that pushed and pulled the students in diverse directions and examins the consequences of these friendship networks.[26] These examples represent only a few of the various options for organizing the presentation of your analysis. Ultimately, the choice depends on your personal style as well as what works best for the material and for the argument you wish to build.

Presenting Interview Findings

Whatever your presentation style may be, it's important to remain attentive to the general principles shared by all methodologies: developing and defining key concepts, describing and documenting patterns, making connections among the patterns, and reaching theoretical conclusions. Using interview material to accomplish these goals raises an obvious challenge—how to use the complex aspects of a relatively small number of cases to make a convincing argument about possible causal relationships. Combining several strategies makes that possible.

First, it is useful to begin with one or more carefully chosen stories that exemplify each analytic "ideal type" that will become a focus in ensuing pages. Take care to include the aspects of each story that illustrate the details to be fleshed out going forward as well as the arguments they support. To illustrate core concepts in our work and show how they take shape in the participants' lives, we like to present condensed life histories that illustrate diverse life paths and destinations.[27]

The next step is to interweave a descriptive narrative with a discussion of the factors, processes, and mechanisms that drive the narrative. The key is to select quotes that best illustrate the range of factors that matter, the reasons they matter, the ways they operate and interact over time, and the responses they prompt. One effective format is to present the major routes taken by each group within the sample of interviewees and then highlight the factors that propelled each group along their distinct path and toward their specific destination. This approach identifies the range of important life events, social contexts, and institutional arrangements that contribute to specific outcomes and shows how they converge and interact with each other in a developing, unfolding process. An analysis of this kind sets the stage for then presenting the range of consequences that ensue for each group. This format demonstrates how specific social arrangements and forces influence the lives of participants and then how the participants react to these forces, often in unexpected ways. It highlights the dynamic process by which social contexts shape experiences that, in turn, provoke mental and behavioral responses. No less important, it provides a framework for presenting your argument via an accessible, concrete, and compelling narrative. Appropriate examples flesh out and provide support for each abstract argument.

Using carefully chosen quotes and related descriptive material to make theoretical arguments about how social forces and contexts are connected to individual worldviews and action strategies provides a forceful way to bring the relationship between structure and agency to life as a dynamic, interactive process. Whether you choose this format or another, you can use your findings to describe the core dimensions of a set of outcomes, explain how and why these outcomes came to be, and explore their consequences for people's life circumstances and psychological orientations.

Selecting Quotes

Vivid quotes are the lifeblood of interview material, but they are meaningful only insofar as they illustrate a broader pattern within and among the interviews. The significance of any quote depends on its role in the analysis. Specifying the social and analytic context gives meaning to each quote or comparable piece of information. (It is also important to identify the person being quoted, but only using a pseudonym and providing generally descriptive information to preserve confidentiality.)[28] It is necessary but never sufficient to select the right quote, even if you know why you selected it. Even the best quote can leave the reader confused and struggling to impute an interpretation. It is thus your job to explain the significance of each quote or set of quotes by providing the analytic context as a guide to its meaning.

If you wish to distinguish between the underlying social forces that con-tribute to the interviewees' life paths and the accounts people give to explain these paths, the text needs to explain this distinction in a prelude (and pos-sibly also a postlude) that introduces the supporting quote. When we present a participant's quote invoking the role of "luck" in determining that person's situation, we clarify that this quote serves to illustrate how some participants draw on a cultural frame stressing the importance of chance, *not* as evi-dence that luck—at least as conceived as disconnected from institutional arrangements and social contexts that distribute resources and advantages unequally—plays the decisive role in explaining the outcome.

Placing Quotes in Analytic and Numerical Context

Even after you have selected the quotes and illustrative stories that move your argument forward and explained their deeper meaning and conceptual sig-nificance, it is also necessary to document that a selected example is not a unique or unusual case. Quotations and descriptive summaries provide the primary evidence, but your readers also need to know how many additional but unreported cases they represent. While numbers alone are never suffi-cient, it is useful to report the proportion of the sample that shares a similar experience or view (as well as to draw on relevant findings from other studies with larger samples).[29] People can reasonably debate the role of numbers, ta-bles, and figures in the presentation of interview material, but it is always useful to let readers know the breakdowns within the sample or the preva-lence of a finding. Even though trends and patterns within your sample need not have any implications for the prevalence of these patterns in the broader population, presenting basic numerical tallies—such as the proportion of the sample that falls into different groups—are additional forms of evidence that help build your argument and add support to your claims.

Even though numerical summaries take a backseat to the qualitative ma-terial, they nevertheless lend added clarity by providing an overview of the sample contours and the size of the group for which each piece of informa-tion applies. If raw numbers or exact percentages seem to imply more than you intend (for example, suggesting a broader prevalence in the wider pop-ulation), an alternative is to cite the general proportion of interviewees—such as a third, a half, or two-thirds—who reported a certain behavior or expressed a particular view. Whether you choose to report proportions or absolute numbers, you should always make it clear that these numerical summaries provide information crucial to making sense of the findings in your sample and are not presented to claim statistical significance or representativeness of a large population.[30]

However you choose to summarize your findings, the key is to let the audience know why and how the selected quotes illustrate a noteworthy pattern, demonstrate a specific point, and fit within your larger argument. Readers need and typically want specific information about the frequency of a particular finding, rather than vague descriptors such as "some," "many," or "few." As Howard Becker has pointed out, such imprecise statements are "quasi-statistics."[31] They do not provide sufficiently precise information for the reader to adequately interpret the findings. For this reason, we prefer to present more precise quantitative information—in the form of either percentages or absolute numbers—along with the qualitative material, while also making it clear that the numbers are included to clarify the contours within the study sample and not to claim statistical representativeness or significance. Presented properly, numerical summaries add valuable information that stories and quotes alone cannot.

The Cutting Room Floor

Since interviews generate a voluminous amount of material, one of the biggest challenges is to decide how much of it to present. To begin, you need to know what you wish to argue in order to find the best supporting evidence. Yet there are likely to be far more illustrative quotes available for each argument than you can include. Too much information can bore the reader and disrupt the narrative flow, while too little can undermine the power of your argument. The interviewing method provides more than enough compelling material to push your larger argument forward. Yet this advantage means that you will have more analytically relevant material, including quotes and stories, than there will be room to include (which is why you should use a "good quote" code during the coding stage).

How then to select a quote or story among all the alternatives? Richness should not be the sole criterion. While it may be tempting to include every especially interesting quote, you should not present a quote when it does not represent a general pattern, for at best this wastes space and at worst it takes readers on a misleading detour. The general rule is to include as much as necessary and no more, but that raises the question of how to judge what is necessary and what is not. A common temptation is to include as many quotes and stories as possible, especially if they seem interesting. Another is to rely on the quotes rather than your analysis to tell the story. Yet brevity is also integral to making a clear argument.[32] A good test is thus to ask what each quote adds to the story and the argument. If you have presented three or four quotes when one or two will do, a good editor is likely to delete a number of them, perhaps including some of your favorites.[33]

Sometimes a quote may seem especially resonant but still leave the reader unclear about its relevance. At these moments, consider what about that quote makes it difficult to ignore. Does the appeal lie in its uniqueness or in its ability to embody a set of widely shared experiences? Does it point in an overlooked analytic direction that might reorient or add to the explanatory frame and is thus worthy of unpacking? If a deeper consideration of such findings points to new analytic insights, it remains possible to make appropriate adjustments even at this late stage.

One relatively simple solution to the problem of what to do with informative material that does not fit in the body of the text is to put some of it in an appendix (as we do in this book). Placing meaningful but not directly relevant information (such as general sample characteristics, methodological insights, feedback from participants, and interesting bits of data that do not advance the core arguments) in an appendix opens up space in the main body of your writing to weave the analysis and interview material into a compelling argument and succinct narrative.

Crafting a Persuasive Conclusion

When you arrive at the conclusion, you have permission to "go big"—as long as you tread carefully and stay within the limits of your evidence. Assuming you originally asked big questions and your research design brought them down to a manageable level, you can now tell readers what your answers are and summarize the evidence that supports them (and not others). Assuming that your analysis has been painstaking and convincing, you have also earned the credibility to reflect on the significance of your answers, speculate about their implications, and take a personal stand.

This is a good time to ask yourself: What do I know now that I didn't know before the research began, and what is surprising and important about these findings? A summary of your empirical work provides the answer, but that is only the first step. To expand on the summary, it's important to discuss clearly and confidently how your findings and analysis reorient, reformulate, or expand theoretical thinking. Do your findings debunk certain theories and support others or help adjudicate between competing approaches? Do they extend or add complexity to a prevailing approach or form the basis for reconceiving theory in a new way? What framework do you propose for making sense of the patterns and relationships your interviews have revealed? Everything you have done to this point gives you permission—and provides an opportunity—to move beyond your findings to explore and articulate the broader theoretical implications.[34] Put simply, a strong conclusion uses the findings to move existing theoretical understanding forward.

A strong conclusion also addresses the limitations of your research and clarifies when and how your arguments do and do not apply. It is neither necessary nor effective to take a defensive posture, but it is also important not to overreach in making your claims. Acknowledging a study's limits lets you allay potential skeptics and clarifies your work's place within a wider body of knowledge. All research has limitations, and recognizing them provides a platform for explaining why and how the study's contributions are nevertheless important and worthy of attention.

Finally, you can now bring your values to bear explicitly on the issues that have motivated your interest from the outset. The conclusion is thus your best opportunity to consider any wider implications of the research, including any political or policy implications you wish to consider. Even beyond these real-world implications, this is the moment when you can use your findings and arguments as a point of takeoff for thinking creatively and speculating more broadly about human society and social theory.

Style as Substance, or Making Your Case by Finding Your Voice

Style is not the same as substance, but it is integral to telling your story precisely and making your argument persuasively. Clear thinking and good writing are inseparable, and your ideas can become influential only if you express them effectively in writing. It is thus important to pay attention to matters of stylistic voice as well as to follow the rules of good writing. The good news is that interviews provide ideal material for combining resonant human detail with analytic rigor. The key is to use the material to tell a story that is grounded in empirical support and adds something new to what we already know or think we know.

Some stylistic principles transcend any specific method or data source. First, show respect for the ideas of others, especially if you disagree with them. You seek to build on past knowledge, not disregard or demolish it. It is also advisable to avoid interpretive overreach—a stylistic technique that can undermine rather than strengthen your credibility. You may be tempted to infer a person's beliefs, opinions, or reactions to specific experiences without clear evidence in support, but we all need to resist the lure of presuming to know about matters left unspoken. Researchers are not mind readers, and we need to limit our analysis to the information interviewees disclose. It is equally important to avoid presenting prevalent findings as if they are ubiquitous. This surrenders one of the strengths of interviewing, which is to pay attention to nuance, including minority as well as majority experiences and views. Rather than smoothing out variation in the search for averages, interview material can use counterexamples to bring this variation into stark relief. While Sarah found that the majority of women framed their work and family decisions as "for the family," not all did so; although most of the young men in Kathleen's study of children growing up during the gender revolution expected to fall back on a neo-traditional pattern, a smaller group anticipated a different fate.[35] Universal patterns are rare in social life, and ignoring the exceptions misses an opportunity to examine the complexity. By reporting minority responses and distinguishing them from more prevalent ones, the analysis becomes more credible as well as more illuminating.

Finally, though it may take courage, you have earned the opportunity to express your distinctive voice, even if that means disagreeing with others you hope to please or impress. Presenting an argument clearly, unambiguously, and without apology can feel risky. Yet the alternative is more perilous, for it can lead you to bury your argument under a blanket of conditionals, equivocations, and apologies. Armed with rich interview material that you have carefully collected and analyzed, you are on safe ground using a clear, straightforward, and forceful presentation style that avoids the passive voice (which obscures who or what is acting), avoids turgid prose and unnecessary jargon (not to be confused with widely accepted technical terms), and eschews vague qualifiers that lack precision and add little to the argument.[36] Without these stylistic burdens, you can sidestep writing in "sociologese" and reach instead for clarity and eloquence.[37]

Letting Go

Unlike a race, the location of the finish line to an interview project is not pre-set. You must ultimately decide when you have reached it. How do you determine you have included the right type and amount of analysis and supporting evidence (and excluded extraneous and unnecessary material)? When enough is enough? The end point of research and writing rarely announces itself. There is always more work that *can* be done. It can be difficult to decide when additional time and effort are no longer worth the payoff or the price. Considering the law of diminishing returns, you must weigh how much improvement additional work will add to the final product. Ask how long this work will take and what other opportunities you will lose by doing it. Are there advantages to meeting an earlier deadline or, alternatively, to extending the deadline to make room for more changes? The answers are necessarily judgment calls, and that makes the process of finishing as much an emotional decision as a cognitive one.

If a reasonable end point seems near but you are reluctant to stop, think about why you are resisting. If there are sound pedagogical reasons to believe the manuscript needs more work, then attend to these concerns. After all, the watchword for good writing is to revise, revise, and revise again. If after several revisions, however, you are still reluctant to let go, it may be time to ask if this is because you are committed to craftsmanship or just fearful of moving on. Are you worried about how your work will be received? About facing the challenge of starting a new project? About whether your work lives up to aspirations of perfection? These concerns are predictable reactions to facing the completion of a project that has taken so much time, effort, and devotion.

If a reluctance to finish is actually a strategy for avoidance, it helps to realize there will be future opportunities to make additional tweaks. To lower anxiety about showing the draft to editors, colleagues, reviewers, or authority figures, ask some trusted friends to read it first. Critical and constructive feedback offers a dose of reality while providing a map for making revisions. It may even help in thinking about how to extend your research in new directions for future projects. Keep in mind the aphorism "Don't let the perfect be the enemy of the good." The paradox of science is that it depends on debate and revision, not on reaching unattainable perfection. If you have done the job well, the results will provide a point of departure on which others can build. All your hard work has added to the pool of knowledge and gives you a platform to inspire others, engage with your professional peers, and (if you wish) contribute to the wider world of public debate and ideas.

Delivering a Presentation with Interview Findings

Once you have written up your findings and arguments (and, perhaps, before), you will likely have opportunities to present your research at a conference, a university colloquium, academic departments, and other settings. For studies that rely on qualitative interviews, presenting your findings and arguments orally poses somewhat different challenges than does writing it up. While the interview material remains central, you must still decide what to present and how to present it within a relatively short time period and on a fairly short canvas. Presentations often require explanations even pithier than what is required to fit in the tight spaces of a journal. This means setting the stage quickly, providing a brief overview of the literature (its limitations and your additions), raising your research question(s), providing enough details about your methods for the audience to have confidence in your findings, and still having enough time to devote most of your talk to presenting your findings, arguments, and conclusions. Daunting? Yes. But definitely feasible.

For short presentations, the kind you might give at a conference, we recommend one of two approaches. One option is to present the "puzzle" (if you are posing a puzzle, as we discussed in Chapter 2) on the first slide(s), discussing the literature—that is, the key theoretical debates and current state of empirical knowledge—in the next one(s), and then introducing your research questions. Another option is to briefly introduce the literature in the first slide(s) and then present the slide(s) that discuss the gaps in the literature you plan to address. Either way, it is good to present the research questions by your third or fourth slide, leaving ample time to present an overview of your methods, data, and findings. For coverage of data and methods, we typically use two to three slides—including one with details about the rationale and contours of the study design and data collection process, one with the sample characteristics, and one with information about how you analyzed your collected material. If you have additional information that you believe people may want to know, it's good to create additional slides that you can refer to in the question-and-answer session.

The next group of slides, which outline your findings and arguments, makes up the most crucial portion of the presentation. At this point, it may be appropriate to return to the research questions as a reminder and as a prelude to demonstrating how you will answer them. We generally like to highlight what conventional thinking has suggested about the answer(s) to our core questions, including the ways these approaches fall short. This sets the stage for presenting our findings and developing a framework that does a better job of explaining them and offers something new by way of theoretical understanding.

A major challenge to presenting findings based on qualitative interviews is the sheer amount of material involved. How best to draw on such voluminous and nuanced material to demonstrate your argument and keep the audience's attention? To avoid the problem of having the audience spend more time reading the slides than focusing on your ideas, it helps to avoid displaying long quotes (or even short ones). Instead, we recommend summarizing the main themes and analytic structure on your slides, incorporating carefully selected examples to illustrate each theme, group, and/or argument. If time allows, you can then read specific quotes to illustrate these findings and themes, taking care not to overdo it since the audience is likely to be waiting for the punchlines these quotes are chosen to represent.

For shorter talks, it's especially important to select core findings, arguments, and examples or, alternatively, brief but powerful quotes. Longer talks make it possible to expand the scope of the presentation, but not (in most instances) to cover everything. In the case of a book, for example, the challenge is to decide what stays and what goes. You can present an overview of the book that covers the highlights without diving too deeply into any one area. The benefit of this approach is that you are able to present most of your material and drive home your main contributions; the drawback is that to achieve this breadth you will likely need to sacrifice some of the nuance and depth in your findings (a major strength of interview material). Another strategy is to select a chapter, section, or core finding and dive deeply into its significance while also explaining how it fits into the overall framework of the book or project. This approach emphasizes depth over breadth. A third strategy is to split the difference by presenting an overview that emphasizes scope, while delving into the details for a limited number of notable findings. This strategy highlights a few of the main findings, but not all of them, using the narrative pull of the book to move the talk along, but pausing to highlight some of the most important parts of the book.

Whatever presentation strategy you choose, the concluding portion should emphasize the main contributions of the research, including your core findings and their theoretical significance. In anticipation of the questions to come, you may also want to note any limitations that need further attention. Finally, to broaden the scope of your work and the next steps it may imply, it is good to end by pointing to the implications of your findings for existing theory and future research and, if applicable, for social trends and public policy.

Final Thoughts

Depth interviewing—as we hope to have demonstrated—offers a method for studying and explaining the social world that is unique and indispensable. Through its ability to illuminate internal cognitive and emotional states, individual and institutional pathways, and the multiple dimensions of meaning that humans give to their experiences, interviews offer information that would otherwise remain unavailable. Through its ability to gather information about the social contexts that give rise to such outcomes and the strategic responses they prompt in individuals, groups, and organizations, the interview is a powerful tool for explaining the links between social structure and human agency. And through its ability to map trajectories over time and to discover the points at which those trajectories may change direction, the interview can uncover the obvious and not-so-obvious reasons that change occurs in some cases but not in others. In sum, interviewing is one of the essential research tools needed to link human perception and action with the structure of social opportunities, to map processes of social and personal change, and thus to account for the full range of human experience and social organization.

While the nature of the empirical findings interviewers collect is unique, the principles of research design and analysis that make it possible to link these findings to theoretical questions and answers are not. Like any research method, depth interviewing relies on a set of tools and rules about how to collect and analyze findings in a systematic, logically coherent, and scientifically sound way. By breaking down the stages—and the many steps within each stage—of this process, we have sought to provide a blueprint for conducting interview-based research that combines the rigor we associate with science and the creativity we associate with art. What's more, by taking you through every step involved in designing and carrying out a research project—from formulating a question and research design to conducting the interviews and analyzing the findings to deciding how to present your arguments and when to know you have come to completion—we have sought to make this process visible. Finally, by addressing the predictable challenges that are likely to arise at each stage and suggesting ways to tackle them, we have endeavored to provide effective strategies that make the journey from beginning to end more manageable and even fun.

Attending to the research principles we have outlined and developing the skills they rely on is as integral to interviewing as it is to any other research method. While it certainly doesn't hurt to possess some combination of enthusiasm and luck, successful interviewing does not depend on forces beyond one's control. Our hope is that understanding the principles that make interviewing a powerful method and having the tools to apply those principles to an exciting project will inspire you to ask "big" questions and seek compelling answers. Interview projects require a level of commitment through all the stages we have outlined that is easy to underestimate. Yet this journey is well worth the time and effort if you choose your projects carefully and tackle the issues and questions that matter most to you. Given the amount of time, attention, and emotional engagement involved, the most effective way to sustain your interest and motivation is to choose a project that sparks your passion. In doing so, you can enjoy the research journey and look forward to making contributions that help us better understand the social world and our place in it and that inspire others to use and build on that knowledge.

Examples of Recruitment Documents and Procedures

Gerson's Letter of Invitation to Potential Participants

Dear (NAME),

It is a pleasure to invite you to participate in a study of work and family life in contemporary America. To introduce myself, I am a (TITLE) at (INSTITUTION), and I am directing this study to learn how people like yourself view work and family life today. As an expression of appreciation, I am happy to offer you (AMOUNT OR TYPE OF GIFT) for your help.

Your name was randomly selected by a careful procedure designed to find a representative group of (AREA NAME) residents between the ages of (AGE) and (AGE). Your views are very important because they provide the best way to get an accurate picture of how people feel about these important matters and are approaching decisions about them as they go about their lives. This information may, in turn, help others who are facing similar situations as well as policymakers who need to understand and respond to the needs of people like yourself.

The interview asks about such matters as your past experiences, activities today, and plans for the future. Your participation is strictly confidential and entirely voluntary. The interview can take place at a time and location that is most convenient for you. It usually lasts about two hours, but the time allotted is also entirely up to you. Most people find the interview quite interesting and enjoyable, and I hope you will, too.

In the next week or so, I will contact you by phone to find out if you are able to participate. At that time, I will answer any questions you may have and, if you agree, arrange a good time and place to get together. If you would like to contact me before then, just give me a call at (PHONE NUMBER) or send me an email at (EMAIL ADDRESS).

Thanks so much, and I look forward to speaking with you soon!

Sincerely,

(SIGNATURE OF RESEARCHER)
(NAME OF RESEARCHER)
(TITLE AND/OR INSTITUTIONAL AFFILIATION OF RESEARCHER)

Gerson's Screening Form and Record of Contacts for Members of Sampling Pool

Name: _____

Address: _____

_____

Phone: _____

Gender: _____   Age: _____   Miscellaneous: _____

Current Living Arrangement: _____

Date Letter Sent: _____

Email Address: _____

RECORD OF CONTACTS: <u>Date and Time</u>   <u>Result</u>

_____
_____
_____
_____
_____
_____
_____
_____
_____
_____

Damaske's Master List for Recruitment Calls and Follow-ups

Following are the categories that head columns in the Excel spreadsheet in Sarah's master list for recruiting for her unemployment project. Since participants were originally invited to participate via announcements at the end of meetings required of the unemployed in Pennsylvania, Sarah had collected some information on potential participants already.[1] This information allowed her to identify who was eligible to participate in the study given the sample parameters, which were being between the ages of twenty-eight and fifty-two, having involuntarily lost a job, and having lost a full-time job. People were also asked to indicate the best time and day to reach them.

Everyone who was eligible to participate was given a permanent ID (Perm_ID) that would replace their name in all future documentation, including transcripts, except for the master recruiting list (to ensure participant confidentiality). All information was stored on a password-protected and encrypted Penn State secure data site. The master list was stored in a separate file folder from the transcribed interviews.

To keep track of recruiting, there was a "called for interview" column in which every phone call was tracked, including information about whether anyone was reached, whether a message was left, and whether the participant agreed to an interview or declined an interview (this was fairly rare and most often occurred when the potential participant had found new work, often out of state).

Once an interview was scheduled, it was noted as "Y" in the "interview scheduled" column, and the time, date, and location of the interview were noted. The interviewer was noted prior to this, as the person who called to invite someone to participate in an interview was almost always the one who conducted the interview. Sarah conducted the majority of the interviews, and a team of wonderful graduate students conducted the rest. The interviewers were assigned depending on when people said they would prefer to be interviewed and how this meshed with the students' and Sarah's class schedules.

Once an interview was completed, it was marked completed in the "interview complete?" column, then securely sent to a transcriptionist or transcribed locally by one of the graduate students on the research team. After the interview was completed, memos about the interview were written and uploaded to the file; these were marked complete once they were in the file, as were the transcriptions. Finally, there was a final check to make sure that all of the necessary files were stored correctly in their permanent location in the Penn State Population Research Institute's secure data site for Sarah's project. At that point that participant's first round of interviewing was complete.

The final step included marking whether the participant had agreed to participate in a follow-up interview on their consent form.

Column Headings for Master List

Perm_ID
First Name
Last Name
Gender
Home Phone
Cell
Email
Street Address
City
Zip
Job Loss Y/N?
FT? Y/N?
Year of Birth
Married or Partnered Y/N?
Children (under 18) Y/N?
Daytime or Evening?
Best Days for Interviews
Site/Date of Recruit
Called for Interview?
Interview Schedule?
Date/Time of Interview
Interviewer
Interview Complete?
Total Completed Count
Memo Uploaded?
Audio File Uploaded
Recording Sent for Transcription?
Transcription Received?
Transcription in PRI Folder
Willing to Participate in Follow-up?

Examples of Consent Forms

Gerson's Consent Form

CONSENT TO PARTICIPATE IN STUDY OF "THE NEW WORLDS OF WORK AND CARE"

You have been invited to participate in a research study to learn more about [STUDY NAME AND/OR DESCRIPTION]. This study will be conducted by [RESEARCHER NAME], who is a [TITLE] at [INSTITUTION].

If you agree to help, you will participate in an in-depth interview that asks a series of questions about your past educational, work, and family experiences, your outlook on life today, and your plans for the future. The interview will be audiotaped and, if you desire, made available for your review. You may then request that any or all portions of the tape be destroyed.

The interview will take approximately one and a half to two hours, and participation is entirely voluntary. You may refuse to participate or withdraw at any time without penalty. You also have the right to decline or skip any questions you prefer not to answer. Although every effort will be made to prevent any discomfort, if you find any questions sensitive or upsetting, I can provide you with a referral to a counselor with whom you may discuss your feelings.

In addition, confidentiality will be strictly maintained. After the interview is completed, it will be assigned an ID number, and this number will replace your name on all interview documents. Any research findings will be presented only in the form of statistical summaries and anonymous quotes that use pseudonyms. No one else will have access to the interviews.

If there is anything about the study or your participation that is unclear or if you have questions or wish to report a research-related problem, you may contact me by phone at (NUMBER), by email at (EMAIL ADDRESS), or by mail at (MAILING ADDRESS).

For questions about your rights as a research participant, you may contact the University Committee on Activities Involving Human Subjects at (INSTITUTION'S NAME AND RELEVANT LOCATION, PHONE NUMBER, AND EMAIL).

You have received a copy of this consent document to keep for your records.

Agreement to Participate

Participant's Signature: _____   Date: _____

Damaske's Consent Form

Title of Project: Inequality, Gender, and Unemployment
Principal Investigator: Dr. Sarah Damaske
                    Associate Professor
                    (INSTITUTIONAL AFFILIATION)
                    (CONTACT PHONE NUMBER AND EMAIL)

Purpose of the Study: The purpose of this research study is to explore the differences in the ways that men and women experience job loss and its effects. Also of interest is how men and women negotiated this job loss.

Procedures to be followed: You will be asked to answer in-depth interview questions about your work and family history. Your interview will be audiotaped. You may review the recording and request that all or any portions of the recording be destroyed.

Discomforts and Risks: There are no risks in participating in this research beyond those experienced in everyday life. Some of the questions are personal and might cause discomfort. If participating in this research causes you to feel concerns beyond normal daily living, please contact (NAME) for assistance. Phone: (PHONE NUMBER). E-mail: (EMAIL).

Benefits: You might learn more about yourself by participating in this study. You might have a better understanding of how the recession impacted you and others. You might realize that others have had similar experiences as you have.

This research might provide a better understanding of how the recession affected men and women differently. This information could help provide policy suggestions that can be tailored to men's and women's differential experiences of unemployment.

Duration: Participation in this study will take approximately 2 hours.

Statement of Confidentiality: Your participation in this research is confidential. The data will be stored and secured in the locked office of (NAME), in a password-protected computer file. Only (NAME) and the transcriptionist will have access to your audio file. Once the file has been transcribed, all identifying data on the transcripts will be removed and the audio file will be destroyed one year after the transcription. The Pennsylvania State University's Office for Research Protections, the Institutional Review Board and the Office for Human Research Protections in the Department of Health and Human Services may review records related to this research study. In the event of a publication or presentation resulting from the research, no personally identifiable information will be shared.

Right to Ask Questions: Please contact (NAME) at (PHONE NUMBER) with questions, complaints, or concerns about this research. You can also call this number if you feel this study has harmed you. If you have any questions, concerns, or problems about your rights as a research participant, or would like to offer input, please contact (INSTITUTIONAL OFFICE) at (PHONE NUMBER). The (INSTITUTIONAL OFFICE) cannot answer questions about research procedures. Questions about research procedures can be answered by the research team.

Payment for Participation: Participants will receive $50 for completing the interview session. If you withdraw before the end of the study, no payment will be given. If participants complete the follow-up interview, they will receive an additional $10. If you withdraw before the end of the follow-up interview, you will not receive the additional $10.

Voluntary Participation: Your decision to be in this research is voluntary. You can stop at any time. You do not have to answer any questions you do not want to answer. Refusal to take part in or withdrawing from this study will involve no penalty or loss of benefits you would receive otherwise.

You may be contacted and invited to participate in a follow-up interview. This interview would last no longer than an hour and you are under no obligation to participate in it, even if you participate in this study. Should you participate in the follow-up interview, this form will serve as notification of your participant rights for both sets of interviews.

At the conclusion of the interview, you may be invited to participate in an audio diary study in which you would be invited to record an audio diary of your job search experiences for a three-month period. You would be under no obligation to participate in the audio diary study even if you participate in this study.

You must be 18 years of age or older to take part in this research study. If you agree to take part in this research study and the information outlined above, please sign your name and indicate the date below.

You will be given a copy of this consent form for your records.

_____   _____

Participant Signature   Date

_____   _____

Person Obtaining Consent   Date

Examples of Interview Guides

Damaske's Job Loss, Unemployment, and Inequality Study

Subject ID Number:
Name:
Location:
Phone:
Date and Time of Interview:
Notes:

Enumeration

First, I'd like to make sure that the information I have about you from your screening is correct.

1. You were _____ years old on your last birthday, is that right?
2. You are (partnered/married/single), is that right?

Now, I'd like to get an idea about who else lives in your household.

3. Who are the other adults who live with you?
4. Now how about the children?
5. Is there anyone else who usually lives here?
6. Have I missed anyone who is temporarily away?

For each person listed, ask as necessary and record:
How is _____ related to you?
What is ____ gender?
How old was ____ on (his/her/their) last birthday?
Is _____ now married, widowed, divorced, separated, or has (s/he/they) never been married?
Is ____ now employed full-time or part-time? (30+ hours)
If not employed: Is _____ looking for work, on layoff from job, or in school?

7. What race/ethnicity do you identify as?

Family and Household History

To start, I'd like to ask you some questions about your family and about the kinds of arrangements you lived in when you were growing up. First, I'd like to get a picture of who you lived with during your childhood.

1. Could you tell me who you lived with while you were growing up? *If necessary:* Did you live with both biological parents throughout your childhood or did

you live with other people at least some of the time? Can you tell me about those arrangements? Did you live with any siblings? Did they always live with you or did those arrangements change?

2. In general, how would you describe your family's financial situation during that time? *If necessary:* Was there more than enough money for the needs of the household, just enough money, or not enough money? How so?

3. What were the sources of family income in your household during that time?

If no father, skip to section on mother.

Father, Stepfather, and/or Surrogate Father

Now I'd like to ask you some questions about your (biological) father (and your stepfather or any father figures you had growing up).

1. What is the highest grade or year your (biological) father completed in school? *If don't know: follow up.*

2. When you were growing up, would you say your father worked for pay all of the time, most of the time, some of the time, a little of the time, or not at all?

If did not work at all, skip to #4.

3. What was the main job(s) your father held while you were growing up? Did your father's work situation change while you were growing up? Did he ever lose a job?

4. *If did not work:* What did your father do instead of working?

If no mother, skip to section on education.

Mother, Stepmother, and/or Surrogate Mother

Now I'd like to ask you some questions about your (biological) mother (and your stepmother or any mother figures you had growing up).

1. What is the highest education level your (biological) mother completed in school? *If don't know: follow up.*

2. When you were growing up, would you say your mother worked for pay all of the time, most of the time, some of the time, a little of the time, or not at all?

If did not work at all, skip to 6.

3. What was the main job(s) your mother held while you were growing up? Did your mother's work situation change while you were growing up? Did she ever lose a job?

4. *If did not work:* What did your mother do instead of working?

Education History, Experiences, and Aspirations

1. First, think back: Growing up, did your mother or father express any expectations or hopes regarding your future?

2. Now, thinking back, did you have any expectations or hopes for what you wanted to do when you grew up? How did your outlook compare with your parents'?

   3. Did you expect to get a job?
      Did you want to get a job?
      Did you think it would be okay not to work? *Probe:* Why/why not?
   4. What is the highest grade or year you completed in school?
   5. Are you taking any classes right now?
      If yes, probe: What taking? What plans?
   6. Did you graduate from high school?
      If yes, graduated: What did you do after you graduated from high school? *Probe:* Did you go to college, go into another kind of training program, go into the military, go to work, have children, or something else? *If no, didn't graduate:* Why do you think you didn't graduate? What was going on in your life?

If College

   7. Why did you choose to go to college at that point?
      Did you consider other options?
   8. What college was it? Where located?
   9. What was your major?
  10. What was the highest degree you got from there? How long did you stay? Why leave?
  11. What did you do after you left that college?
      Did you go to another college? *If so, repeat questions 7–10.*
  12. Did you get any degrees or certificates after that point? *If yes, probe.*
  13. So what is the highest degree you've received at this point?
  14. Are you in school now? *If yes:* For what? Why?
      Now go to work section.

If Training Program

  15. Why did you choose to go into a training program at this point?
  16. What kind of program was it?
  17. Where was it located?
  18. What was your field of specialty?
  19. Did you get a degree or certificate? *If yes:* What was it?
  20. What did you do after you left this program?
  21. Did you get any other degrees after this point? *If went to college, go to college section.*
  22. Are you in school now? *If yes:* For what? Why?
      Now go to work section.

If Military

  23. Why did you choose to go into the military at this point?
  24. Which branch of the military did you join? Why?
  25. When did you first enter active military service?
  26. Other than basic training, how many specialized training programs or schools did you complete?

If Straight to Work

  27. Why did you decide to go straight to work at this point?
  28. Was this your first full-time job?

Work History, Experiences, and Current Situation

Now, I'd like to talk about the kinds of jobs you've worked at over the years. *Note: We want to get a general idea of their work history, but it's okay to say that it's too much detail if they get stuck on something and focus instead on getting a general overview.*

1. Have you always worked since (either high school or college), sometimes worked, rarely worked, never worked?
2. When did you have your first full-time job?
3. What kind of work was it?
4. Why did you decide on this kind of work?
5. What were your most important activities or duties there?
6. How long did you work there?
7. How did you feel about that job? Did you like it or not? What did you like best or worst about your job?
8. Did you leave this job? *If no, skip ahead to next section. If yes:* Why did you leave?

If this was when lost job, skip ahead to the unemployment section questions. I'm going to get a general work history from you, going over these questions for your different jobs. *If currently employed:* When we hit your current position, let me know, as I have some specific questions that we'll go into in a bit about what you are doing now, but we'll save that for later. Before that, I want to know when we hit the job you most recently lost. (*Get general work history, repeat questions as needed.*)

Job Loss and Unemployment

1. What kind of work were you doing when you lost your job?
2. Did you expect that you would be fired or w as it a surprise?
3. Did other people that you worked with lose their jobs at the time? *If yes:* How many?
4. How did the company give you the news?
5. How did you react when you found out?
6. How did your family react when they heard the news?
7. Did you receive any kind of severance pay? *Be sure to disentangle difference between severance and being paid for any outstanding vacation or sick days.*
8. How much severance did you receive? How long did you receive it?
9. How did you feel about how the company treated you?
   Probe: Why did you feel that way? Have your feelings changed?
10. Has your family struggled financially after your job loss?
    Why/why not?
    If yes: How so?
    If no, probe for details.
    Do you anticipate that you will if you don't find a job soon?
11. Now, it's pretty common for families to have to tighten their belts after a job loss. Did you or anyone in your family ever have to forgo or reduce the following after your job loss? *If yes for any of the following, probe and ask for more details about what happened (clarify if reduce or forgo and for whom for each of the following).*
    a. Food
    b. Medications

c. Doctor's visit

d. Children's necessities

e. Timely bill paying

f. Household supplies

g. Electricity

h. Phone service

i. Vacation

j. Saving for the future

    i. Do you have any savings?

    ii. Have you stopped saving?

    iii. Do you have any retirement savings?

    iv. *If yes:* Have you had to dip into your retirement?

k. Do you have any credit card debt? *If yes:* May I ask how much?

    i. Have you been able to keep up with the minimum payments?

    ii. Has your credit card debt increased since your job loss?

12. Did you find that you changed any of the following behaviors after you lost your job? *If so, how—probe for details on each.*

    a. Taking care of minor health problems you took care of in the past more easily, like taking daily medication/getting prescriptions filled.

    b. Taking care of ongoing chronic problems you took care of in the past more easily.

    c. Eating differently. *If yes:* Are you eating more or less comfort food or fast food? Are you no longer cooking at home or cooking more at home? Are you eating less expensive food or has your spending on food not changed?

    d. Have there been any changes in your sleep? *If yes:* Nighttime sleep? Daytime sleep?

    e. Any changes in your drinking habits? What about other recreational substances?

    f. Any changes in exercise?

    g. Have you found yourself avoiding other things you used to enjoy, maybe spending time with friends or visiting family?

    h. Hanging out with friends.

        i. Did you have many friends at your job? Did losing your job change these relationships? If so, how?

        ii. After you lost your job, did you notice any changes in your relationships with friends outside of work? *If necessary, prompt:* Did anyone help you out after your job loss? Did anyone stop hanging out with you? Did you stop hanging out with anyone? What do you think prompted these changes or why don't you think things changed?

13. Did you apply for unemployment?

    If yes: What happened?

    Did you receive it? Was it enough to cover bills?

    How long did you (or do you expect to) receive unemployment?

14. Did anyone in your family go to work (or try to go to work) to make up for your job loss?

    Did anyone increase their work hours to make up for your lost income?

    If yes: What happened?

    How did you feel about this?

    How did they feel about this?

15. *If partnered/married:* Do you think your job loss affected your relationship with your spouse? *If yes:* how so? *If no:* why not?

16. *If partnered/married:* Now, in some households, it is common for spouses/partners to pool their money together. But in others, spouses/partners each have their own pot of money. How would you characterize your household? Since you lost your job, has this changed? Have you found that you needed to ask for money to use?

17. *If has kids:* Did losing your job affect your relationship with your children? If so, how?

18. Was this the only time you lost a job? *Second time around, ask:* Now, have you experienced any other job losses?
    Very important to get accurate count of total job losses and the history of them. If had experienced a prior (or post) job loss, repeat questions 1–13 in unemployment section until you've gotten a complete history of their experiences of job loss. If had no other job loss experience, move on.

19. After your most recent job loss, did you start looking for a new job?
    If no, skip ahead to question 30.

20. *If yes:* When did you starting looking for a new job?

21. What kind of job were you looking for?

22. How many job applications did you end up sending out?

23. How did you hear about the jobs that you applied for?

24. Did your friends or family members or anyone that you know have leads on jobs?

25. Why do you think you took the steps that you took following your job loss?

26. Were you successful in finding a new job?
    If no, skip ahead to question 30.

27. Was it the kind of job that you were looking for?

28. How long were you out of work before you found your new job?

29. Are you currently employed by the same company that hired you after your job loss in the recession? *If yes, go to current work section. If no, go back to work history section and get the general work info for that job.*

30. *If not working:* What are the main reasons you are not working a paying job right now?

31. How do you feel about not working?

32. Are you currently looking for work? *If yes: probe, ask them to tell you about the process.*
    What do you think have been the main barriers to finding a new job?
    Why do you keep looking?
    Have you changed your search in any way?
    How are you supporting yourself in the meantime?

33. Has not working had any effect on your outlook? If so, how?

34. Has it affected your plans for the future? If so, how?

35. Has it affected your family? If so, how?
    Of everyone: In your job search or in your work experience:

36. Do you think that you have been discriminated against because of your race during your career? Please describe.

37. Do you think that you have ever been discriminated against because of your gender during your career? Please describe.

Current Work

Now, I have some specific questions for you about your current employment situation.

1. Do you have work now? *If no, skip ahead.*

2. When did you start your current job?

3. What do you do?
4. Why did you decide on this kind of work?
5. Do you work there full-time? How many hours a week would you say you spend working at this job?
6. Do you work anywhere else in addition to this job?
7. How many hours a week do you work at that job?
8. What would you say is the total number of hours you spend at all of your jobs, total, on average for each week?
9. Are you paid hourly or are you a salaried worker?
10. Do you get paid for overtime?
11. What is a typical day at work like for you? *Probe on this—be sure to get a detailed account.*
12. What are your most important activities or duties there?
13. What are the most important skills someone in your position needs to do your job well?
14. Do you feel appreciated at work or not appreciated or in between?
15. What do you find most annoying about your job?
16. What would you say you find most rewarding about your job?
17. All things considered, how satisfied are you with the job as a whole—very satisfied, fairly satisfied, somewhat dissatisfied, or very dissatisfied? *Probe:* Why?
20. Does your workplace offer childcare? *If yes:* Did/would you use it?
21. Does your workplace offer maternity or paternity leave? *If yes:* Did/would you use it?

Past and Current Relationships

1. You are (partnered/married/not), is that right?
2. Have you ever been married or in a long-term partnership before your current relationship? If yes, can you tell me a little bit about that relationship and what happened and how it ended?
3. How long have you known your partner?
   When did this relationship start?
   How long have you been together?
4. How would you describe your relationship?
5. What are your future plans?
6. Is partner employed? *If yes:* What does s/he/they do?
7. How does s/he/they feel about job?
8. How do you feel about his/her/their work (or staying at home)?
9. What is the race of your partner? And ethnicity?

Childbearing Decisions

Now, along these same lines, I'd like to ask you some questions about children.
1. When you were growing up, did you have any expectations or hopes about having children? *If necessary, probe:* What were they?

2. Did you have any thoughts about how you would like to combine having children with working outside the home?

3. How old were you when your (first) child was born?

4. What was your financial situation like when you found out you were going to have a child?

5. What was your living situation like? *Probe:* Were you living with someone? Where did you live—near parents, in an apartment, a house? Get details about what life was like.

6. Thinking back to that time, how did you feel about the prospect of being a parent?
   Did you plan to have a child or was it an accident?
   Did you consider not having the child?

7. How did having a child affect your life?
   Did it change your plans?
   Did it make things better or worse or about the same?

Division of Labor in the Household

I'm going to read you a list of chores, and you tell me who is primarily responsible for them.

1. How are chores divided in the house for each of the following tasks?
   a. Grocery shopping
   b. Cooking
   c. Meal cleanup
   d. Laundry
   e. House cleaning
   f. Bills
   g. Repairs
   h. Other chores (specify)

2. When it comes to childcare, who is regularly responsible for the following?
   a. Looking after the kids
   b. Bathing the kids
   c. Feeding the kids
   d. Playing with the kids
   e. Disciplining the kids
   f. Doctor visits
   g. School visits
   h. Other (please specify)

3. Did these arrangements change after your job loss? (Go back through lists again and discuss each item.) What changed? What didn't change? If nothing changed, why do you think nothing changed? If something changed, how did it change? Why?

4. How much leisure time would you say you have each week? Has that changed since your job loss?

5. How much leisure time would you say your partner has each week? Has that changed since your job loss?

6. Do you think there is a difference in the amount of leisure time you each have? Has the amount of leisure time you each have changed since your job loss? Why or why not?

7. How satisfied are you with these arrangements? How satisfied do you think your partner is? *Probe: Try to understand how feels about arrangements.*

Then, Now, and the Future

Now, I've just got some general questions for you about your past, present, and future.

1. If you could have things just the way you wanted, what would be your ideal balance between family, work, and the rest of your life?
2. What do you think the chances are that you will achieve this balance?
3. In thinking about the future, what do you think your life will be like five or ten years from now?
4. When you compare your life to that of your parents, do you think you are better off, worse off, or relatively the same?
   If isn't clear from above answer: Do you think you are financially similar to your parents or financially different? *Probe:* Why do you think that is?
5. Do you think that you have different goals for your life than your parents had for theirs? Please specify.
6. Do you think you have different goals for your children than your parents had for you? Please describe.

Opinions

1. In your opinion, what is an ideal job?
   Probe: Why? How does this job compare to yours?
2. What do you think about changes in American families such as more working mothers?
3. Do you think someone should be most responsible for providing the family income?
   If yes, who and why?
   If no, why not?
4. Do you think someone should be most responsible for taking care of the children?
   If yes, who and why?
   If no, why not?
5. Do you think someone should be most responsible for doing the housework?
   If yes, who and why?
   If no, why not?
6. In your opinion, is there anything the government can do to make life easier for families?
7. Do you think women have it better or worse today than in the past? Why?
8. Do you think men have it better or worse today than in the past? Why?

Background

We're almost done. Just a few short questions about your background.

1. Were you raised in a religion? Which one? Do you belong now?
2. In politics, do you consider yourself a Democrat, independent, or Republican?

3. Remembering that this is confidential, will you share what you receive in unemployment benefits from the state? *Clarify if it's weekly/biweekly/monthly. Ask if capped.*
4. Remembering that this is confidential, will you share your personal annual income before taxes?
   If doesn't have new job, ask: Remembering that this is confidential, what was your income before you lost your job?
   Follow up: What do you think are the chances that you can find a job that will bring in a similar salary?
5. Remembering that this is confidential, will you share your spouse/partner's personal annual income before taxes? How does this compare to before you lost your job?
6. Those are all of my questions. What would you like to ask or to say that I haven't asked about?

Conclusion

1. If I need to contact you again, what is the best time and place to contact you? Would you like to receive a report of our findings when the study is completed?
2. *Snowball screening:* Do you know anyone between the ages of 25 and 45 who lost a full-time job between 2007 and now and is married/partnered with kids in the household? Would you be willing to share their contact information in case they would like to participate in the study, too? *Get out contact sheet.*
3. *If currently unemployed and searching for work:* Would it be okay if we checked in with you in six months to see how your job search is going? Also, if you want to give us a call to let us know if you've found a job, we would love to hear from you!
4. *If currently working:* Would it be okay if we checked back in with you in six months to see how your job has been? Also, if you want to give us a call to let us know how things are going, we would love to hear from you!

Thank you very much for your help!

Interview observations: Remember to note anything important that will not be apparent by reading a verbal transcription (details of participant, details of meeting location, etc.).

INSTRUCTIONS FOR OTHER INTERVIEWERS:

Remember, this is an open-ended interview, not a survey. It is best to allow interviewees time to think and respond. They may, or may not, stay exactly on target when they respond. Allow them to respond to each question in their own words. If you feel like they have not answered the original question, use your best judgment as to whether you should rephrase and ask again (was it not clear to them?) or hang in there and see if you get the answer at some later point (is this a question they aren't comfortable answering right now?).

Even if they do answer the question, you may often want to follow up on their response (when it appears that they may have given a partial answer or when it seems like the story is incomplete or when it seems like there may be additional layers to their response). In this case, probe, by asking questions such as, "Could you tell me a bit more about that?" or "What did X mean to you?" or "Interesting. Do you have anything else you want to add here?"

Gerson's Work and Care Study

ID Number:
Name:
Location:
Phone:
Date and Time of Interview:
Notes:

Enumeration

E.1. First, I'd like to just get some basic information or make sure the information I have is correct.
   a. Your first name is _____, is that right?
   b. You were _____ years old on your last birthday, is that right?
   c. What is your marital status—are you never married, married, separated, divorced, widowed? Do you have a live-in relationship?
   d. How about your work situation—are you are currently employed full-time, employed part-time, not employed, going to school, or something else? What kind of work do you do? *Count 30 or more hours per week as full-time.*
   If not employed: Are you looking for work or on layoff from a job?
E.2. Now, I'd like to get an idea about who else lives in your household.
   a. What are the first names of all the other adults who live here?
   b. Now, how about the children? What are their first names in order, beginning with the oldest? Any others?
   c. Is there anyone else who usually lives here, like a roomer or boarder, or anyone who is away temporarily?

For each person listed, ask as necessary and record in table:

1. How is _____ related to you?
2. Does _____ identify as a (woman/man/other gender)?
3. How old was _____ on (his/her/their) last birthday?
   If over 16:
4. Is _____ married, widowed, divorced, separated, or has (he/she/them) never been married?
5. Is _____ employed full-time or part-time? *Count 30 hours or more per week as full-time.* What kind of work does (he/she/they) do?
   If not employed: Is _____ looking for work, on layoff from a job, or going to school?

ID NUMBER: _____

Relation to Respondent	Gender	Age	Marital School/Labor Force Status Status (circle all that apply)	If employed: Job Title
Respondent	_____		NvM Mar Sep Div Wid Live-in	In school Emp full Emp part Looking Not emp

Spse/LI Prtnr	NvM	Inschool
Child _____	Mar	Emp full
Parent	Sep	Emp part
Other rel	Div	Looking
Not related	Wid	Not emp
	Live-In	

Spse/LI Prtnr	NvM	Inschool
Child _____	Mar	Emp full
Parent	Sep	Emp part
Other rel	Div	Looking
Not related	Wid	Not emp

Spse/LI Prtnr	NvM	Inschool
Child _____	Mar	Emp full
Parent	Sep	Emp part
Other rel	Div	Looking
Not related	Wid	Not emp

Spse/LI Prtnr	NvM	Inschool
Child _____	Mar	Emp full
Parent	Sep	Emp part
Other rel	Div	Looking
Not related	Wid	Not emp

Spse/LI Prtnr	NvM	Inschool
Child _____	Mar	Emp full
Parent	Sep	Emp part
Other rel	Div	Looking
Not related	Wid	Not emp

Spse/LI Prtnr	NvM	Inschool
Child _____	Mar	Emp full
Parent	Sep	Emp part
Other rel	Div	Looking
Not related	Wid	Not emp

Family Background

Now, I'd like to find out a little bit about the arrangements you lived in growing up, and especially any changes in your family's situation, including how your parents or other caretakers divided work and caretaking.

F.1. *Preschool years: before first grade or started school.*

First, let's discuss arrangements when you were a preschooler.

a. What region of the country—or the world—did you live in? *Specify ages if more than one.*

b. What type of neighborhood(s) did you live in? *Specify ages if more than one.*

c. What parents or other adult guardians did you live with? *If more than one arrangement, specify ages for each.*

d. Did you have a parent or other guardian that you did <u>not</u> live with?
   If so, who?
   Why didn't you live with (him/her/them)?
   When and how often did you see (him/her/them)?

e. What siblings or other relatives did you live with?

f. What were the work arrangements in your household?
   Father worked full-time/part-time/not employed.
   Mother worked full-time/part-time/not employed.
   Another arrangement: *specify.*

If father worked:	What job(s) did your father hold?
	About how many hours did he work on weekdays?
	About how many hours did he work on the weekends?
If mother worked:	What job(s) did your mother hold?
	About how many hours did she work on weekdays?
	About how many hours did she work on the weekends?

g. What were the caretaking arrangements for you (and your siblings)?
   Mother did all/most/half/less than half/none of caretaking. Who did the rest?
   Father did all/most/half/less than half/none of caretaking. Who did the rest?
   Another person did all/most/half/less than half of caretaking? Who? Paid or unpaid?
   Another arrangement: *specify.*

h. How did you view your household's arrangements—did you prefer the way things were or prefer a different situation? Why do you say that?

i. Have your views changed? How do you see things today? Why do you say that?

F.2. *Primary school years: roughly grades 1 through 6.* Now, how about arrangements when you were in primary school?

a. Were things still the same, or had anything changed?
   Specify any changes in location, household members, parents' relationship, jobs, breadwinning, and caretaking arrangements.

b. How did you view these changes? Were there improvements or disadvantages?
   If so, how?
   If not, why not?

c. Have your views changed since then? How do you see things today? Why do you say that?

F.3. *Middle school: roughly grades 7 through 9.* Now, how about arrangements when you were in middle school?

a. Were things still the same, or had anything changed?
   Specify any changes in location, household members, parents' relationship, jobs, breadwinning, and caretaking arrangements.

b. How did you view these changes? Were there improvements or disadvantages?
   If so, how?
   If not, why not?

c. Have your views changed since then? How do you see things today? Why do you say that?

F.4. *High school: roughly grades 10 through 12.* Now, how about arrangements when you were in high school?

    a. Were things still the same, or had anything changed?

      Specify any changes in location, household members, parents' relationship, jobs, breadwinning, and caretaking arrangements.

    b. How did you view these changes? Were there improvements or disadvantages?

      If so, how?

      If not, why not?

    c. Have your views changed since then? How do you see things today? Why do you say that?

F.5. *After left home.* Now, how about arrangements after you left home to (go to college/ live on your own)?

    a. Did things stay the same, or did anything change?

      Specify any changes in location, household members, parents' relationship, jobs, breadwinning, and caretaking arrangements.

    b. How did you view these changes? Were there improvements or disadvantages?

      If so, how?

      If not, why not?

    c. Have your views changed since then? How do you see things today? Why do you say that?

Education

Now, I'd like to find out a bit more about your educational and other experiences growing up as well as any expectations or aspirations you had.

E.1. a. First, thinking back as far as you can remember, did your mother, father, or anyone else who was important in your life express any expectations or hopes regarding your future—whether that involved education, work, marriage, or childbearing and childrearing?

    Probe: Did they agree with each other, or did they have different ideas? Specify who expressed expectations and whether or not they agreed.

    Follow up as necessary.

    Did (they/she/he) have any hopes or expectations about education?

    Probe: How much or little did (they/she/he) stress education? How high did (they/ she/he) want you to go?

    What about work?

    Probe: How much or little did (they/she/he) stress getting a job? Did (they/she/he) stress any particular kind of work?

Did (they/she/he) have any expectations or hopes about marriage?

Probe: How much or little did (they/she/he) stress getting married? Did (they/she/he) talk about a good age for getting married or any particular kind of partner or family lifestyle?

    Did (they/she/he) have any expectations or hopes about your having children?

    Probe: How much or little did (they/she/he) stress having children? Did (they/she/ he) talk about a good age, or a good number, or how to raise children?

b. In general, how would you describe (their/her/his) approach to childrearing?
Probe for strategies of "concerted cultivation" vs. "natural growth": high or low on pressures to do well in school, participate in extracurricular and after-school activities, etc.
Follow up as necessary: Can you give me examples of what you mean?

E.2. Now, thinking back as far as you can remember, did you have any expectations or hopes for what you wanted to be doing (at the age you are now/when you grew up)?

a. Did you have any hopes or expectations regarding paid work? Did you think (they/she/he) (were/was) realistic or not so realistic?

    Probe: Did you think you would work:
              Full-time throughout adulthood
              Part-time work throughout pre-retirement adulthood
              Not in a paid job in adulthood
              Not in a paid job if/when have young children
              Part-time if/when have young children

Follow up: Did you think about whether you would work, and if so, what occupation you would like to enter? *If needed:* Describe work or career goals.
Follow up: Why do you think you had these hopes or expectations?
Did you see any conflicts between what you wanted and what you expected?

b. Did you have any hopes or expectations regarding long-term relationships? Did you think they were realistic or not so realistic?
Probe: Did you think you would be:
Married
In a "marriage-like" relationship
Single
In some other kind of arrangement?
Follow up: If you hoped to marry or establish a committed relationship, did you think about what age you thought this would happen or wanted this to happen?
Follow up: Why do you think you had these hopes and expectations? Did you see any conflicts between what you wanted and what you expected?

e. Did you have any hopes about having or not having children? Any expectations?
No children
1 or more children
Follow up if wished to have children: Did you think about how many you wanted? What about the age you wanted to be when you had your first child?

f. Why do you think you had these hopes? Expectations? Did you see any conflicts between what you wanted and what you expected? Why?

g. *If wished to have children:* How did you hope to divide childrearing and working with a partner? How did you expect to divide things?
I would be primary caretaker and wouldn't work or would work part-time
I would be primary caretaker and combine with full-time work
I would share caretaking equally with a partner, and we would both work full-time
I would share caretaking equally with a partner, and we would both work part-time
My partner would be primary caretaker, and I would focus primarily on paid work
Follow up: Why do you think you had these hopes and expectations? Did you see any conflicts between what you wanted and what you expected? Why?

h. How did your hopes and expectations compare with your parents' arrangements?
Generally similar to own family

Generally different than own family

Similar in some ways, different in others

Follow up: Why do you think your aspirations and/or expectations were (similar to/ different than) your parents or other family members? *Probe:* Was there any other person, either an adult or someone your age, who made a difference? Were there any experiences outside your home that made a difference?

    i. How did your hopes and expectations for work, marriage, and parenthood compare with your parents' expectations or desires for you?

Generally similar:

Generally different:

Similar in some ways, different in others :

Follow up: How were your aspirations and/or expectations (similar to/different than) your parents' expectations? Why? Did anyone else express expectations that made a difference to you?

Did you think about how you would put work and family together?

Now, just a few questions about your education.

E.3. a. What is the highest grade or year you completed in school?

Grade school:

High school:

College :

Graduate (*specify degree*):

Technical/trade (*specify*):

    b. *If quit school at any point before college graduation:* Why did you leave school when you did? *Probe:* Did you consider going on? Why did you decide against it? How did you feel about the decision to leave school? How do you feel now?

    If continued school beyond college graduation: Why did you continue in school after graduation from college? *Probe:* What graduate program did you attend? Why?

    c. Are you in school or taking any classes right now, or do you have any plans to return to school?

    d. *If yes:* What (are you taking/do you plan to study)? What is the highest grade you plan to complete in school? *Probe:* What degree would you like to get? What are the main reasons you want to get this degree?

    e. By the time you finished school, had your expectations or hopes for the future become clearer or changed in any way? *Probe:* Did you have any clearer ideas about what you wanted to do or what you expected your life to be like in the future? What about work, marriage, or children? Why did you want or expect that? Did your hopes and expectations seem to be more or less in conflict?

Work History

Now, I'd like to talk about the kinds of jobs you've worked at over the years, especially since you left school.

W.1. Since you left school, about how many jobs have you worked at?

If never held a paid job since leaving school, skip to W.3.

For those with jobs prior to current job, ask series of questions below for each job.

W.2. a. What kind of jobs did you work at? *Probe:* Could you name each job? What was your position or job task?

  b. If more than three, which of these jobs would you say are most important? *Probe:* Why do you say that?

  c. Different people want different things from paid work. When you first started working, what, if anything, did you hope to get from work?

   Probe: What did an ideal job look like then?

   Probe: How did you rate the importance of:

   Advancement prospects

   Pay

   Financial security

   Enjoyable work

   Personal control and autonomy about how, where, and when to do work

   Flexibility in scheduling, demands, or work location

   Number of hours

   A supportive environment

   Boss/supervisor

   Colleagues

   Owner

   Ability to combine with private life—especially family, children, caring for others

  d. Now, I'd like to ask you some questions about your past jobs.

   For important jobs, ask:

   What were your main reasons for taking this job? About how many hours a week did you work? Would you call this part-time or full-time?

   How did you feel about this job?

   Probe: What were the best aspects? The worst aspects?

   How long did you work at this job?

   Probe: Did your position change while you were there?

   Did you consider this job to be part of a career or not?

   Why did you leave?

   Did you consider this a step up, a step down, or a lateral move?

   How did this job experience affect you?

   Probe: Did it change your outlook on yourself or your plans for the future? On what you wanted from a job or the rest of your life?

  e. Has there ever been a time, including now, when you wanted to work, but could not? *If yes:* When was that? What (were/are) the reasons? How (did/does) that feel? How (did/does) that experience affect you—including your outlook on yourself or the future?

  f. Has there ever been a time when you didn't want to take a job but had to anyway? *If yes:* Why did you have to? Why didn't you want to? Did that experience change your outlook?

   If never held a paid job after leaving school:

W.3. a. What are the main reasons you have not worked (at a paid job) since leaving school?

  b. How do you feel about not working during that time?

  c. Has not working (or not having to work) had any effect on your outlook, your morale, or your plans for the future?

Relationship History

Now I'd like to switch the subject for a moment and ask you some questions about any special personal relationships and family experiences over the years.

R.1. You said you were (married/divorced/separated/widowed/never married), right?

If married, skip to R.3.

R.2. *If not currently married:* Are you seeing someone steadily right now? *If necessary:* Is there one special person you are seeing? What is their first name? Are you living with them?

R.3. Have you had any (other) serious relationships over the years—that is, with someone you considered to be a special partner like a boyfriend or girlfriend? About how many would you say you have had?

If one or more serious involvements, skip to R.5.

R.4. *If never had a special relationship:* Why do you think you've never been in a serious relationship? Have you ever wanted one?
If yes: About how many times has this happened? What happened?
If no: Why not? Do you have any special reasons?

If no serious involvements, skip to next section: Parental, Fertility, and Care History.

R.5. *If had any serious involvements:* How old were you the first time you had a relationship?
Now, I'd just like to spend some time talking about your experiences in these situations.
For each past involvement, including current relationship, ask the following questions (if more than five involvements, ask about most serious ones):
   a. When and how did this relationship start? *Probe:* How did you meet? What was going on in your life at the time? Why did you get involved at that point in your life?
   b. What made this person special to you? *Probe:* What kind of partner were you looking for?
   c. Did you ever live with or marry this person? *If no:* Did you consider it? Why not?
   d. What did you like most about the relationship? What did you like least?
   e. How long did this relationship last? Why did it break up? What were your reactions?
   f. Did this experience change you in any way? *Probe:* Did it change your outlook on relationships or what you wanted in a partner? Did it change your outlook on other things in life, such as work or family?

Parental, Fertility, and Care History

Now, along these same lines, I'd like to ask some questions about any decisions you have made about whether or not to become a parent.

C.1. a. You said you had (no/number of) children living with you—is that right?
   b. Do you have any children who don't live with you or are being raised by someone
      else? *If yes:* Is that a son or a daughter? How old (is/are) (he/she/they)? Why (don't
      they/doesn't she/he) live with you? How long ago was that? Where (does/do) (he/
      she/they) live? Who is primarily responsible for raising (them/him/her)? How
      often do you see (them/him/her)?
   c. Is there anyone you are responsible for taking care of? Who is that? How did that
      happen? Why? What do you do?

If interviewee has no children or care dependents, skip to C.4.

C.2. a. *If has children/dependents:* How old were you when your (first) child was born?
   b. What were you doing when you found out you were going to have a child/someone
      to care for—were you going to school, working, or doing something else?
   c. What was your living situation when you found out you were going to have a child/
      someone to care for? *Probe:* Who were you living with? What was going on in your
      life at the time? Who was the (mother/father)? How did (she/he/they) feel?
   d. Thinking back to that time, what were your reactions to the prospect of becoming
      a (mother/father/caretaker)? *Probe:* Were you excited or concerned? What were
      your main reasons for having a child? Did you plan it or not?
   e. How did having a child/dependent affect your life? Did it change your plans? Did it
      make things better or worse?

If has one child/dependent, skip to C.5.
If has more than one child, repeat question series below
for all subsequent children.

C.3. a. How old were you when (your other child/each of your other children) was born?
   b. What were you doing at the time (this child/each of these children) was born?
   c. What was your living situation? *Probe:* Did (this child/these children) have the
      same or a different (father/mother)?
   d. How did you feel about having (this child/each of these children)?
   e. How did having (this child/these children) affect your life?

Skip to C.5.

C.4. *If has no children:* Have you ever seriously considered having—or tried to
   have—a child?
   If yes: What happened? How did you feel? Did your outlook change?
   If no: Why not? Any special doubts or fears about having children or raising them?
C.5. a. *Everyone:* Have you ever been in a situation where you faced a decision about
      whether or not to have a child/take care of someone?
      If no, skip to b.
      If yes: When did this happen? *Probe:* What was going on at the time? What did you
      decide? Why?

Current Work Situation

Okay, so now that we've talked about your past experiences, let's talk about what things are like in your life today, both at work and in your personal life.

You said you were (employed full-time/employed part-time/not employed) at the moment, right?

If not currently employed, skip to W.9.

W.4. a. What kind of work do you do? *If necessary:* What is your job title or position? What are some of your main duties? What kind of business do you work for?

    b. How long have you been (working at that job/in that line of work)?

    c. What are the main reasons you chose that line of work? *If necessary:* Why that job in particular? Did you consider doing something else at the time? Did you consider not working? How did you get this job?

    d. About how many hours do you usually work in an average week?
    Follow up: Are there weeks when you work more, and others when you work less? Would you say that is full-time or part-time? Why?

    e. Do you work on a regular schedule, or is it different?
    Is this the schedule you prefer, or would you prefer a different one? What would be your ideal schedule? *Follow up:* How much flexibility do you have in deciding when and where to work? Are you permitted to change your schedule or work at home? If so, how often do you do these things?

W.5. If you could arrange things just the way you wanted, what would you prefer to be doing—working at your current job, working at another job, or not working at all? *Probe:* What would be your ideal situation?

    If prefers different situation: Why do you say that? *Probe:* What would you like to be doing instead? Why aren't you doing that?

    If prefers current job: Why do you say that? *Probe:* What do you like best about your current job? Is there anything you dislike?

W.7. How would you say working affects you—especially your morale and outlook on yourself? *Probe:* Has working affected your feelings about yourself in any way?

W.8. a. Different people want different things from paid work. What, if anything, would you like to get from work?

    Probe for identity: Is work important for how you see yourself? *If yes:* How? Why? *If no:* Why?

    Probe for time vs. money trade-offs: Compared to what you thought an ideal job would be before you started working, how does that compare today? What brought about the change? What would an ideal job look like now?

    Probe: How would you rate the importance of:

    Material rewards: advancement prospects, future security, pay

    Intrinsic rewards: enjoyable work, doing something "worthwhile"

    Structure: personal control, autonomy, flexibility about how/where/when to work

    Culture: boss/supervisor, colleagues, owner, people you supervise

    Social: being with people outside the home

    Balance, time demands: ability to combine with private life—especially family, children, caring for others

    b. Considering these priorities, how would you describe your current situation? What are the best aspects? The worst aspects?

    c. Compared to what you thought an ideal situation would be growing up, how does that compare today? What brought about the change? What would an ideal situation look like now?

If employed full-time, skip to next section:

Current Relationship/Domestic Situation

W.9. a. *If not currently employed full-time:* What are the main reasons you are not working (full-time) right now?

b. What do you spend most of your time doing when you are not on the job—going to school, looking for work, looking after the (children/house), or doing something else?

c. On the whole, do you prefer not working (full-time), or would you prefer to be working at a paid job (full-time)? *Probe:* Why do you say that? What are the advantages and drawbacks? What would be your ideal situation? Why?

d. How would your life be different if you had a (full-time) job? *Probe:* Would it change your relationships or affect your morale or feelings about yourself?

W.10. a. If you had a paid job, what would you look for? How would you rate the importance of:

Material rewards: advancement prospects, future security, pay

Intrinsic rewards: enjoyable work, doing something "worthwhile"

Work structure: personal control, autonomy, flexibility about how, where, and when to do work

Work culture: boss/supervisor, colleagues, owner, people you supervise

Social: being with people outside the home

Balance, time demands: ability to combine with private life—especially family, children, caring for others

b. Is not working important or not for how you see yourself?

If yes: How? Why? *If no:* Why?

Probe for identity, time vs. money trade-offs.

c. Compared to what you thought an ideal situation would be growing up, how does that compare today? What brought about the change? What would an ideal situation look like now?

Current Relationship/Domestic Situation

If in a relationship, skip to R.6.

R.1. a. *If not currently involved:* What are the main reasons you are not seeing someone steadily right now?

b. Would you like to have a steady relationship or not?

If yes: What kind of things would you look for in a relationship?

If no: Why not?

Probe for trade-offs between self-reliance and commitment.

c. Have your views changed over the years?

If yes: How? Why? Were there particular turning points?

If no: Why not? Have things happened to reinforce your views? Would anything need to happen to change your mind?

Probe for trade-offs between self-reliance and commitment.

If currently in a relationship (including seeing someone steadily, cohabiting, or married): Now some questions about your relationship today.

R.2. a. How long have you known (first name of partner)? When did this relationship start? *Probe:* How did you meet? What was going on in your life at the time? Why did you get involved at that point in your life? What kind of partner were you looking for?

   b. Has your relationship changed since you got together? Have there been any crises, ups and downs, or turning points over the years? Any big issues or decisions? *If yes:* About what? What happened? How did you handle these situations? How did it change the relationship?

   c. *If married:* How long have you been married? What are the main reasons you got married?
   If cohabiting: How long have you been living together? Have you ever considered getting married?
   If not married or cohabiting: Have you ever considered getting married or living together? *Probe:* Why (not)?

   d. How would you describe your relationship today? *Probe:* What works best? Anything you would like to change?

   e. Has this relationship changed you in any way? *Probe:* Has it changed your outlook on relationships, work, or caretaking?

   f. Do you have any plans for the future? *Probe:* Do you expect your situation to change in any way? How? Why?
   If married, skip to R.4.

R.3. a. *If not married or in a long-term relationship:* Would you like to have a long-term re-lationship or get married someday—or not? *Probe:* Why (not)? How would you feel if you (never) got married (again)? Has your outlook changed? How? Why?
   If prefers to never marry, skip to d.

   b. *If wants to get married/find a long-term relationship:* Ideally, when would you like to get married? *Probe:* Why then? Do you have any definite plans or not?

   c. In thinking about marriage, what kind of relationship would you like to have? What do you look for in a partner? *Probe for "egal" vs. "neo-trad" vs. "self-reliance":* How would you like to relate to each other? How would you like to divide up responsibil-ities/tasks? What do you think are the chances of creating this?

Skip to R.9.

   d. *If prefers not to marry/find a long-term relationship:* Why do you prefer to not get married? *Probe:* What are the benefits? Are there any drawbacks? Did anything happen to make you feel this way? What about other relationships you have seen or been in?

   e. How would you like to live (instead of getting married)? *Probe for "self reliance" vs. "egal":* Why do you prefer that? Would you like to live alone or with someone else? With whom?

Skip to R.9.

R.4. a. *If married:* In thinking about marriage, how would you describe your relationship? *Probe for "egal" vs. "neo-trad" vs. "self-reliance":* How do/would you like to relate to each other? How do/would you like to divide up responsibilities/tasks? Has it changed over time? How does this compare with your ideal?

    b. In thinking about the future, would you like your relationship to remain pretty much the same, or would you like it to change in any way? *Probe:* Why? What kind of changes would you like? What are the chances these changes will occur?

R.5. a. *If has a partner:* What is the highest grade (first name of partner) completed in school?

    Grade school:

    High school:

    College :

    Graduate:

    Trade/technical:

    b. Did (first name of partner) grow up in a family situation similar to yours, or was (his/her) family different? *Probe:* How? Do you think this affects your relationship?

    c. Is (first name of partner) working full-time, working part-time, or not working for pay right now?

If partner not employed, skip to R.11.

R.6. a. *If partner currently employed:* What kind of work does (first name of partner) do? *If necessary:* What is (his/her) job title or position? What are some of (his/her) main duties? What kind of business does (he/she) work for?

    b. About how many hours does (she/he/they) usually work in an average week? Does (she/he/they) have a regular schedule or some other kind of schedule? *Probe:* What is it?

    c. How long has (she/he/they) been (working at that job/in that line of work)? *If couple has children over two:* Did (she/he/they) work when the child(ren) (was/were) younger?

    d. How do you think (she/he/they) feels about (her/his/their) job—does (she/he) find it satisfying or do you think (she/he/they) would prefer to be doing something else? *If prefers something else:* Would (she/he/they) prefer another job or not to work at all? What would (she/he/they) prefer to be doing? Why doesn't (she/he/they) do that?

R.7. a. *If partner not currently employed:* What does (first name of partner) spend most of (her/his) time doing—keeping house, going to school, looking for work, or something else? *Probe:* What is the main reason (she/he/they) (is/are) not working?

    b. How do you think (first name of partner) feels about what (she/he/they) (is/are) doing now—(does/do) (she/he/they) find it satisfying or would (she/he/they) prefer to be doing something else? *Probe:* Why is that? What would (she/he/they) prefer to be doing? Why (isn't/aren't) (she/he/they) doing that now?

    c. (Does/do) (she/he/they) have any plans to change (his/her/their) situation? *If yes:* What does (she/he/they) plan to do? When? How definite are these plans?

    d. Would you like to have (more) children/others to care for?

    If yes: How many? When? Do you have any specific plans? What are your main reasons? *Probe:* How will your life and outlook be different? Did anything happen to change your outlook?

    If no: Why not? *Probe:* Why not? How would your life and outlook be different? Did anything happen to change your outlook?

Current Work-Personal Balance

WF.1. a. First, can you generally describe your daily life and current responsibilities at home (and at work) and in the wider community? *Probe for balance between home and work.*

     b. What about your responsibilities at home? Do you have any responsibilities for taking care of other people, including children, a partner, a housemate, a relative, or anyone else? About how much time does that take daily or weekly? *Specify caregiving and financial responsibilities.*
      If not employed, skip to WF.3.

WF.2. a. Now, can you describe your current responsibilities at work? About how much time does that take?

WF.3. a. What about any responsibilities you have beyond those at work and at home—are you responsible for anyone else, either in terms of caregiving or financial help? *Probe for unpaid caregiving and financial contributions.*

     b. *If yes:* Who do you do that for? *Probe for nonresidential children, parents, relatives, friends.*

     c. What do you do for (this/these) (person/people)? *Probe for caregiving and financial contributions.*

WF.4. a. Is there anyone who provides help to you, either in terms of caregiving or financial help?

     b. *If yes:* Who is that? *Probe for nonresidential children, parents, relatives, friends.*

     c. What (does this person/do these people) do for you? *Probe for caregiving and financial contributions.*
      If lives without another adult and has a child/dependent, skip to WF.6.
      If lives alone with no dependents, skip to WF.7.
      If not living alone: Now, just a few questions about how things get done for the household.

WF.5. a. First, I'd like to get an idea of how chores are divided. Can you tell me what things you mainly do, what things someone else mainly does, and if there are any things you divide fairly equally? *Probe for:*
      Housework
      Grocery shopping
      Cooking
      Meal cleanup
      Laundry
      House cleaning
      Repairs (or yard work)
      Other chores (specify)

     b. How (do/did) you decide to divide things this way? *Probe for allocation principles: gender appropriate, dividing equally, according to preferences/skills.*

     c. Are you satisfied with these arrangements, or would you like them to be different in any way? *Probe for perceptions of fairness, justice.*
      If prefers different arrangement: Why? How? What are the obstacles?

     d. *If married or cohabiting:* How do you feel about this arrangement? How does your (partner/housemate) feel about these arrangements? *Probe:* Would (she/he/they) like it to be different? How? Why?

If single: How do you feel about this situation? Would you like or expect these arrangements to change (if/when) you (get married/move in with someone else)? *Probe:* How? Why?

e. What would be your ideal arrangement? *Probe:* Have your ideas changed over the years? How? What brought about the change? How do these arrangements compare with the way you were raised?

If no dependents, skip to WF.7.

WF.6. a. *If has a child:* What about caretaking? Who is regularly responsible for various activities—mainly you, mainly someone else (*specify who*), mainly shared, or do you have a different arrangement?

Would you say caretaking is divided 50/50, 60/40, 70/30, 80/20, 90/10, or 100/0? Time divisions: looking after the kid(s) in the morning, during the day/after school, in the evenings, during the night, on the weekends. Activities: bathing and dressing, feeding, playing, disciplining, helping with homework, doctor visits, teacher visits, shopping.

b. How (do/did) you decide to divide things this way? *Probe for allocation principles: gender appropriate, dividing equally, according to preferences/skills.*

c. Are you satisfied with these arrangements, or would you like them to be different in any way? *Probe for perceptions of fairness, justice.*

If prefers different arrangement: Why? How? What are the obstacles?

d. *If married or cohabiting:* How does your (partner/housemate) feel about these arrangements? *Probe:* Would (she/he//they) like it to be different? How? Why?

If single: How would you expect these arrangements to change (if/when) you (get married/move in with someone else)? *Probe:* How? Why?

e. What would be your ideal arrangement? *Probe:* Have your ideas changed over the years? How? What brought about the change? How do these arrangements compare with the way you were raised?

WF.7. a. Now, can you tell me how you handle financial matters—that is, what things you mainly do, what things someone else mainly does, and if there are any things you divide fairly equally?

Would you say bringing in income is divided 50/50, 60/40, 70/30, 80/20, 90/10, or 100/0? *Probe for responsibility for bringing in income, decisions about spending, keeping books, paying bills, etc.*

b. How (do/did) you decide to divide things this way? *Probe for allocation principles: gender appropriate, dividing equally, according to preferences/skills.*

c. Are you satisfied with these arrangements, or would you like them to be different in any way? *Probe for perceptions of fairness, justice.*

If prefers different arrangement: Why? How? What are the obstacles?

d. *If married or cohabiting:* How does your (partner/housemate) feel about these arrangements? *Probe:* Would (she/he/they) like it to be different? How? Why?

If single: How would you expect these arrangements to change (if/when) you (get married/move in with someone else)? *Probe:* How? Why?

e. What would be your ideal arrangement? *Probe:* Have your ideas changed over the years? How? What brought about the change? How do these arrangements compare with the way you were raised?

WF.8. a. Now, some general questions about how you feel about work, family, leisure, and how they all fit together. If you could have things just the way you wanted, what would be your ideal balance? *Probe for balance of paid work, caregiving, and personal or leisure pursuits.* Would you like to make anything your first priority, and if so, what?

Paid work first

Caregiving first

Equal balance

Other

b. How does your current situation compare with this ideal balance? What do you think are the chances that you will achieve this balance? *Probe:* Why do you say that? What are the obstacles?

c. Now, how (have you arranged/would you like to arrange) things with a partner or with other people? *Probe:* Who (has/will/would) be primarily responsible for earning money, caregiving, or other things? *Probe for differences between hopes and expectations. If necessary, get order of preferences.*

Primarily me breadwinning/partner caregiving

Primarily me caregiving/partner breadwinning

Sharing of breadwinning and caregiving

I do it all

Other arrangement (specify)

d. (Will/Do) you get either paid or unpaid help from anyone else on a regular basis for anything? *If no:* Why not? *If yes:* From whom? What/will they do?

e. Why (will/do) you divide up the responsibilities this way? *Follow up:* Do you see any difficulties or drawbacks to this arrangement? What are they?

f. How does this arrangement compare with the way you were raised or the way your friends manage things? *Probe:* How do you feel about that?

WF.9. a. Is there anyone, including children, parents, relatives, friends, or anyone else, that you feel especially responsible for—either in terms of financial support or taking care of them?

b. Do you ever feel that you have to choose between what is best for anyone you feel responsible for and what is best for yourself?

If yes: How often? When does that happen? What are those circumstances? What do you do? How does that make you feel? *If no:* Why do you think that doesn't happen?

WF.10. a. Do you ever feel you have to choose between (obligations at work/what is best for your job) and what is best for yourself?

If yes: How often? When does that happen? What are those circumstances? What do you do? How does that make you feel? *If no:* Why do you think that doesn't happen?

b. Do you ever feel that you have to choose between obligations at or to work and obligations to care for others?

If yes: What are these circumstances? What do you do? How does that compare with what you feel you should do? With what you like to do? *Probe for time vs. money, self-development vs. care.*

c. Do you ever feel any conflict between these responsibilities and your own needs or goals as an individual?

If yes: What kinds of conflicts? How do you respond to these conflicts? How do you feel about these conflicts? *If no:* Why do you think you don't feel a conflict? How do you feel about that? Would you like more responsibilities or do you like things the way they are? How about five to ten years from now?

WF.11. a. When it comes to how you see yourself, how would you describe yourself to your-self? *Probe:* In terms of your place in the world, the kind of person you are, and your relationships to other people such as family members, friends, or co-workers?

    b. How does your description compare with your ideal?

The Future

Now, I'd like to ask you some questions about your hopes and plans for the future.

F.1. a. What would you like to be doing five or ten years from now in terms of work? *Probe:* Would you like to be working full-time, part-time, or not working?

    b. *If wants to be working:* Ideally, what kind of work would you like? *Probe:* Do you see it as a career or not? What would an ideal job look like in terms of:

Number of hours (full vs. part time)

Flexibility and autonomy in scheduling, etc.

Advancement

Combining with caregiving and personal life

    c. *If does not want to be working:* What would you like to be doing instead? *Probe:* Why?

    d. What do you think are the chances of reaching this goal—high, low, or somewhere in between? *Probe:* Do you foresee any obstacles?

F.2. a. Now, what would you like to be doing outside of work? *Probe:* Would you like to have (more) children someday, or would you prefer not to have any (more) children? Any desires to increase or lighten your caregiving activities? For whom?

    b. Ideally, what would your personal life look like? *Probe:* How would it combine with your work life? What would be your ideal balance?

    c. What do you think are the chances of reaching this goal—high, low, or somewhere in between? *Probe:* Do you foresee any obstacles?

F.3. a. In thinking about the future in general and taking everything together, what do you think your life will be like five or ten years from now? *Probe:* Why do you say that? Have you ever thought about what you would like to be doing or to have done by then?

    b. How does this compare with what you would like your life to be like—is it the same or are there differences? *Probe for relationship, paid work, and caretaking ideals and expectations.*

Follow up: What is your best-case scenario? Your worst-case scenario? The most probable scenario?

    c. What do you think are the chances of achieving your ideals—high, low, or some-where in between? *Probe:* Why do you say that? What are the things that might prevent you? Do you see any of these ideals in conflict? Are you taking any steps to achieve any of them?

F.4. a. Looking back, is there anything you wish had been different?

What would you say to your twenty-year-old self? Any advice, regrets, surprises? *Probe:* If a younger person asked, "What have you learned in your years in this world?" what would you tell him or her? What kind of advice might you give to others about love, work, or related matters?

    b. Are there any things you would do differently if you had the chance? *Probe:* How do you wish things had gone vs. how they have gone? Why? What difference would that have made?

F.5. a. In thinking about your goals for the future, have they changed since you were a child? *If yes:* How? Why? *If no:* Why not?

   b. Do you think you will have to give up anything important to pursue your goals? *If yes:* What things? *If no:* Why not? *Probe for perceived obstacles and trade-offs.*

   c. Looking forward, what do you think you need to do in the future to see yourself and your life as "successful"? What about "failure"? *Probe:* What does "successful" mean to you? Does it involve any particular work goals? Any family or personal goals? Do you see any of these in conflict? What do you think you know now about living a successful life that you didn't know when you were younger? Why do you think your ideas have changed?

   d. Some people think the best way to find happiness is by setting and achieving personal goals, especially through work. Others believe the best way is by taking care of other people. For yourself, what do you feel is the best way? *Probe for specifics:* In what arena, public or private? Can you give some examples?

Influences and Identity

Before we finish, I'd like to make sure you've mentioned all the people or experiences that have been important influences—especially when it comes to work and caretaking.

I.1. Is there any person or experience not already mentioned that has had an important influence on your past decisions or plans for the future—especially when it comes to family and work?

   a. Were there turning points in your life—key events or experiences, both positive and negative—that you haven't mentioned that changed its course and sent you in a different direction? *Probe for positive and negative influences.*
   Follow up: Is there an event you would single out? *Probe:* What did you learn from these experiences? Many people derive important lessons from both good and difficult or stressful experiences. If this applies to you, can you give some examples?

   b. Are there important choices or decisions you made? What did you learn from these decisions? *Probe:* What are some of the most important lessons you have learned over the course of your life?

   c. Is there a person or anyone (else) whose life you would like to emulate or avoid being like? *Probe:* Who is that? Why do you want to be like (him/her/them)? In what ways?
   If necessary: Is there anyone (else) who you would like to emulate or avoid being like? *Probe:* Who is that? Why do you want to be different? In what ways? *Ask as applicable:* What about your mother, father, or other relatives? Your friends growing up or today? Any past or current relationships? Any special teachers, coaches, counselors, employers, or people like that? Any important experiences or events?

I.2. At this point in your life, how would you describe yourself to yourself? Does that differ from how you would have described yourself growing up? In your twenties? *If yes:* What are the differences? Why do you think you've changed? *Probe for identity in work pursuits and care of/connections to others.*

I.3. Sometimes people face a situation when they have to choose between fulfilling their own needs or aspirations, such as pursuing a job opportunity, and caring for someone else, such as a child, a parent, another relative, or a friend. Have you ever felt you had to choose between what was best for yourself and the needs or wishes of a partner, child, or other person you are close to? *Follow up:* When was that? What did you do? Why did you do that? How did you feel? How did that affect you?

Opinions

Now, I'd like to get your opinions on various matters concerning work and family life today.

O.1. a. Some people think happiness is best found through taking care of others, while other people think happiness is best achieved through personal pursuits and achievements. What do you think is more likely to bring happiness to most people?

    b. What about for a man, in general?

    c. What about for a woman, in general?

    d. What about for yourself?

O.2. a. Sometimes people are asked to choose between seeking a personal goal, such as a job opportunity, and caring for someone else, such as a child, a parent, or a friend. When a person is faced with such a choice, what should they do—fulfill a personal aspiration or put the needs of others first?

    b. What if the person is a man?

    c. What if the person is a woman?

O.3. a. *If in a breadwinner-homemaker or neo-traditional household:* When you see other people about your age who live in a family where both parents work outside the home, does that bring out any response in you? *Probe:* What do you imagine their lives to be like? Compared to your own situation?

    b. What about people in a family where the man stays home and the woman works?

    c. What about people in a single-parent family?

    d. What about people who are not married and don't have children?

Skip to O.7.

O.4. a. *If in a dual-earner or reversed household:* When you see other people about your age who live in a family where (one person/the woman) stays home most of the time and the (other/man) is the main breadwinner, does that bring out any response in you? *Probe:* What do you imagine their lives to be like? Compared to your own situation?

    b. What about people in a single-parent family?

    c. What about people who are not married or don't have children?

Skip to O.7.

O.5. a. *If in a single-parent family:* When you see other people about your age who live in a family where one person stays home most of the time and the other is the main breadwinner, does that bring out any response in you? *Probe:* What do you imagine their lives to be like? Compared to your own situation?

    b. What if the man stays home and the woman works?

    c. What about people in a dual-earner family, where both parents work outside the home?

    d. What about people who aren't married and don't have children?

Skip to O.7.

O.6. a. *If single and childless:* When you see other people about your age who live in a family where there is a married couple, and one person stays home most of the time and the other is the main breadwinner, does that bring out any response in you? *Probe:* What do you imagine their lives to be like? Compared to your own situation?

e. What about people who live in a dual-earner family, where both parents work outside the home?

f. What about people in a single-parent family?

O.7. a. *Everyone:* How would you describe an ideal man? *Probe:* What about an ideal partner, father? *Probe for achievement vs. caretaking, gender similarities/differences.*

b. How would you describe an ideal woman? *Probe:* What about an ideal partner, mother? *Probe for achievement vs. caretaking, gender similarities/differences.*

O.8. a. In an ideal situation, who do you think should be responsible for providing the family income? *Probe:* Why do you say that?

b. Who do you think should be responsible for taking care of others, such as children or relatives? *Probe:* Why do you say that?

O.8. a. In your opinion, is there anything that can be done to make it easier for you to create the combination/strike the balance you prefer or meet the challenges of work, family, and the rest of life, or not? *If yes:* What should it do? *If no:* Why not?

b. What about the government? *If yes:* What should it do? *If no:* Why not?

c. What about employers? *If yes:* What should they do? *If no:* Why not?

Background

We're almost finished now. Just a few short questions, and we're done.

B.1. a. Were you raised in a particular religion?

Yes

No (*skip to B.3*)

B.2. a. *If yes:* Which one?

b. Was your mother a (name of religion)?

If no: Was she a member of any other religion?

c. Was your father a (name of religion)?

If no: Was he a member of any other religion?

d. Do you consider yourself a (name of religion) today?

If no: Do you consider yourself a member of any (other) religion at present? *If yes:* Which one?

e. Do you belong to a place of worship? *If yes:* Which one?

B.3. a. Growing up, how important was religion in your life?

Very important

Somewhat important

Not very important

Not at all important

Probe: How important was religion in your family? How often did your family attend religious services?

Very important

Somewhat important
Not very important
Not at all important
b. How important is religion in your life today?
Very important
Somewhat important
Not very important
Not at all important
B.4. a. *If necessary:* Where did you live most of your life up to age eighteen? *If mentions more than three places:* Name the three places where you spent most of your time.
b. *For the one place where lived most of time:* Would you call (name of place) a large city, a small city, a suburb, a small town, or what?
B.5. a. From what country or part of the world did your mother's ancestors come?
b. From what country or part of the world did your father's ancestors come?
c. In terms of race and ethnicity, how do you identify yourself? *Probe:* Choose all that apply:
Non-Hispanic white
Latinx or Hispanic
Black or African American (or Caribbean)
Asian (including Indian subcontinent and Philippines)
American Indian or Alaska Native
Native Hawaiian or other Pacific Islander
B.6. a. In politics, generally speaking, do you usually think of yourself as a Democrat, a Republican, or an independent?
Democrat
Republican
Independent

(skip to B.4.c)

b. *If Democrat or Republican:* Would you say you are a strong (Democrat/Republican) or a not very strong (Democrat/Republican)?
Strong
Not strong
Can't say

Skip to B.6.d.

c. *If independent:* Would you say you are closer to the Democratic Party or closer to the Republican Party?
Closer to Democratic
Closer to Republican
Can't say
d. *Everyone:* In politics, would you say that you are strongly liberal, liberal, middle-of-the-road, conservative, or strongly conservative?
Strong liberal
Liberal
Middle-of-the-road
Conservative
Strong conservative
Other (specify)

e. In politics, would you say you are:
Very active (specify)
Somewhat active (specify)
A little active
Not at all active
If very or somewhat active: What kinds of political issues or activities are you active in? Do you vote on a regular basis?

B.7. a. Please look at this card (*hand income card*) and give me the letter of the group that includes your total household income before taxes—that is, all the money you (and your partner) made last year from any sources, including wage and salary income, profits, rental income, interest, and off-the-books income. *If necessary:* If you aren't sure, just give an estimate.

b. Now, what letter represents your own personal income before taxes—that is, all the money you made last year from any sources, including wage and salary income, profits, rental income, interest, and off-the-books income. *If necessary:* If you aren't sure, just give the group for last year.

c. Does that letter represent your personal earnings? *If no:* What other sources of income do you have? What letter represents your personal earnings?

d. *If married or living with partner:* What group includes your partner's personal income before taxes? *If necessary:* Is that figure included in the letter you gave me for your total family income?

e. *If additional earners in the household:* Which group includes the total income before taxes of everyone living here? *If uncertain:* What would be your best guess?

B.8. a. Well, that's all the questions I have. Is there anything you would like to ask or anything you would like to add to what you have already said?
That's all. Thanks very much for your help! Please don't hesitate to stay in touch and get back to me if you have anything else you'd like to add or anything new to report.

Notes

Chapter 1

1. Glaser and Strauss (1967). See also Timmermans and Tavory (2012) and Tavory and Timmermans (2014). Charmaz (2006) provides an in-depth consideration of how to apply the principles of grounded theory to the analysis of qualitative material.
2. Merton et al. (1956); Weiss (1994).
3. Luker (2008).
4. This framework offers a way to augment methods that highlight the "determinants" of social and individual outcomes with explanations that specify the interaction of social-structural arrangements and innovative human agency. Wrong (1961) and Giddens (1984), among others, have contributed incisive critiques of overly determinist social theories that ignore or underplay the role of agency. And even though Bourdieu (1990) stresses the power of "habitus" to shape individual action, he also recognizes that contending pressures in an organizational field can create tensions and contradictions that necessitate new agentic responses.
5. Researchers use various terms, including "qualitative," "depth," "in-depth," and "focused," to refer to the kind of interviewing we consider. We use these terms interchangeably, although more often we rely on the simple descriptor "depth."
6. Among the many excellent studies that rely on interviews to illumine sexual practices, see Armstrong and Hamilton's (2013) study of partying on campus and Wade's (2017) study of the college hookup culture, both of which combine ethnographic immersion and depth interviews.
7. Chapter 5 considers these issues in greater detail.
8. Chapter 3 contains a thorough discussion of sampling issues, including how to decide what constitutes a sufficient sample size.
9. Wingfield (2013); Dow (2019). Also see Lacy's (2007) study of the "new" Black middle class.
10. Thomas (2017).
11. Pfeffer (2016) and Meadow (2018) offer impressive examples of this process in their studies of queer families and parents raising transgender children. In a similar way, Corse and Silva (2017) and Silva (2013) demonstrate how a changing economy shapes the intimate relationships formed by heterosexual working- and middle-class couples. Ray and Rosow's (2010) interviews also offer insight into how the structure of fraternity spaces and communities shape how white and Black men in those fraternities differentially approach women for intimate relationships college campuses.
12. Hondagneu-Sotelo (2001).
13. See, for example, Ladner (1972), Higginbotham (2001), and Moore (2011).

14. See C. Williams (1992) and J. Williams (2000). Moen and Roehling (2004) refer to a similar social formation, which they call the "career mystique."

15. Hays (2003) and Lipsky (2010).

16. Vaughn (1986).

17. To name only some of the many fine examples of how to combine interviews with ethnographic methods, see Hochschild's study of dual-earner families (1989), Lareau's research on class differences in childrearing (2003), Desmond's portrayal of families coping with eviction (2016), Pascoe's inquiry into the culture of masculinity in high school (2007), Haney's study of formerly incarcerated fathers (2018), and studies conducted by Beaman (2017) and Rao (2020). Torres uses follow-up interviews to enrich and expand ethnographic findings about the importance of "elastic ties" for personal survival and social integration among elderly working-class New Yorkers aging in place in a gentrifying neighborhood (2017). And in their study of the immigrant second generation, Kasinitz, Mollenkopf, and Waters (2009) combine interviews with surveys and ethnographies.

18. Kang (2010); Tavory, Prelat, and Ronen (2020).

19. This standardization presumes all respondents interpret a question in the same way and their verbalized responses have the same meaning, a presumption that values reliability at the expense of validity—what Cicourel (1982) termed the "ecological validity problem."

20. Moore (2011).

21. Lee (2019).

22. Edin and Kefalas (2005). Numerous interview studies seek to discover the reasons for well-documented demographic trends. To name a few on the issue of single motherhood alone, see Luker's research on young unmarried mothers (1996) and Hertz's study of older, middle-class unmarried mothers (2006).

23. Smith (2007).

24. Damaske (2011).

25. Pedulla and Thébaud (2015); Gerson (2010). This finding also points to how apparently conflicting statements can be used to discover deeper meanings, especially about the ways people cope with structural and cultural conflicts over which they have little control.

26. See Collins (1998), Crenshaw (1991), and McCall (2005), among many others.

27. Gerson (2002).

28. Gonzales (2011).

29. Schilt (2010).

30. Tavory (2020).

31. Geertz (1973).

32. Cherlin (2019).

33. Cerulo (2006) considers how "envisioning the future" affects actions and views in the present.

34. Glaser and Strauss (1967).

35. Stinchcombe (1968).

36. Fisher (1993) defines social desirability bias as "the desire of respondents to avoid embarrassment and project a favorable image to others."
37. Jerolmack and Khan (2014). For incisive critiques of this argument, see Cerulo (2014), DiMaggio (2014), and Vaisey (2014). Indeed, in a notable (and somewhat ironic) twist, Khan's co-authored book about sexual assault on campus (Hirsch and Khan 2020) relies heavily on depth interviews that detail students' reports of their sexual experiences.
38. Martin (2010) and Vaisey (2009).
39. Smith (1990); Ladner (1972); Thornton Dill (1979).
40. It is important to note that Thornton Dill's critique was aimed at both white men and white women, whom she rightly critiqued for drawing conclusions about "all" women when they often mean white women, thus subsuming the concerns of women of color within that group. As white women who study gender issues, we couldn't agree more that it is essential to acknowledge the vast diversity among women and to avoid overgeneralizations that ignore or stereotype marginalized groups. It is all too easy for researchers to presume to account for all members of a large, socially diverse group rather than to specify precisely which members of that group are the focus of the analysis. To avoid this peril, a good rule of thumb is to consciously and consistently steer clear of any approach that, wittingly or unwittingly, lumps together all members of a diverse group.
41. Jacobson (2016).
42. Scott and Lyman view "accounts" as "a linguistic device employed whenever an action is subjected to valuative inquiry" (1968, p. 46).
43. Damaske (2011); Branch (2017).
44. Luker (1984).
45. DeLuca, Clampet-Lundquist, and Edin make a similar point (2016, Appendix A).
46. Gerth and Mills (1953).
47. Pugh (2013, p. 50).
48. Jerolmack and Khan (2014).
49. Thomas and Thomas (1928) as quoted by Merton (1995). We would, of course, add every type of gender identification to the category of social actors whose beliefs have consequences for action.
50. Lamont and Swidler (2014) argue that the "challenge for those using interview . . . methods [is] to take [institutional contexts] sufficiently into account."
51. Burawoy (2019).
52. Hays (1998).
53. Lamont (2020).
54. Warikoo (2016).
55. Abdelhadi (2019).
56. This approach can help interviewers discover—using Hirschman's (1970) frame—when social conditions encourage "loyalty" and when they instead encourage "exit" or "voice." In a more literary vein, Emerson (1908) famously remarked, "Foolish consistency is the hobgoblin of little minds," and Fitzgerald said, "The test of a first-rate

intelligence is the ability to hold two opposed ideas in mind at the same time and still retain the ability to function" (1945).

57. Shoda, Mischel, and Peake (1990).

58. Watts, Duncan, and Quan (2018); Calarco (2018b); Perry and Calarco (2017).

59. The problem of positionality can work in complicated ways that are difficult to de-cipher. Goffman's (2014) high-profile study of inner-city African American men created controversy for several reasons. Some researchers expressed doubts about a white woman's ability to understand the experiences of poor Black men, while others expressed concern that her sympathy for their plight biased her account of their criminal behavior. Additionally, unconscious bias can influence reviewers' as well as researchers' conclusions. Since a work's reception can be—and often is—affected by who writes it, it is also possible that Goffman's position as a junior woman (and whose work garnered a great deal of media attention) played a role in drawing attention to the controversy about her findings and methods.

60. Smith (1990). Also see Hartstock (1998) and Collins (2009).

61. Ladner (1972).

62. Becker (1967).

63. In this sense, interviewers rely on collecting and making sense of the many versions of reality offered by their participants, in contrast to the ethnographer's reliance on their own observational lens.

64. Mead (1934) argued that we should strive to "take the role of the other," a goal that may not be entirely attainable but is nevertheless worth striving for. See also Berger and Luckmann (1966).

65. See Gerth and Mills (1953).

66. Luker (2008, p. 169).

67. Pugh (2013).

68. For more on the theoretical significance of future visions, aspirations, ideals, and/or expectations, see Cerulo (2006, 2019); Tavory and Eliasoph (2013). Tavory (2020) refers to a "promissory structure of talk" that can also signal possibilities for future action.

69. Mills (1959).

70. Rickey is generally quoted as saying "Luck is the residue of design." See Shapiro and Epstein (2006). Another apt sports metaphor about how luck emerges from prior planning and effort, usually attributed to the golfer Gary Player, declares that "the more I practice, the luckier I get."

71. Burawoy (2019). A number of ethnographers have also argued that deductive the-orizing is insufficient. See Burawoy (1998), Small (2009, 2018), Timmermans and Tavory (2012), and Tavory and Timmermans (2014).

72. The timing of each stage in an interview project may differ from that of other methods. Ethnographers may choose a research site before developing a clear set of questions, while interviewers must decide whom to interview before they can begin talking with people. Quantitative analysts typically depend on existing data sets that exclude the option of formulating their own questions, while interviewers must construct an in-terview guide, with a clear set of questions, before they can interview participants.

Chapter 2

1. As we will discuss in depth in Chapter 3, before deciding whom to interview and how many participants to include, it is necessary to know what information to collect.
2. Robinson and Schulz (2016).
3. For an overview of how "unconscious bias" operates and how we can address it, see Eberhardt (2019).
4. Luker (2008, p. 52). Luker offers less detail about depth interviewing but provides an excellent guide to conducting qualitative work.
5. Although elaborate statistical analyses require a larger sample size than a depth interview study can handle, interview studies often employ simple quantitative techniques, such as tabular analyses that present bivariate or trivariate relationships. Qualitative studies can also apply significance tests to the relationships if random selection techniques were used to draw the sample.
6. While the question or set of questions should focus on a puzzling or problematic "social fact," this term has a broad meaning. A social fact is not confined to actions or institutions that can be observed or easily counted; it also includes social formations that cannot be observed or easily counted, such as mental states and cultural practices (Durkheim 1982).
7. Reich (2016).
8. Wade (2017, p. 17).
9. Both of us have addressed such puzzles in our research. In *For the Family*, Sarah asked why working-class women are not as likely as their middle-class peers to hold a paid job if their employment results from "need" rather than "choice" (Damaske 2011). In Kathleen's research on the new economy, she seeks to explain why some trends point to a stalled gender revolution while others point toward women outpacing men in education and career aspirations (Gerson 2017). Stone (2007) and Stone and Lovejoy (2019) address a related puzzle: Do professional women who leave the workforce "opt out" (to use a phrase coined by Belkin in 2003), or do employment and domestic constraints push them out and then set the conditions for how they can opt back in?
10. Davis (1971).
11. Dow (2019); Barnes (2016).
12. Chung (2016).
13. Gillespie (1971).
14. Connell (2018). This essay can be found in an important collection, *Other, Please Specify: Queer Methods in Sociology* (Compton, Meadow, and Schilt [2018]).
15. Mills (1959).
16. Ryder (1965) provides the classic rationale for looking at cohorts in order to understand processes of social change. In addition to our own work, Blair-Loy's (2003) study comparing two generations of women finance workers is an excellent example of this technique.
17. Pedulla (2020).
18. McMillan Cottom (2017).
19. Shedd (2015).

20. Edin and Nelson (2013).
21. Ibid., 16.
22. Ibid.
23. Roth (2006).
24. See Burawoy (1998).
25. See Haney (2002).
26. For an overview of theories of family life and how historical changes required paradigm shifts to account for new family forms, see Gerson and Torres (2015). Parsons (1974) presents a summary of the "sex roles" theory of family formation.
27. In *The Structure of Scientific Revolutions* (1962), Thomas Kuhn famously argued that new theoretical paradigms do not replace older ones; they subsume them. In physics, Einstein's theory of relativity did not replace Newtonian physics but instead placed Newton's laws within the context of a higher-order theory.
28. Explanatory theories, Karl Popper argued, are logically connected "falsifiable" arguments rather than statements of ultimate truth (1959). Their worth is measured by their usefulness—that is, their ability to explain the phenomena they aim to explain.

Chapter 3

1. In rare instances, surveys that seek to study "hidden" populations may use snowballing techniques to find members who cannot be reached via random sampling procedures.
2. Small (2009). Small discusses the challenges ethnographers face selecting a sample of cases that, while necessarily small in size, can meet "scientific" criteria.
3. Luker (2008, p. 103); Glaser and Strauss (1967).
4. Creswell (2014) refers to this approach to sampling as "purposive," and Small (2009) uses the term "inferential logic." Glaser and Strauss (1967), Luker (2008), and Small (2009) are especially helpful in thinking through issues of sampling in qualitative research. As Small notes, too often quantitative researchers press qualitative researchers to mimic quantitative methods in order to receive funding or publish in top journals, leading to larger sample sizes that some have argued can be generalizable to a broader public. While we both typically use larger sample sizes than does Small, we do not do so in order to claim that the samples are "generalizable" to the larger population. We do so, instead, to gather a sufficiently large group of participants to generate within-sample variation in order to make useful comparisons (which we discuss later in the chapter) and discover the mechanisms that explain differences and similarities among the comparison groups. We also argue that the sampling strategy should emphasize the issues and groups in question rather than an abstract rule about generalizing to a broader population. When writing about the findings, however, it is useful to consider how the theoretical insights might apply to other groups and the population at large.
5. In the language of statistics, this means you wish to seek internal validity (which bolsters confidence in the patterns within the sample) rather than external validity (which involves claims to representativeness). Stinchcombe (1968) explains

that the goal of theory building is to identify the consequential forces and specify the mechanisms that link them to defined outcomes. Since the *rate* of an outcome will change in response to changes in the underlying social forces and conditions that produce it, the challenge in theory construction is to discover those underlying conditions and their relationships, not to predict the specific rate at which an outcome occurs at any particular moment in time.

6. The good news is that since interviewers collect their material one interview at a time, there will be future opportunities to adjust the sampling criteria in response to unanticipated findings in the field.

7. Klinenberg (2013).

8. Collins (2019).

9. Calarco (2018a); Lareau (2003).

10. A study of this kind, which includes interviews with a "protected group" (in this case, children under eighteen), requires permission from an institutional review board.

11. Royster (2003).

12. Utrata (2015).

13. Lareau, Weininger, and Cox (2018).

14. Jack (2019).

15. Viscelli (2016).

16. Jacobson (2008).

17. Soto-Márquez (2018). In a similar way, Imoagene (2017) compares the experiences of second-generation Nigerians in the United States and Britain. In contrast, Waters's classic studies of white ethnic identities (1990) and Black identities (2001) stay focused on the United States, but they make systematic comparisons within a diverse racial grouping.

18. Practical considerations are not inconsequential. Although India also sends a large number of high-skilled workers to other countries, Soto-Márquez's knowledge of Spanish culture and language made Spain a better choice.

19. Glaser and Strauss (1967, p. 61).

20. Small (2009).

21. Damaske (2020 and forthcoming). Ultimately, Sarah was not able to find the racial variation originally sought.

22. Ryder (1965) presents the classic rationale for investigating the experiences of a cohort (or cohorts) in the best position to illuminate processes such as demographic change.

23. Klinenberg (2013).

24. Collins (2019).

25. Compton (2018) offers a thoughtful approach about how to think through sampling design for depth interviewing and especially for studying queer or other marginalized populations.

26. Though it is difficult to specify an ideal sample size, some guidelines are helpful. A sample should be large enough to contain a minimally acceptable number of cases in each comparative cell, but not so large that your time and resources are stretched too thin to collect rich interviews and conduct a systematic analysis of them. There

are few rules—and little agreement—about a minimum or maximum number, although we would argue for a sample that contains *at least* ten to fifteen interviewees in each comparison group. When considering the total sample size, it is difficult to conduct a convincing analysis with fewer than fifty interviewees, and more than that is preferable. Yet if the interviews are lengthy, it is difficult to analyze more than 150 to 200 transcripts. Within that range, there lies a great deal of discretion. Deterding and Waters's (2018) analysis of interview studies published in the top sociology journals found that only 20 percent relied on interviews alone and that the median number of interviews is eighty-five in the *American Journal of Sociology* and fifty-five in the *American Sociological Review*, but the authors also note that the numbers are much higher for studies that relied on interviews alone.

27. Even though comparisons among children with differing family experiences is central to Kathleen's analysis in *The Unfinished Revolution* (Gerson [2010]), it was not necessary to use variation in family structure as a criterion for sample selection because the ubiquity of family change meant the needed variation would "naturally" emerge though random sampling techniques.

28. Hagedorn (2018).

29. Some possible sources (which we have used) include voter registration rolls and lists compiled by polling firms, which can usually be purchased for a nominal price, or membership lists of large organizations.

30. Ecklund (2010).

31. Gerson (1985). It is worth noting that the original sampling criteria for this study, which screened for married women, expanded after the first interview, when a single woman asked to participate. This early, exploratory interview made it clear that excluding women who did not have a steady partner would obscure one important reason women cited for choosing to pursue a career or deciding not to have a child.

32. Although the rise of cellphones and caller ID have complicated the process of contacting people, our response rates among those we contact are quite high, ranging from 70 percent to well over 90 percent.

33. De Graauw (2016).

34. Luker (1978).

35. Royster (2003). If random sampling fails to provide a sufficient number of participants for a specific category, randomly chosen participants can suggest others who fit the category you are seeking. In this way, snowballing can help complete the sample without compromising the sampling process as long as it is used sparingly and carefully.

36. Chambliss (1996).

37. Miller-Idriss (2018).

38. A procedure that selects participants based on the outcome in question is considered "sampling on the dependent variable," an approach that risks predetermining the findings before the research begins. Limiting a sample in this way forecloses the possibility of discovering unknown outcomes or looking for counterfactuals that could disconfirm original assumptions and thus precludes developing an explanation to address the reasons for differences between included and excluded groups.

39. Wingfield (2013, p. 171).
40. Moore (2018). Other examples that use creative methods to secure hard-to-find samples include Steinburgler's study of interracial gay relationships (2012) and Twine's examination of white mothers raising Black children.
41. McPherson, Smith-Lovin, and Cook (2001). Jennifer Patrice Sims took a similar approach to recruit multiracial interview participants in the US and the UK (2016).
42. Gonzales (2011, p. 607).
43. Schilt (2010).
44. The internet has spawned new sampling sources, such as Amazon's Mechanical Turk, which provides paid volunteers for surveys and other types of opinion research. These new services offer easy accessibility but contain considerable drawbacks. It is virtually impossible to know whom a sample represents when it relies on volunteers who participate for a fee.

Chapter 4

1. We use the terms "questionnaire" and "interview guide" interchangeably. Some people might prefer answering a set of questions, while others might prefer a conversational interaction. While in its most structured form an interview can consist of a series of questions and answers, most interviews become a conversation as they proceed. Just as people vary in their interactional styles, there is no one "right" way to gather information. For each interviewee, the best approach is the one that evokes an open and comfortable interaction. What matters is that the form and wording of the questions elicit high-quality answers that are sufficiently comparable across all the interviews.
2. Goffman (2014).
3. Cohen (2015); Lubet (2015). Goffman's response (2015) to this critique—that she had burned her notes as a way to ensure her participants' privacy—is not typical among ethnographic researchers. Yet whether or not ethnographers retain their notes and other data, most do not release them publicly. Indeed, many institutional research boards require that research notes be destroyed after a specified period of time.
4. Jerolmack and Murphy (2017).
5. Pratt, Kaplan, and Whittington (2019).
6. See Burawoy (2019) and Khan (2019) for compelling considerations of the dangers posed by requiring researchers to turn over their field notes, which are presumed to be confidential, to legal authorities or the public at large. As Khan states, "Complying with a subpoena would have destroyed my relationship with my subjects. . . . It also would have violated the condition under which the undergraduates at Columbia had consented to be part of my research" (Khan 2019, p. 255).
7. In *The Fine Line*, Eviatar Zerubavel (1993) makes a similar distinction between the overly "rigid" mind and the overly "fuzzy" mind, arguing that the "flexible" mind strikes a balance between these extremes.
8. Economic approaches to studying time use, for example, tend to presume that the amount of time people devote to market and domestic work reflects their

preferences—or, as economists term it, their "tastes" (Becker [1981]; Hammermesh and Pfann [2002]). Rather than presuming that behavior can serve as a measure of preferences, sociological approaches distinguish between the two in order to investigate how preferences develop and change as well as the social conditions that either prevent or allow people to enact their preferences (Jacobs and Gerson [2004]; Gerson [2010]).

9. Pugh (2009).
10. Wingfield (2013); Kanter (1993); Williams (1992).
11. Parreñas (2001).
12. Whitaker (2016).
13. Comey (2018).
14. DeLuca, Clampet-Lundquist, and Edin (2016) make a similar point, arguing that phrasing questions as "how" rather than "why" and seeking detailed examples increases the ability of interviewers to gather accurate information grounded in concrete experiences.
15. The General Social Survey is a national survey administered annually by the National Opinion Research Council at the University of Chicago. These questions have been asked since the 1970s, with the same wording preserved to facilitate comparisons over time.
16. For a detailed analysis of the strengths and limits of these question wordings, see Jacobs and Gerson (2016).
17. While "follow-ups" are always asked, "probes" seek a fuller response when an answer is incomplete.
18. Pedulla and Thébaud (2015).
19. Jacobs and Gerson (2016).
20. See Bettie (2003) for a discussion of how subjects are not necessarily able to talk back in observational studies.
21. We draw from Nadirah Farah Foley's (2018) recent call to use this terminology in place of the words "women and people of color" to recognize the ways that women of color are marginalized as both women and as people of color.
22. Our approach of using events as a prime for recalling details of social context, experiences, reactions, and longer-term consequences resembles Robinson and Schulz's (2016) iterated questioning approach, which consists of sequenced iterations of a baseline question designed to elicit multiple forms of talk. It involves four distinct steps: (1) establishing the baseline iterated question, (2) eliciting frontstage talk, (3) going backstage, and (4) eliciting backstage talk.
23. For the specific versions used in our research projects, see Appendix C as well as Damaske (2011); Damaske (2020); Gerson (1985, 1993, 2010, 2017).
24. Vaisey (2009) argues that surveys are better able to tap people's snap judgments (or what he calls "hot cognitions"). Yet interviews can contain the best of both worlds by combining closed- and open-ended questions and moving from the more specific to the more general. Starting with narrowly constructed questions, an interviewer can pursue a line of questioning by probing for the broader significance of the original answers.
25. See Elder and Giele (2009).

26. DeLuca, Clampet-Lundquist, and Edin (2016) refer to an interview structure based on sequential ordering as "narrative interviewing."
27. Survey researchers call this beginning segment an "enumeration." More sensitive information, such as income or political leanings, should be postponed to the end, when any disclosure cannot influence the course of the interview.
28. Weiss (1994).
29. Abbott (2017) discusses how a core insight of sociological analysis is seeing individuals, groups, and institutions not as fixed in time but rather as a series of events and social processes.
30. Giddens (1979, 1984) discusses how contradictory institutional arrangements require social actors to invent new scripts that give concrete shape to social change. Kathleen's analysis also emphasizes how conflicts between institutional domains— such as work and family—set up socially structured dilemmas that require innovative responses (1986, 1993, 2010, 2016).
31. Friedman (2018).
32. Meadow (2018).
33. Kathleen used this question series for her interviews with "the children of the gender revolution" (2010). The appendix presents examples of full questionnaires, including questionnaires that include sections on work, relationship, and other histories.
34. In several studies, Kathleen uses the comparison between changers and non-changers to analyze women's and men's life paths (Gerson [1985, 1993]).
35. In Chapter 6, we will discuss strategies for confronting and minimizing the potential bias posed by selective memory.
36. Like a good therapeutic strategy, the neutral format of these follow-ups should help interviewees think and speak more openly about their experiences without concern about being judged.
37. Giddens (1984) contrasts purposeful "discursive consciousness" with "practical consciousness," which is so internalized and taken for granted that it guides behavior by remaining unnoticed. Also see Tavory and Eliasoph (2013), Mische (2009), and Cerulo (2006).
38. Tavory (2020).
39. Kathleen developed these questions for her study of work and caregiving in the new economy (Gerson 2017).
40. We use questions of this kind in all our projects, regardless of the topic or sample.

Chapter 5

1. Von Pfetten (2016) stresses the importance of practicing how to listen actively. She suggests using your eyes as well as your ears by facing and looking at the interviewee. Hsiung (2018) is a good source of examples (drawn from interviews with immigrants to Canada) exploring issues of data collection, reflexivity, and analysis.
2. To assess how well her interview guide worked for people with different kinds of family experiences, Kathleen sought pre-test subjects who grew up in families that

exemplified the "ideal types" prevailing in current theories, including single-parent, dual-earner, and breadwinner-caregiver homes, even though these categories ultimately proved to be more fluid and complex than much of the literature acknowledged.

3. Since institutions do not all follow the same procedures, check the guidelines at your home institution. Although the rules can vary, most institutions agree there is no need for prior approval to conduct provisional interviews when the findings will not be disseminated to the public

4. This process resembles the model used in medical training, where a medical student or intern first observes an experienced physician at work and then administers medical treatment under the guidance of a seasoned practitioner.

5. We also encourage beginning interviewers to listen to their audio recordings for clues about what went well and what adjustments they might wish to make. Taking the time to transcribe the early interviews, though time-consuming, also highlights findings that may have gone unnoticed during the interview as well as interview strategies that worked well or poorly.

6. Risman (2018).

7. When Kathleen began interviewing in the 1970s and 1980s, people who received a letter often called her before she had a chance to contact them. When she did call, almost everyone answered the phone and agreed to participate. As people's lives have become busier and requests from unknown sources have become more frequent, this ease in recruiting is certainly no longer the case.

8. Mead (1934); Cooley (1902).

9. To manage the payment process, we recommend placing the payment, whether cash or a gift card, in an envelope with the interviewee's name on the front. It is a simple matter to give the gift envelope at the start of the interview, when the participant signs the release form. If needed, you ask for a signed receipt as well. If an interviewee tries to decline, it helps to suggest using it to buy a gift for a loved one or to donate to a favorite charity. Even if symbolic, a small gift provides a tangible way to underline the importance of a person's participation and to express your appreciation for the time and effort it requires.

10. As an example of creative recruiting, Sabrina Dycus (2018) needed to recruit former inmates for a study of "jailhouse lawyers." To reassure potential participants, who are likely to harbor strong suspicions about the motives of researchers and the uses of research, she developed a web page that included her photo, contact information, a description of the research, and a field for people to enter their name, email address, and a brief personal message about how to reach them.

11. Even if it proves difficult to make an initial contact with many of your potential participants, we find that the rate of participation among those whom we successfully contact is quite high and much higher than survey researchers have come to expect. Kathleen's studies have yielded 80 to 90 percent participation rates among the people she is able to contact, while Sarah's unemployment study (which focused on a group that it is known to be difficult to recruit) had a participation rate of 67 percent. To keep tabs on your sampling results, be sure to keep a record of the fate of each attempted contact, including when the letter was sent, when and how many phone

calls were made, the result of each call, and the details of all contacts that were made. It is also important to pay attention to how many letters need to be sent and to create a steady flow of interviews that is neither insufficient nor too taxing for your schedule. This record facilitates the recruitment process and makes it easy to calculate the ultimate response rate after all the interviews have been completed.

12. Gottlieb (2019).

13. Like the therapeutic relationship, interviewers need to strike a balance by presenting themselves as neutral, professional, and trustworthy while also making a personal connection by conveying our shared humanity. The key is to offer personal details that help interviewees feel comfortable without disclosing information that might influence their responses.

14. Over several decades and hundreds of interviews, only one person—a lawyer—has declined Kathleen's request to record, and only one person has asked Sarah to delete a recording after completing the interview.

15. Also see Weiss (1994).

16. Tavory (2020) distinguishes between "open" questions that seek factual information and "closed" questions that seek interpretation. Asking questions in a chronological sequence helps interviewers avoid what he calls "hindsight bias," and gathering information about the context in which interpretation emerges helps avoid what he calls "agency bias."

17. As we discussed in Chapter 4, Robinson and Schulz's (2016) iterative questioning approach is similar to our format of nested questions. These strategies provide a format for establishing rapport as well as for pursuing an informative line of questioning.

18. Poniewozik (2016).

19. Weiss (1994).

20. Scott and Lyman (1968); Damaske (2011). See Blair-Loy (2003) for an example of using interviews to explain the shape and influence of cultural schemas for women executives.

21. Pugh (2013).

22. We disagree with Vaisey (2009), who argues that snap judgments (which he terms "hot cognitions") are a better measure of people's "true" beliefs than are consciously considered ones (which he terms "cold cognitions"). When institutions are in flux or intersect in contradictory ways, such superficial responses are unlikely to offer a good guide to learning about the uncertain, ambiguous strategies people pursue.

23. Gerson (2010).

24. Timmermans and Tavory (2012) refer to the tacking between deductive and inductive reasoning as "abductive" analysis. In contrast to grounded theory, which depends on the inductive emergence of theoretical insight rather than imposing an analytic framework in advance, they propose a "creative inferential process aimed at producing new hypotheses and theories" through the collection and analysis of "surprising research evidence." To avoid sacrificing comparability, it is best to seek unexpected insights and incorporate changes in the interview guide as soon as possible. Fortunately, prior interviews are likely to contain comparable information, although it will be embedded in the answers to different questions. For this reason, the

need to reinterview some participants is unlikely. In the rare case when crucial information is missing, a brief follow-up conversation can follow via the phone, computer video session, or email.

25. Glaser and Strauss (1967).

26. Gerson (2017).

27. Often attributed to the ancient Greek physician Hippocrates, the phrase "do no harm" is commonly included in the oath medical students take when they graduate from medical school.

28. See Jones (1981), Milgram (1974), and Zimbardo (2007).

29. Humphreys (1970). For an insightful critique of the Humphreys study, see Williams (2002).

30. Blee (2002); Luker (1984).

31. Newman (1988).

32. Hochschild (2016).

33. Take the cases discussed in Chapter 4, including Goffman's study of inner-city youth (2014) and Khan's (2019) experiences when his ethnographic data on an elite boarding school were subpoenaed for use in a legal suit.

34. In some cases, an interviewee may not define an action or belief as sensitive, even though you may find it ethically and morally distasteful (or worse). In Sarah's study of job loss, some white working-class interviewees expressed racially based critiques that they did not consider biased. In these instances, participants assume you share views they take for granted.

35. Berger and Luckmann (1966). In some, hopefully very rare, instances, you may encounter a person whom you deem a threat to themselves or others. If this occurs, it is important to consult the rules of your institutional review board for advice about how to handle the case.

36. Jerolmack and Murphy (2017).

37. Institutional review boards use the term "human subjects" to refer to research participants, and their legal mandate is to ensure that researchers maintain both privacy and confidentiality.

38. Pratt, Kaplan, and Whittington (2019).

39. If the research topic is one that is especially likely to explore potentially sensitive territory, it may be worthwhile to have a list of appropriate services available on request.

40. We use the term "in-person" rather than "face-to-face" to make a distinction between interviews that take place in a shared space and interviews that take place online even if the meetings might technically be considered two (or more) people facing each other.

41. According to a Pew Research Center survey, one in five American parents with school-age children reported that it was somewhat or very likely their children could not complete their classwork online. That figure rises to 40 percent among low-income households, where children are more likely to lack access to a computer or internet connection (Pew Research Center, 2020). Also see Moyer (2020).

42. Bianchi, Robinson, and Milkie (2006).

43. Theodosius (2006, p. 901); Worth (2009).

44. Hislop et al. (2005).

45. To enlarge the sample size, both of us have relied on research assistants for selected projects, but only after conducting the bulk of the interviews ourselves.

46. For women, both skirts and pants are fine. Sarah generally prefers pants, which can be more comfortable in any seating arrangement. Michelle Lamont (1992) reports that being slightly less formally dressed can be an advantage in some contexts, such as interviews with successful businessmen who might feel more comfortable if your clothes convey you are not seeking to be seen as a peer, although that is clearly a judgment call. Dress codes vary widely across cultural groups and social settings, so it is best to weigh each situation and select a style that balances what you think will make the interviewee comfortable with your personal standards of self-presentation. When interviewing American Muslims, for example, Eman Abdelhadi (2019) concluded that wearing a hijab not only would send too strong a message but also would interfere with her ability to feel comfortable in the interview setting.

47. Haney (2018).

48. Anner (2015).

49. Rivera (2017).

50. Emerson, Fretz, and Shaw (2011) include a discussion on note-taking that is useful for interviewers.

51. Calarco (2018c).

Chapter 6

1. Small (2009).

2. Deterding and Waters (2018). Also see Pugh (2013).

3. The "Rashomon effect" refers to the classic Kurosawa film *Rashomon,* where four witnesses offer conflicting accounts of how a rape and murder took place.

4. The argument that interviews can only measure perceptions is in itself suspect. Like surveys, interviews collect "facts" such as age, income, marital status, occupation and work status, work history, and other "hard" data. Even if the answers to these questions contain some inaccuracies, this does not make them "perceptions." A carefully constructed interview guide, along with diligence in conducting the interviews, can minimize the degree of inaccuracy as well as any bias in the overall results it might pose.

5. All social science involves the measurement and analysis of perceptions. Observational methods rely on the ethnographer's perceptions, much as a play-goer observes the action onstage and infers the inner motives of the characters. Interviews, in contrast, rely on participants to describe and discuss their perceptions, so they bear more resemblance to a novel in which the reader infers motives and meanings based on the actions and inner thoughts of the characters. The challenge is then to make sense of these varying perspectives and points of view.

6. Even if a small number of interviewees are willfully dishonest, this becomes a problem only if there are systematic differences in who is truthful and who isn't. The key is to stay alert to this possibility and not allow it to bias the results.

7. Allison Pugh presents a thoughtful discussion of the tension between acknowledging one's bias and striving for scientific neutrality in the appendix of *Longing and Belonging* (2009).

8. Mills (1959).

9. Although theirs is a minority opinion, some researchers recommend against recording interviews or using a qualitative analysis program. See, for example, Back (2012). In contrast, not only do we recommend recording and transcribing interviews, we also recommend uploading the transcripts as soon as possible, thus easing the process of organizing the interviews and attaching related memos as they are constructed. Sarah often begins working with a transcriber as soon as she enters the field, which makes it possible to include the review of transcriptions as part of the iterative process between conducting interviews and analyzing them. If the costs of hiring a transcriber or transcription service are prohibitive, another option is using low-cost voice recognition software (for example, Otter or Trint), which is rapidly improving in accuracy and efficiency.

10. Most qualitative software programs, such as Atlas.ti, Nvivo, and Dedoose, allow the analyst to add notes in the margin of each transcript file as well as in a separate file attached to each transcript.

11. Unless there is reason to doubt the accuracy of the transcript or you need to hear the tone of an answer to understand its meaning, you need not listen to every recording.

12. For an excellent discussion of how to adapt grounded theory coding precepts to twenty-first-century technology, we recommend Deterding and Waters (2018).

13. Deterding and Waters (2018).

14. Taking our own research as an example, Kathleen begins with codes for basic demographic categories, key areas of childhood and family life, education, job history, relationship history, current circumstances, future plans, and opinions.

15. Timmermans and Tavory (2014) call this process "abductive analysis."

16. A number of packages, such as SPSS, Excel, and Stata, can be used to construct a spreadsheet with codes for all the participants, and this can summarize the sample, sort variables, construct tables and cross tabs, and, if pertinent, ascertain measures of association. SPSS is well suited to this task because (in addition to its quantitative tools) it allows the analyst to sort codes that use nominal as well as numeric categories.

17. See Zerubavel (1996) on "lumping and splitting" as a central task of theory building.

18. Ramirez (2018).

19. Among the many studies of how policies adopted by lawmakers are transformed when they are applied in practice, see Pressman and Wildavsky (1984). For a classic analysis of how an organization's founding principles shape its path going forward, see Stinchcombe (1965).

20. This approach led Kathleen to distinguish between "ideals" and "fallback positions" in her analysis of women's and men's outlooks on the future (Gerson 2010).

21. Damaske (2020).

22. See Scott and Lyman (1968), Orbuch (1997), and Damaske (2011).

23. Timmermans and Tavory make a similar point, arguing that ethnographers can find "meaning in observations" (2012, 2014).

24. Damaske (2011).
25. Ann Swidler (1980) documents the many ways American conceptions of love contain contradictory ideals, such as the importance of both unfettered choice and lasting commitment.
26. The bias in favor of publishing studies that show a statistically significant finding, while failing to publish research that confirms a null hypothesis, leads to overemphasizing some results—i.e., significant findings—and underemphasizing others that can have equally important implications for theory. To take one example, every time an article reporting a gender difference is published, even as a finding of no difference is ignored, the belief that gender differences are large, pervasive, and immutable is reinforced. See Rothstein, Sutton, and Borenstein 2005.
27. Life-course analysts use a variety of qualitative and quantitative methods. See Elder and Giele (2009) and Moen and Roehling (2005), among many others.
28. See Powell and DiMaggio (1991) for a consideration of Bourdieu's concept of institutional fields.
29. As Eviatar Zerubavel (2006) points out, an inability to see the "elephant in the room" is as much a product of social arrangements as is the ability to see it.
30. Chapter 4 discusses how to construct the interview guide to minimize participants' efforts to avoid inconsistent or contradictory statements and encourage a clear recounting of past experiences and current outlooks.
31. Proposing a new way of understanding accepted "facts" means challenging taken-for-granted assumptions. Questioning common theoretical wisdom invites controversy, but confidence in the analysis can be a source of courage for finding and expressing your sociological voice. See Mills (1959).

Chapter 7

1. Merriam-Webster (2019) defines a method as "a systematic procedure, technique, or mode of inquiry."
2. Becker (1986); Luker (2008); Zerubavel (1999).
3. Strunk and White (1959).
4. Lamott (2007).
5. Rabiner and Fortunato (2003); Germano (2001).
6. Goldberg and Allen (2015).
7. Those with a humanities background may find this format stilted, and it certainly removes the element of surprise. A straightforward presentation style, however, does not in itself require a stilted writing style.
8. Cooper (2014).
9. Besen-Cassino (2014); Kalleberg (2011).
10. McCabe (2016).
11. Not coincidentally, Lynne Haney is a colleague with whom both of us have worked closely.
12. Kuhn (1962).

13. Whooley (2013).
14. Yukich (2013)
15. Sharone (2013).
16. Edin and Kefalas (2005), for example, effectively combine all three goals by using stories from the popular media to establish a connection between their research on single mothers and ongoing political and academic debates.
17. One caution is to avoid presenting hypotheses. Qualitative interviewing does a better job by interrogating existing paradigms in order to pose research questions. Quantitative approaches, in contrast, are much better suited to testing hypotheses.
18. Sarah, for example, likes to walk readers through the coding process, offering a brief description of how coding works (beginning with known concepts and adding new codes through an iterative process) and then providing an example of how a code used in the manuscript was constructed.
19. Sherman (2017).
20. See Gerson (1985, 1993, and 2010) and Damaske (2011).
21. Sherman (2009).
22. Pamela Kaufman collected the interviews used to develop the argument in Patterson, Damaske, and Sheroff (2017).
23. Gerson (2011).
24. Sherman (2009).
25. Sharone (2013).
26. McCabe (2016).
27. Gerson (2011, pp. 33–43); Damaske (2011, pp. 24–39).
28. There may be some instances when the institutional review board and the interviewees grant permission to provide identifying information, but these are rare circumstances and they are rarely necessary to accomplish the research goals.
29. Balancing the need to present sufficient evidence within the page limitations (for an article) or readers' attention spans (for a book) can be a challenge with qualitative material, which requires more space than quantitative findings. Drawing on relevant prior research can be helpful, especially for journal articles, where three to four examples are generally accepted as supporting evidence.
30. We agree with Maxwell (2010), who also makes this argument.
31. Becker (1970, 1998).
32. As a quote commonly attributed to Einstein famously declared, "A theory should be as simple as possible, but no simpler" (https://en.wikiquote.org/wiki/Albert_Einstein).
33. Thanks to Claude Fischer, who many years ago described Kathleen's inclination to include every interesting detail as "an overgrown garden in need of pruning."
34. As members of numerous editorial boards and reviewers for a wide range of journals, we have found that many submissions that are strong in the presentation and analysis of findings then conclude with a short discussion that fails to explain why the findings are important for addressing larger theoretical issues.
35. Damaske (2011); Gerson (2011).
36. Bernoff (2016) calls vague and unnecessary prose "weasel words." In addition, there is no need to use introductory phrases such as "I argue" or "it seems." Not only does

the reader know you are the person making the argument, but such phrases dilute the prose without adding anything to the argument.

37. The term "sociologese" is used to describe a stilted style of writing held to be characteristic of sociologists (Merriam-Webster [2019]).

Appendix A

1. For details on the recruiting process, see Damaske (2020).

<u>Damaske's Script and Eligibility Sheet for In-Person Recruitment</u>

As part of Sarah's unemployment study, she and her team of graduate student research assistants recruited participants from unemployment centers in five counties in Pennsylvania. Below is a copy of the recruitment script approved by Penn State's institutional review board and by the unemployment centers that was read at the end of the meetings.

If people were interested, they would approach the recruiter and the recruiter then handed them the eligibility form. This form collected information that would allow Sarah to determine if people fit the study criteria (were between the ages of twenty-eight and fifty-two, had lost a job recently, and had lost a full-time job).

Unemployment and Job Loss Research Study

Hello, my name is _____ and I am from a research team at Pennsylvania State University that is here to invite you to participate in a research project about job loss and unemployment. We're doing this study because we really want to understand people's experience of their job loss, and we greatly appreciate your consideration of the project.

We are inviting people to fill out a short survey about themselves and their job loss. It should take less than five minutes to fill out, and you are under no obligation to do so. If you're interested, I'll be outside after you've completed your Prep meetings; please just stop by to see me.

If you are eligible for participation in the study, you may be contacted and invited to participate in an in-depth interview about your work experiences to help us better understand your experience of job loss and unemployment.

If chosen for participation in the in-person interview, you will receive $50 for completing the in-person interview session.

I want you to know that you do not have to participate in this study. Your study participation is voluntary. You may refuse to participate or withdraw from the study at any time without penalty.

I want to assure you that should you decide to participate, your information will be kept strictly confidential.

I also wanted to let you know that we can arrange to hold the interview at a location of your choice—your house, a local Starbucks where we can buy you a cup of coffee, or an alternative location. You decide.

Finally, we understand that everyone has busy lives today and that it might be hard to fit us into your busy schedule. We appreciate this challenge and will work to make the interview fit your schedule. We hope that you'll consider participating, because we truly can't understand what your experience of job loss and unemployment has been like unless we talk to you.

Again, thanks for listening. I'll be outside after the meeting if you have any questions or if you want to sign up. I'm looking forward to meeting you!

First Name: _____ Last Name: _____

Phone: _____ Cell: _____

Email: _____

Street Address: _____

City: _____

- Did you experience job loss between 2007 and the present? Please circle one: Yes or No
- Prior to your job loss, were you employed full-time? Please circle one: Yes or No
- In what year were you born? _____
- Are you currently married or partnered and living with someone with whom you are in a relationship? Please circle: Yes or No
- Do any children under the age of 18 live in your household? Please circle one: Yes or No
- When are you generally available for an interview? Circle all that apply: Daytime or Evening
- What days are BEST for you for an interview? Circle all that apply:
  Monday, Tuesday, Wednesday, Thursday, Friday, Saturday, Sunday

Bibliography

Abbott, Andrew. 2017. *Processual Sociology*. Chicago: University of Chicago Press.

Abdelhadi, Eman. 2019. "Departures, Detours and the Counterfactual Self: Gendered Community and Identity Pathways Among Second Generation American Muslims." Unpublished manuscript.

Anner, Mark. 2015. "Labor Control Regimes and Worker Resistance in Global Supply Chains." *Labor History* 56 (3): 292–307.

Armstrong, Elizabeth A., and Laura T. Hamilton. 2013. *Paying for the Party: How College Maintains Inequality*. Cambridge, MA: Harvard University Press.

Back, Les. 2012. Untitled contribution. In *How Many Qualitative Interviews Is Enough? Expert Voices and Early Career Reflections on Sampling and Cases in Qualitative Research*, edited by Sarah Elsie Baker and Rosalind Edwards, 12–14. Brighton, UK: National Centre for Research Methods, Economic and Social Research Council. http://eprints.brighton.ac.uk/11632/1/how_many_interviews.pdf.

Barnes, Riché Daniel. 2016. *Raising the Race: Black Career Women Redefine Marriage, Motherhood, and Community*. New Brunswick, NJ: Rutgers University Press.

Beaman, Jean. 2017. *Citizen Outsider: Children of North African Immigrants in France*. Berkeley: University of California Press.

Becker, Gary S. 1981. *A Treatise on the Family*. Cambridge, MA: Harvard University Press.

Becker, Howard S. 1998. *Tricks of the Trade: How to Think About Your Research While You're Doing It*. Chicago: University of Chicago Press.

Becker, Howard S. 1986. *Writing for Social Scientists: How to Start and Finish Your Thesis, Book, or Article*. Chicago: University of Chicago Press.

Becker, Howard S. 1970. "Field Work Evidence." In *Sociological Work: Method and Substance*, 39–62. New Brunswick, NJ: Transaction Books.

Becker, Howard S. 1967. "Whose Side Are We On?" *Social Problems* 14 (3): 239–247.

Belkin, Lisa. 2003. "The Opt-Out Revolution." *New York Times Magazine*, October 26, 2003.

Bellah, Robert N., Richard Madsen, William M. Sullivan, Ann Swidler, and Steven M. Tipton. 2007. *Habits of the Heart: Individualism and Commitment in American Life*. Berkeley: University of California Press.

Berger, Peter L., and Thomas Luckmann. 1966. *The Social Construction of Reality: A Treatise in the Sociology of Knowledge*. Garden City, NY: Anchor Books.

Bernoff, Josh. 2016. *Writing Without Bullshit: Boost Your Career by Saying What You Mean*. New York: HarperCollins Publishers.

Besen-Cassino, Yasemin. 2014. *Consuming Work: Youth Labor in America*. Philadelphia: Temple University Press.

Bettie, Julie. 2003. *Women Without Class: Girls, Race, and Identity*. Berkeley: University of California Press.

Bianchi, Suzanne M., John P. Robinson, and Melissa A. Milkie. 2006. *Changing Rhythms of American Family Life*. New York: Russell Sage Foundation.

Blair-Loy, Mary. 2003. *Competing Devotions: Career and Family Among Women Executives*. Cambridge, MA: Harvard University Press.

Blee, Kathleen M. 2002. *Inside Organized Racism: Women in the Hate Movement*. Berkeley: University of California Press.

Bourdieu, Pierre. 1990. *The Logic of Practice*. Stanford, CA: Stanford University Press.

Branch, Enobong Hannah. 2017. "Racialized Family Ideals: Breadwinning, Domesticity, and the Negotiation of Insecurity." In *Beyond the Cubicle: Job Insecurity, Intimacy, and the Flexible Self*, edited by Allison J. Pugh, 179–201. New York: Oxford University Press.

Brown, Eliza, and Mary Patrick. 2018. "Time, Anticipation, and the Life Course: Egg Freezing as Temporarily Disentangling Romance and Reproduction." *American Sociological Review* 83 (5): 959–982.

Burawoy, Michael. 2019. "Empiricism and Its Fallacies." *Contexts* 18 (1): 47–53.

Burawoy, Michael. 1998. "The Extended Case Method." *Sociological Theory* 16 (1): 4–33.

Calarco, Jessica McCrory. 2019. "Flexible Coding for Fieldnotes." *Scatterplot: The Unruly Darlings of Public Sociology* (blog), March 29, 2019. https://scatter.wordpress.com/2019/03/29.

Calarco, Jessica McCrory. 2018a. *Negotiating Opportunities: How the Middle Class Secures Advantages in School*. New York: Oxford University Press.

Calarco, Jessica McCrory. 2018b. "Why Rich Kids Are So Good at the Marshmallow Test." *The Atlantic*, June 1, 2018.

Calarco, Jessica McCrory. 2018c. "Notes from the Field: Show How You Know What You Know." *Scatterplot: The Unruly Darlings of Public Sociology* (blog), November 6, 2018, https://scatter.wordpress.com/2018/11/06/notes-from-the-field-show-how-you-know-what-you-know.

Cavna, Michael. 2015. "How Pixar Enchants Us, and Moves Us, with Close-Up Emotional Magic." *Washington Post*, June 20, 2015.

Cerulo, Karen. 2019. "Dreams of a Lifetime: Society, Culture and Our Wishful Imaginings." Paper presented at New York University Sociology of Culture Workshop, September 12, 2019.

Cerulo, Karen. 2014. "Re-Assessing the Problem: Response to Jerolmack and Khan." *Sociological Methods & Research* 43: 219–226.

Cerulo, Karen. 2006. *Never Saw It Coming: Cultural Challenges to Envisioning the Future*. Chicago: University of Chicago Press.

Chambliss, Daniel. 1996. *Beyond Caring: Hospitals, Nurses, and the Social Organization of Ethics*. Chicago: University of Chicago Press.

Charmaz, Kathy. 2006. *Constructing Grounded Theory: A Practical Guide Through Qualitative Analysis*. Thousand Oaks, CA: Sage Publications.

Chen, Victor Tan. 2015. *Cut Loose: Jobless and Hopeless in an Unfair Economy*. Berkeley: University of California Press.

Cherlin, Andrew J. 2019. "In the Shadow of Sparrows Point: Racialized Labor in the White and Black Working Classes." Working paper, Russell Sage Foundation, October 2019.

Chung, Angie Y. 2016. *Saving Face: The Emotional Costs of the Asian Immigrant Family Myth*. New Brunswick, NJ: Rutgers University Press.

Cicourel, Aaron V. 1982. "Interviews, Surveys, and the Problem of Ecological Validity." *American Sociologist* 17 (1): 11–20.

Cohen, Philip. 2015. "Comment on Goffman's Survey." *Family Inequality* (blog), August 26, 2015. https://familyinequality.wordpress.com/2015/06/19/on-goffmans-survey.

Collins, Caitlyn. 2019. *Making Motherhood Work: How Women Manage Careers and Caregiving*. Princeton, NJ: Princeton University Press.

Collins, Patricia Hill. 2009. *Black Feminist Thought: Knowledge, Power and the Politics of Empowerment*. New York: Routledge.

Collins, Patricia Hill. 1998. "It's All in the Family: Intersections of Gender, Race and Nation." *Hypatia* 13 (3): 62–82.

Comey, James. 2018. "The F.B.I. Can Do This." *New York Times*, September 30, 2018.

Compton, D'Lane. 2018. "How Many (Queer) Cases Do I Need? Thinking Through Research Design." In *Other, Please Specify: Queer Methods in Sociology*, edited by D'Lane Compton, Tey Meadow, and Kristen Schilt, 185–200. Oakland: University of California Press.

Compton, D'Lane, Tey Meadow, and Kristen Schilt, eds. 2018. *Other, Please Specify: Queer Methods in Sociology*. Oakland: University of California Press.

Connell, Catherine. 2018. "Thank You for Coming Out Today: The Queer Discomforts of In-Depth Interviews." In *Other, Please Specify: Queer Methods in Sociology*, edited by D'Lane Compton, Tey Meadow, and Kristen Schilt, 126–139. Oakland: University of California Press.

Cooley, Charles Horton. 1902. *Human Nature and the Social Order*. New York: Transaction.

Cooper, Marianne. 2014. *Cut Adrift: Families in Insecure Times*. Oakland: University of California Press.

Corse, Sarah M., and Jennifer M. Silva. 2017. "Intimate Inequalities: Love and Work in the 21st Century: Job Insecurity and the Flexible Self." In *Beyond the Cubicle: Job Insecurity, Intimacy, and the Flexible Self*, edited by Allison J. Pugh, 283–303. New York: Oxford University Press.

Crenshaw, Kimberlé. 1991. "Mapping the Margins: Intersectionality, Identity Politics, and Violence Against Women of Color." *Stanford Law Review* 43 (6): 1241–1299.

Creswell, John W. 2014. *A Concise Introduction to Mixed Methods Research*. Thousand Oaks, CA: Sage Publications.

Damaske, Sarah. Forthcoming. *The Tolls of Uncertainty: How Privilege and the Guilt Gap Shape Unemployment in America*. Princeton, NJ: Princeton University Press.

Damaske, Sarah. 2020. "Job Loss and Attempts to Return to Work: Complicating Inequalities Across Gender and Class." *Gender & Society* 34 (1): 7–30.

Damaske, Sarah. 2011. *For the Family? How Class and Gender Shape Women's Work*. New York: Oxford University Press.

Damaske, Sarah, and Adrianne Frech. 2016. "Women's Work Pathways Across the Life Course." *Demography* 53 (2): 365–391.

Daminger, Allison. 2019. "The Cognitive Dimension of Household Labor." *American Sociological Review* 84 (4): 609–633.

Davis, Murray S. 1971. "Towards a Phenomenology of Sociology and a Sociology of Phenomenology." *Philosophy of the Social Sciences* 1 (2): 309–344.

de Graauw, Els. 2016. *Making Immigrant Rights Real: Nonprofits and the Politics of Integration in San Francisco*. Ithaca, NY: Cornell University Press.

DeLuca, Stefani, Susan Clampet-Lundquist, and Kathryn Edin. 2016. *Coming of Age in the Other America*. New York: Russell Sage Foundation.

Desmond, Matthew. 2016. *Evicted: Power and Profit in the American City*. New York: Crown/Archetype.

Deterding, Nicole M., and Mary C. Waters. 2018. "Flexible Coding of In-Depth Interviews: A Twenty-First-Century Approach." *Sociological Methods & Research* 47.

Dill, Bonnie Thornton. 1979. "The Dialectics of Black Womanhood." *Signs: Journal of Women in Culture and Society* 4 (3): 543–555.

DiMaggio, Paul. 2014. "Comment on Jerolmack and Khan, 'Talk Is Cheap.'" *Sociological Methods & Research* 43 (2): 232–235.

Dobbs, David. 2015. "Review of Galileo's Finger by Alice Dreger." *New York Times Book Review*, April 17, 2015.

Dow, Dawn Marie. 2019. *Mothering While Black: Boundaries and Burdens of Middle-Class Parenthood*. Oakland: University of California Press.

Draaisma, Douwe. 2001. *Why Life Speeds Up as You Get Older: How Memory Shapes Our Past*. Cambridge: Cambridge University Press.

Duckworth, Angela. 2016. *Grit: The Power of Passion and Perseverance*. New York: Scribner.

Durkheim, Emile. 1982. *The Rules of Sociological Method and Selected Texts on Sociology and Its Method*. Edited by Steven Lukes. New York: Free Press.

Dycus, Sabrina. 2018. "Jailhouse Lawyers: On Both Sides of the Law." Unpublished manuscript, New York University.

Eberhardt, Jennifer L. 2019. *Biased: Uncovering the Hidden Prejudice That Shapes What We See, Think, and Do*. New York: Penguin Random House.

Ecklund, Elaine Howard. 2010. *Science vs. Religion: What Scientists Really Think*. New York: Oxford University Press.

Edin, Kathryn, and Maria Kefalas. 2005. *Promises I Can Keep: Why Poor Women Put Motherhood Before Marriage*. Berkeley: University of California Press.

Edin, Kathryn, and Timothy J. Nelson. 2013. *Doing the Best I Can: Fatherhood in the Inner City*. Berkeley: University of California Press.

Elder, Glen H., and Janet Z. Giele. 2009. *The Craft of Life Course Research*. New York: Guilford Press.

Emerson, Ralph Waldo. 1908. *The Essay on Self Reliance*. East Aurora, NY: Elbert Hubbard.

Emerson, Robert M., Rachel I. Fretz, and Linda L. Shaw. 2011. *Writing Ethnographic Fieldnotes*, 2nd edition. Chicago: University of Chicago Press.

Engel, David, Anita Woolley, Lisa Jing, Christopher Chabris, and Thomas Malone. 2014. "Reading the Mind in the Eyes or Reading Between the Lines? Theory of Mind Predicts Collective Intelligence Equally Well Online and Face-to-Face." *PloS* 9 (12): e115212.

Fisher, Robert J. 1993. "Social Desirability Bias and the Validity of Indirect Questioning." *Journal of Consumer Research* 20 (2): 303–315.

Fitzgerald, F. Scott. 1945. *The Crack-Up*. New York: New Directions.

Foley, Nadirah Farah. 2018. "Reconsidering the Use of 'Women and People of Color.'" *Scatterplot: The Unruly Darlings of Public Sociology* (blog), October 24, 2018. https://scatter.wordpress.com/2018/10/24/reconsidering-the-use-of-women-and-people-of-color.

Friedman, Richard A. 2018. "Why Sexual Assault Memories Stick." *New York Times*, September 20, 2018.

Geertz, Clifford. 1973. *The Interpretation of Cultures: Selected Essays*. New York: Basic Books.

Germano, William. 2001. *Getting It Published*. Chicago: University of Chicago Press.

Gerson, Kathleen. 2017. "Different Ways of Not Having It All." In *Beyond the Cubicle: Job Insecurity, Intimacy, and the Flexible Self*, edited by Allison J. Pugh, 155–179. New York: Oxford University Press.

Gerson, Kathleen. 2010. *The Unfinished Revolution: Coming of Age in a New Era of Gender, Work, and Family*. New York: Oxford University Press.

Gerson, Kathleen. 2009. "Changing Lives, Resistant Institutions: A New Generation Negotiates Gender, Work, and Family Change." *Sociological Forum* 24 (4): 735–753.

Gerson, Kathleen. 2002. "Moral Dilemmas, Moral Strategies, and the Transformation of Gender: Lessons from Two Generations of Work and Family Change." *Gender & Society* 16 (1): 8–28.

Gerson, Kathleen. 1993. *No Man's Land: Men's Changing Commitments to Family and Work.* New York: Basic Books.

Gerson, Kathleen. 1985. *Hard Choices: How Women Decide About Work, Career and Motherhood.* Berkeley: University of California Press.

Gerson, Kathleen, and Ruth Horowitz. 2002. "Interviewing and Observation: Options and Choices in Qualitative Research." In *Qualitative Research in Action*, edited by Timothy May, 199–224. London: Sage Publications.

Gerson, Kathleen, and Stacy Torres. 2015. "Changing Family Patterns and the Future of Family Life." *Emerging Trends in the Social and Behavioral Sciences*, edited by Robert A. Scott and Stephen M. Kosslyn. Hoboken, NJ: Wiley and Sons.

Gerth, Hans, and C. Wright Mills. 1953. *Character and Social Structure: The Psychology of Social Institutions.* Orlando, FL: Harcourt, Brace & World.

Giddens, Anthony. 1984. *The Constitution of Society: Outline of the Theory of Structuration.* Cambridge: Polity Press.

Giddens, Anthony. 1979. *Central Problems in Social Theory: Action, Structure, and Contradiction in Social Analysis.* Berkeley: University of California Press.

Gillespie, Dair L. 1971. "Who Has the Power? The Marital Struggle." *Journal of Marriage and Family* 33 (3): 445–458.

Glaser, Barney G., and Anselm L. Strauss. 1967. *The Discovery of Grounded Theory: Strategies for Qualitative Research.* New Brunswick, NJ: Transaction Publishers.

Goffman, Alice. 2015. "A Reply to Professor's Lubet's Critique." https://web.archive.org/web/20160304201335/http:/www.ssc.wisc.edu/soc/faculty/docs/goffman/A Reply to Professor Lubet.pdf.

Goffman, Alice. 2014. *On the Run: Fugitive Life in an American City.* Chicago: University of Chicago Press.

Goldberg, Abbie E., and Katherine R. Allen. 2015. "Communicating Qualitative Research: Some Practical Guideposts for Scholars." *Journal of Marriage and Family* 77 (1): 3–22.

Gonzales, Roberto. 2011. "Learning to Be Illegal: Undocumented Youth and Shifting Contexts in the Transition to Adulthood." *American Sociological Review* 76 (4): 602–619.

Goodwin, Jeff, and Ruth Horowitz. 2002. "Introduction: The Methodological Strengths and Dilemmas of Qualitative Sociology." *Qualitative Sociology* 25 (1): 33–47.

Gottlieb, Lori. 2019. "How Much Should You Know About Your Therapist's Life?" *New York Times*, March 30.

Hagedorn, Annelise. 2018. "'If We Were Valued More': A Study of Childcare Providers in Rural Southwest Pennsylvania." Doctoral dissertation, Pennsylvania State University, University Park.

Hammermesh, Daniel S., and Gerard A. Pfann. 2002. *The Economics of Time Use.* Bingley, UK: Emerald Group.

Haney, Lynne. 2018. "Incarcerated Fatherhood: The Entanglements of Child Support Debt and Mass Imprisonment." *American Journal of Sociology* 124 (1): 1–48.

Haney, Lynne. 2002. *Inventing the Needy: Gender and the Politics of Welfare in Hungary.* Berkeley: University of California Press.

Hartstock, Nancy. 1998. *The Feminist Standpoint Revisited and Other Essays*. Boulder, CO: Westview Press.

Hays, Sharon. 2003. *Flat Broke with Children: Women in the Age of Welfare Reform*. New York: Oxford University Press.

Hays, Sharon. 1998. *The Cultural Contradictions of Motherhood*. New Haven, CT: Yale University Press.

Hertz, Rosanna. 2006. *Single by Chance, Mothers by Choice: How Women Are Choosing Parenthood Without Marriage and Creating the New American Family*. New York: Oxford University Press.

Higginbotham, Elizabeth. 2001. *Too Much to Ask: Black Women in the Era of Integration*. Chapel Hill: University of North Carolina Press.

Hirsch, Jennifer S., and Shamus Khan. 2020. *Sexual Citizens: A Landmark Study of Sex, Power, and Assault on Campus*. New York: W. W. Norton.

Hirschman, Albert O. 1970. *Exit, Voice, and Loyalty: Responses to Decline in Firms, Organizations, and States*. Cambridge, MA: Harvard University Press.

Hislop, Jenny, Sara Arber, Rob Meadows, and Sue Venn. 2005. "Narratives of the Night: The Use of Audio Diaries in Researching Sleep." *Sociological Research Online* 10 (4).

Hochschild, Arlie R. 2016. *Strangers in Their Own Land: Anger and Mourning on the American Right*. New York: The New Press.

Hochschild, Arlie R. 1989. *The Second Shift: Working Parents and the Revolution at Home*. New York: Viking.

Hondagneu-Sotelo, Pierrette. 2001. *Domestica: Immigrant Workers Cleaning and Caring in the Shadow of Affluence*. Berkeley: University of California Press.

Hsiung, Ping-Chun. 2018. "Lives and Legacies: A Guide to Qualitative Interviewing." University of Toronto, Scarborough. http://www.utsc.utoronto.ca/~pchsiung/LAL.

Humphreys, Laud. 1970. "Tearoom Trade." *Trans-Action* 7 (3): 10–25.

Imoagene, Onoso. 2017. *Beyond Expectations: Second-Generation Nigerians in the United States and Britain*. Oakland: University of California Press.

Jack, Anthony Abraham. 2019. *The Privileged Poor: How Elite Colleges Are Failing Disadvantaged Students*. Cambridge, MA: Harvard University Press.

Jacobs, Jerry A., and Kathleen Gerson. 2016. "Unpacking Americans' Views of the Employment of Mothers and Fathers Using National Vignette Survey Data." *Gender & Society* 30: 413–441.

Jacobs, Jerry A., and Kathleen Gerson. 2004. *The Time Divide: Work, Family, and Gender Inequality*. Cambridge, MA: Harvard University Press.

Jacobson, Heather. 2016. *Labor of Love: Gestational Surrogacy and the Work of Making Babies*. New Brunswick, NJ: Rutgers University Press.

Jacobson, Heather. 2008. *Culture Keeping: White Mothers, International Adoption, and the Negotiation of Family Difference*. Nashville, TN: Vanderbilt University Press.

Jerolmack, Colin, and Shamus Khan. 2014. "Talk Is Cheap: Ethnography and the Attitudinal Fallacy." *Sociological Methods & Research* 43 (2): 178–209.

Jerolmack, Colin, and Alexandra Murphy. 2017. "The Ethical Dilemmas and Social Scientific Trade-offs of Masking in Ethnography." *Sociological Methods & Research* 48 (4): 1–27.

Jones, James H. 1981. *Bad Blood: The Tuskegee Syphilis Experiment*. New York: Free Press.

Kalleberg, Arne. 2011. *Good Jobs, Bad Jobs: The Rise of Polarized and Precarious Employment Systems in the United States, 1970s–2000s*. New York: Russell Sage Foundation.

Kang, Miliann. 2010. *The Managed Hand: Race, Gender, and the Body in Beauty Service Work*. Berkeley: University of California Press.

Kanter, Rosabeth Moss. 1993. *Men and Women of the Corporation*. New York: Basic Books.

Kasinitz, Philip, John H. Mollenkopf, and Mary C. Waters. 2009. *Inheriting the City: The Children of Immigrants Come of Age*. New York: Russell Sage Foundation.

Khan, Shamus. 2019. "The Subpoena of Ethnographic Data." *Sociological Forum* 34 (1): 253–263.

Klinenberg, Eric. 2013. *Going Solo: The Extraordinary Rise and Surprising Appeal of Living Alone*. New York: Penguin.

Kuhn, Thomas. 1962. *The Structure of Scientific Revolutions*. Chicago: University of Chicago Press.

Lacy, Karen. 2007. *Blue-Chip Black: Race, Class, and Status in the New Black Middle Class*. Berkeley: University of California Press.

Ladner, Joyce. 1972. *Tomorrow's Tomorrow: The Black Woman*. New York: Doubleday.

Lamont, Ellen. 2020. *The Mating Game: Courtship in an Era of Gender Upheaval*. Oakland: University of California Press.

Lamont, Michelle. 1992. *Money, Morals, and Manners: The Culture of the French and American Upper Middle Class*. Chicago: University of Chicago Press.

Lamont, Michelle, and Ann Swidler. 2014. "Methodological Pluralism and the Possibilities and Limits of Interviewing." *Qualitative Sociology* 37 (2): 153–171.

Lamott, Anne. 2007. *Bird by Bird: Some Instructions on Writing and Life*. New York: Anchor Books.

LaPiere, Richard. 1934. "Attitudes vs. Actions." *Social Forces* 13 (2): 230–237.

Lareau, Annette. 2003. *Unequal Childhoods: Class, Race and Family Life*. Berkeley: University of California Press.

Lareau, Annette, Elliot Weininger, and Amanda Cox. 2018. "Parental Challenges to Organizational Authority in an Elite School District: The Role of Cultural, Social, and Symbolic Capital." *Teachers College Record* 120 (1): 1–146.

Lee, Kevin. 2019. "Augmenting or Automating? Breathing Life into the Uncertain Promise of Artificial Intelligence." Unpublished manuscript, New York University Stern School of Business.

Lipsky, Michael. 2010. *Street-Level Bureaucracy: Dilemmas of the Individual in Public Service*, expanded edition. New York: Russell Sage Foundation.

Lubet, Steven. 2015. "Ethics on the Run." *The New Rambler*. http://newramblerreview.com/book-reviews/law/ethics-on-the-run.

Luker, Kristen. 2008. *Salsa Dancing into the Social Sciences: Research in an Age of Info-Glut*. Cambridge, MA: Harvard University Press.

Luker, Kristen. 1996. *Dubious Conceptions: The Politics of Teenage Pregnancy*. Cambridge, MA: Harvard University Press.

Luker, Kristen. 1984. *Abortion and the Politics of Motherhood*. Berkeley: University of California Press.

Luker, Kristen. 1978. *Taking Chances: Abortion and the Decision Not to Contracept*. Berkeley: University of California Press.

Lukes, Steven. 2014. "Thinking, Saying, and Doing." Puck Methods Symposium, NYU Department of Sociology, April 28, 2014.

Martin, John Levi. 2010. "Life's a Beach but You're an Ant, and Other Unwelcome News for the Sociology of Culture." *Poetics* 38 (2): 228–243.

Maxwell, Joseph A. 2010. "Using Numbers in Qualitative Research." *Qualitative Inquiry* 16 (6): 475–482.

McCabe, Janice M. 2016. *Connecting in College: How Friendship Networks Matter for Academic and Social Success.* Chicago: University of Chicago Press.

McCall, Leslie. 2005. "The Complexity of Intersectionality." *Journal of Women in Culture and Society* 30 (3): 1771–1800.

McMillam Cottom, Tressie. 2017. *Lower Ed: The Troubling Rise of For-Profit Colleges in the New Economy.* New York: The New Press.

McPherson, Miller, Lynn Smith-Lovin, and James M. Cook. 2001. "Birds of a Feather: Homophily in Social Networks." *Annual Review of Sociology* 27: 415–444.

Mead, George Herbert. 1934. *Mind, Self and Society.* Chicago: University of Chicago Press.

Meadow, Tey. 2018. *Trans Kids: Being Gendered in the Twenty-First Century.* Oakland: University of California Press.

Merriam-Webster Inc. 2019. The Merriam-Webster.com Dictionary. https://www.merriam-webster.com.

Merton, Robert K. 1995. "The Thomas Theorem and the Matthew Effect." *Social Forces* 74 (2): 379–422.

Merton, Robert K. 1976. *Sociological Ambivalence and Other Essays.* New York: Free Press.

Merton, Robert K., Marjorie Fiske, and Patricia L. Kendall. 1956. *The Focused Interview: A Manual of Problems and Procedures.* Glencoe, IL: Free Press.

Milgram, Stanley. 1974. *Obedience to Authority.* New York: HarperCollins.

Miller-Idriss, Cynthia. 2018. *The Extreme Gone Mainstream: Commercialization and Far-Right Youth Culture in Germany.* Princeton, NJ: Princeton University Press.

Mills, C. Wright. 1959. *The Sociological Imagination.* New York: Oxford University Press.

Mische, Anne. 2009. "Projects and Possibilities: Researching Futures in Action." *Sociological Forum* 24 (3): 694–704.

Moen, Phyllis, and Patricia Roehling. 2005. *The Career Mystique: Cracks in the American Dream.* Lanham, MD: Rowman and Littlefield.

Moore, Mignon R. 2018. "Challenges, Triumphs, Praxis: Collecting Qualitative Data on Less Visible and Marginalized Populations." In *Other, Please Specify: Queer Methods in Sociology,* edited by D'Lane Compton, Tey Meadow, and Kristen Schilt, 169–184. Oakland: University of California Press.

Moore, Mignon R. 2011. *Invisible Families: Gay Identity, Relationships, and Motherhood Among Black Women.* Berkeley: University of California Press.

Moyer, Melinda W. 2020. "Not Everyone Can Write Off a School Year: Who Should Be Worried About Their Kids Falling Behind?" *Slate,* April 9, 2020.

Newman, Katherine S. 1988. *Falling from Grace: The Experience of Downward Mobility in the American Middle Class.* New York: Free Press.

Orbuch, Terri L. 1997. "People's Accounts Count: The Sociology of Accounts." *Annual Review of Sociology* 23 (1): 455–478.

Parreñas, Rhacel Salazar. 2001. *Servants of Globalization: Women, Migration, and Domestic Work.* Stanford, CA: Stanford University Press.

Parsons, Talcott. 1974. "Family Structure in the Modern United States." In *The Family: Its Structures and Functions,* edited by R. L. Coser, 243–253. London: Macmillan.

Pascoe, C. J. 2007. *Dude, You're a Fag: Masculinity and Sexuality in High School.* Berkeley: University of California Press.

Patterson, Sarah E., Sarah Damaske, and Christen Sheroff. 2017. "Gender and the MBA: Differences in Career Trajectories, Institutional Support, and Outcomes." *Gender & Society* 31 (3): 310–332.

Pedulla, David S. 2020. *Making the Cut: Hiring Decisions, Bias, and the Consequences of Nonstandard, Mismatched, and Precarious Employment.* Princeton, NJ: Princeton University Press.

Pedulla, David S., and Sarah Thébaud. 2015. "Can We Finish the Revolution? Gender, Work-Family Ideals, and Institutional Constraint." *American Sociological Review* 80 (1): 116–139.

Percheski, Christine. 2008. "Opting Out? Cohort Differences in Professional Women's Employment Rates from 1960 to 2005." *American Sociological Review* 73 (3): 491–517.

Perry, Brea L., and Jessica McCrory Calarco. 2017. "Let Them Eat Cake: Socioeconomic Status and Caregiver Indulgence of Children's Food and Drink Requests." In *Food Systems and Health,* edited by Sara Shostak, 121–146. Advances in Medical Sociology, volume 18. Yorkshire, UK: Emerald Publishing.

Pew Research Center. 2020. "Fifty-Three Percent of Americans Say the Internet Has Been Essential During the COVID-19 Outbreak." April 30, 2020.

Pfeffer, Carla. 2016. *Queering Families: The Postmodern Partnerships of Cisgender Women and Transgender Men.* New York: Oxford University Press.

Poniewozik, James. 2016. "Matt Lauer Loses the War in a Battle Between the Candidates." *New York Times,* September 8, 2016.

Popper, Karl. 1959. *The Logic of Scientific Discovery.* New York: Hutchinson & Co.

Powell, Walter W., and Paul J. DiMaggio, eds. 1991. *The New Institutionalism in Organizational Analysis.* Chicago: University of Chicago Press.

Pratt, Michael G., Sarah Kaplan, and Richard Whittington. 2019. "The Tumult over Transparency: Decoupling Transparency from Replication." *Administrative Science Quarterly,* November 6, 2019, 1–19.

Pressman, Jeffrey, and Aaron Wildavsky. 1984. *Implementation: How Great Expectations in Washington Are Dashed in Oakland,* 3rd edition. Berkeley: University of California Press.

Pugh, Allison. 2015. *The Tumbleweed Society: Working and Caring in an Age of Insecurity.* Chicago: University of Chicago Press.

Pugh, Allison J. 2013. "What Good Are Interviews for Thinking About Culture? Demystifying Interpretive Analysis." *American Journal of Cultural Sociology* 1 (1): 42–68.

Pugh, Allison J. 2009. *Longing and Belonging: Parents, Children and Consumer Culture.* Berkeley: University of California Press.

Rabiner, Susan, and Alfred Fortunato. 2003. *Thinking Like Your Editor: How to Write Great Serious Nonfiction and Get It Published.* New York: W. W. Norton & Company.

Ramirez, Michael. 2018. *Destined for Greatness: Passions, Dreams, and Aspirations in a College Music Town.* New Brunswick, NJ: Rutgers University Press.

Rao, Aliya Hamid. 2020. *Crunch Time: How Married Couples Confront Unemployment.* Berkeley: University of California Press.

Ray, Rashawn, and Jason A. Rosow. 2010. "Getting Off and Getting Intimate: How Normative Institutional Arrangements Structure Black and White Fraternity Men's Approaches Toward Women." *Men and Masculinities* 12 (5): 523–546.

Reich, Jennifer. 2016. *Calling the Shots: Why Parents Reject Vaccines.* New York: New York University Press.

Risman, Barbara. 2018. *Where the Millennials Will Take Us: A New Generation Wrestles with the Gender Structure*. New York: Oxford University Press.

Rivera, Lauren A. 2017. "When Two Bodies Are (Not) a Problem: Gender and Relationship Status Discrimination in Academic Hiring." *American Sociological Review* 82 (6): 1111–1138.

Rivera, Lauren A. 2016. *Pedigree: How Elite Students Get Elite Jobs*. Princeton, NJ: Princeton University Press.

Robinson, Laura, and Jeremy Schulz. 2016. "Eliciting Frontstage and Backstage Talk with the Iterated Questioning Approach." *Sociological Methodology* 46 (1): 53–83.

Roth, Louise Marie. 2006. *Selling Women Short: Gender and Money on Wall Street*. Princeton, NJ: Princeton University Press.

Rothstein, Hannah R., Alexander J. Sutton, and Michael Borenstein. 2005. *Publication Bias in Meta-Analysis: Prevention, Assessment and Adjustments*. Hoboken, NJ: John Wiley & Sons.

Royster, Deirdre A. 2003. *Race and the Invisible Hand: How White Networks Exclude Black Men from Blue-Collar Jobs*. Berkeley: University of California Press.

Ryder, Norman. 1965. "The Cohort as a Concept in the Study of Social Change." *American Sociological Review* 30 (6): 843–861.

Schilt, Kristen. 2010. *Just One of the Guys? Transgender Men and the Persistence of Gender Inequality*. Chicago: University of Chicago Press.

Schulte, Brigid. 2015. *Overwhelmed: How to Work, Love and Play When No One Has the Time*. New York: Picador.

Scott, Marvin, and Stanford Lyman. 1968. "Accounts." *American Sociological Review* 33 (1): 46–62.

Shapiro, Fred R., and Joseph Epstein. 2006. *The Yale Book of Quotations*. New Haven, CT: Yale University Press.

Sharone, Ofer. 2013. *Flawed System/Flawed Self: Job Searching and Unemployment Experiences*. Chicago: University of Chicago Press.

Shedd, Carla. 2015. *Unequal City: Race, Schools, and Perceptions of Injustice*. New York: Russell Sage Foundation.

Sherman, Jennifer. 2009. *Those Who Work, Those Who Don't: Poverty, Morality, and Family in Rural America*. Minneapolis: University of Minnesota Press.

Sherman, Rachel. 2017. *Uneasy Street: The Anxieties of Affluence*. Princeton, NJ: Princeton University Press.

Shoda, Yuichi, Walter Mischel, and Philip K. Peake. 1990. "Predicting Adolescent Cognitive and Self-Regulatory Competencies from Preschool Delay of Gratification: Identifying Diagnostic Conditions." *Developmental Psychology* 26 (6): 978–986.

Silva, Jennifer M. 2013. *Coming Up Short: Working-Class Adulthood in an Age of Uncertainty*. New York: Oxford University Press.

Sims, Jennifer Patrice. 2016. "Reevaluation of the Influence of Appearance and Reflected Appraisals for Mixed-Race Identity: The Role of Consistent Inconsistent Racial Perception." *Sociology of Race and Ethnicity* 2 (4): 569–583.

Small, Mario Luis. 2018. "Rhetoric and Evidence in a Polarized Society." Coming to Terms with a Polarized Society Lecture Series. Columbia University Institute for Social and Economic Research and Policy, March 1, 2018.

Small, Mario Luis. 2009. "How Many Cases Do I Need? On Science and the Logic of Case Selection in Field-Based Research." *Ethnography* 10 (1): 5–38.

Smith, Dorothy. 1990. *Conceptual Practices of Power: A Feminist Sociology of Knowledge.* Toronto: University of Toronto Press.

Smith, Sandra S. 2007. *Lone Pursuit: Distrust and Defensive Individualism Among the Black Poor.* New York: Russell Sage Foundation.

Soto-Márquez, José G. 2019. "'I'm Not Spanish, I'm from Spain': Spaniards' Bifurcated Ethnicity and the Boundaries of Whiteness and Hispanic Panethnic Identity." *Sociology of Race and Ethnicity* 5 (1): 85–99.

Sprague, Joey. 2005. *Feminist Methodologies for Critical Researchers: Bridging Differences.* Lanham, MD: AltaMira Press.

Steinbugler, Amy C. 2012. *Beyond Loving: Intimate Racework in Lesbian, Gay, and Straight Interracial Relationships.* New York: Oxford University Press.

Stinchcombe, Arthur. 1968. *Constructing Social Theories.* New York: Harcourt, Brace & World.

Stinchcombe, Arthur L. 1965. "Social Structure and Organizations." In *Handbook of Organizations*, edited by James G. March, 142–192. Chicago: Rand McNally.

Stone, Pamela. 2007. *Opting Out? Why Women Really Quit Careers and Head Home.* Berkeley: University of California Press.

Stone, Pamela, and Meg Lovejoy. 2019. *Opting Back In: What Really Happens When Mothers Go Back to Work.* Oakland: University of California Press.

Streib, Jessica. 2015. *The Power of the Past: Understanding Cross-Class Marriages.* New York: Oxford University Press.

Strunk, William, Jr., and E. B. White. 1959. *The Elements of Style.* New York: Macmillan.

Swidler, Ann. 2001. *Talk of Love: Why Culture Matters.* Chicago: University of Chicago Press.

Swidler, Ann. 1986. "Culture in Action: Symbols and Strategies." *American Sociological Review* 51 (2): 273–286.

Swidler, Ann. 1980. "Love and Adulthood in American Culture." In *Themes of Work and Love in Adulthood*, edited by Neil J. Smelser and Erik H. Erikson, 120–147. Cambridge, MA: Harvard University Press.

Tavory, Iddo. 2020. "Interviews and Inference: Making Sense of Interview Data in Qualitative Research." *Qualitative Sociology* (July 7).

Tavory, Iddo, and Nina Eliasoph. 2013. "Coordinating Futures: Toward a Theory of Anticipation." *American Journal of Sociology* 118 (4): 908–942.

Tavory, Iddo, Sonia Prelat, and Shelly Ronen. 2020. "Advertising for Good: Pro Bono Campaigns and the Profusion of Causes." Unpublished manuscript.

Tavory, Iddo, and Stefan Timmermans. 2014. *Abductive Analysis: Theorizing Qualitative Research.* Chicago: University of Chicago Press.

Theodosius, Catherine. 2006. "Recovering Emotion from Emotion Management." *Sociology* 40 (5): 893–910.

Thomas, Kevin J. A. 2017. *Contract Workers, Risk, and the War in Iraq: Sierra Leonean Labor Migrants at US Military Bases.* Montreal: McGill-Queen's University Press.

Thomas, William Isaac, and Dorothy Swaine Thomas. 1928. *The Child in America: Behaviour Problems and Programs.* New York: Knopf.

Timmermans, Stefan, and Iddo Tavory. 2012. "Theory Construction in Qualitative Research: From Grounded Theory to Abductive Analysis." *Sociological Theory* 30 (3): 167–186.

Torres, Stacey. Forthcoming. *Old New York: Late Life in the City.* Oakland: University of California Press.

Twine, France Winddance. 2010. *A White Side of Black Britain: Interracial Intimacy and Racial Literacy*. Durham, NC: Duke University Press.

Utrata, Jennifer. 2015. *Women Without Men: Single Mothers and Family Change in the New Russia*. Ithaca, NY: Cornell University Press.

Vaisey, Stephen. 2014. "The 'Attitudinal Fallacy' Is a Fallacy: Why We Need Many Methods to Study Culture." *Sociological Methods and Research* 43 (2): 227–231.

Vaisey, Stephen. 2009. "Motivation and Justification: A Dual-Process Model of Culture in Action." *American Journal of Sociology* 114 (6): 1675–1715.

Vaughn, Diane. 1986. *Uncoupling: Turning Points in Intimate Relationships*. New York: Oxford University Press.

Viscelli, Steve. 2016. *The Big Rig: Trucking and the Decline of the American Dream*. Oakland: University of California Press.

von Pfetten, Verena. 2016. "Read This Story Without Distraction (Can You?)." *New York Times*, April 29, 2016.

Wade, Lisa. 2017. *American Hookup: The New Culture of Sex on Campus*. New York: W. W. Norton.

Warikoo, Natasha K. 2016. *The Diversity Bargain: And Other Dilemmas of Race, Admissions, and Meritocracy at Elite Universities*. Chicago: University of Chicago Press.

Waters, Mary C. 2001. *Black Identities: West Indian Immigrant Dreams and American Realities*. Cambridge, MA: Harvard University Press.

Waters, Mary C. 1990. *Ethnic Options: Choosing Identities in America*. Berkeley: University of California Press.

Watts, Tyler W., Greg J. Duncan, and Haonan Quan. 2018. "Revisiting the Marshmallow Test: A Conceptual Replication Investigating Links Between Early Delay of Gratification and Later Outcomes." *Psychological Science* 29 (7): 1159–1177.

Weiss, Robert. 1994. *Learning from Strangers: The Art and Method of Qualitative Interview Studies*. New York: Free Press.

Whitaker, Elizabeth Anne. 2017. "Moving On to Stay Put." In *Beyond the Cubicle: Job Insecurity, Intimacy, and the Flexible Self*, edited by Allison J. Pugh, 203–228. New York: Oxford University Press.

Whooley, Owen. 2013. *Knowledge in the Time of Cholera: The Struggle over American Medicine in the Nineteenth Century*. Chicago: University of Chicago Press.

Williams, Christine L. 2002. "To Know Me Is to Love Me? Response to Erich Goode." *Qualitative Sociology* 25 (4): 557–560.

Williams, Christine L. 1992. "The Glass Escalator: Hidden Advantages for Men in the 'Female' Professions." *Social Problems* 39 (3): 253–267.

Williams, Joan. 2000. *Unbending Gender: Why Family and Work Conflict and What to Do About It*. New York: Oxford University Press.

Wingfield, Adia Harvey. 2013. *No More Invisible Man: Race and Gender in Men's Work*. Philadelphia: Temple University Press.

Woolf, Virginia. 1929. *A Room of One's Own*. New York: Harcourt.

Woolley, Anita Williams, Christopher Chabris, Alex Pentland, Nada Hashmi, and Thomas Malone. "Evidence for a Collective Intelligence Factor in the Performance of Human Groups." *Science* 330 (6004): 686–688.

Worth, Nancy. 2009. "Making Use of Audio Diaries in Research with Young People: Examining Narrative, Participation and Audience." *Sociological Research Online* 14 (4).

Wrong, Dennis H. 1961. "The Oversocialized Conception of Man in Modern Sociology." *American Sociological Review* 26 (2): 183–193.

Yukich, Grace. 2013. *One Family Under God: Immigration Politics and Progressive Religion in America.* New York: Oxford University Press.

Zerubavel, Eviatar. 2006. *The Elephant in the Room: Silence and Denial in Everyday Life.* New York: Oxford University Press.

Zerubavel, Eviatar. 1999. *The Clockwork Muse: A Practical Guide to Writing Theses, Dissertations, and Books.* Cambridge, MA: Harvard University Press.

Zerubavel, Eviatar. 1996. "Lumping and Splitting: Notes on Social Classification." *Sociological Forum* 11 (3): 421–433.

Zerubavel, Eviatar. 1993. *The Fine Line: Making Distinctions in Everyday Life.* Chicago: University of Chicago Press.

Zimbardo, Phillip. 2007. *The Lucifer Effect: Understanding How Good People Turn Evil.* New York: Random House.

Index

Abdelhadi, Eman, 21, 249n46
abductive analysis, 247n24
abortion, 19, 60, 124–125
accounts
  belief statements, 115–116
  causal, 154
  construction of, 19
  contradictory, 20–21, 167–168
  definitions of, 18, 165, 237n42
  explanations vs., 165–166
  personal, 115–116, 166
active listening, 109, 114, 115, 245n1
agency, structure and, 12–14, 88, 155,
    170–171, 183, 192
agency bias, 13, 247n16
aha moments, 97, 119, 120, 150, 171
American Community Survey, 46
analysis, 143–171. See also coding
  abductive, 247n24
  attributing meaning in, 144–146
  categories for, 69–70, 149–155, 180
  comparative, 26, 27, 160, 170, 171
  conceiving outcomes in, 160–164
  concepts in, 69–70, 148–155, 159
  explaining outcomes in, 164–171, 181
  factors for, 28, 145, 164–170, 180–181
  goals of, 144, 145
  historical, 51
  immersion process in, 146–148, 171
  intersectional, 13, 158
  lumping and splitting process in,
    158, 163
  memos and matrices in, 155–160
  predictive, 14
  process for, 144, 147, 150, 155, 156
  qualitative, 158, 161, 164, 250n9
  quantitative, 69, 173
  statistical, 15, 164
  strategies for, 145, 155, 159, 160,
    166–171

  systematic, 16, 47, 121, 143,
    145–148, 171
  techniques for, 143, 155, 158–160, 174
  in writing projects, 179–183
Anner, Mark, 140
art, interviews as, 26–29, 100, 172–174
attitudinal fallacy, 17
audio diaries, 135
audio recordings. See recordings

Barnes, Riché Daniel, 36
Becker, Howard, 22, 24, 185
belief statements, 115–116
Besen-Cassino, Yasemin, 176
Bettie, Julie, 79
biases
  agency, 13, 247n16
  determinist, 13
  heteronormative, 55
  hindsight, 13, 247n16
  interviewer, 21–24, 33, 58, 123–127
  management of, 124–127
  publication, 166, 251n26
  sampling, 64, 134
  selection, 15, 46, 62, 63, 65
  self-selection, 58
  social desirability, 16–18, 237n36
  systematic, 8, 58
Blair-Loy, Mary, 239n16, 247n20
Blee, Kathleen, 124
Branch, Enobong Hannah, 19
Burawoy, Michael, 20, 27, 40

Calarco, Jessica, 49, 140
categories
  analytic, 69–70, 149–155, 180
  for coding, 147, 149–155
  conceptual, 14, 71, 121, 149–150, 153,
    162–163
  emergent, 147, 148, 158

categories (*cont.*)
    general, 48, 149–151, 153–154
    matrix, 156–158
    mental, 165
    original, 162–164
    sampling, 53–54
    theoretical, 55, 149
    variation within, 149
causal accounts, 154
Cerulo, Karen, 236n33, 237n37,
        238n68, 245n37
Chambliss, Daniel, 61
Cherlin, Andrew, 14
chronological organization,
        82–83, 247n16
Chung, Angie, 36
Cicourel, Aaron V., 236n19
class. *See* race, class, and gender
closed-ended questions, 16, 17
clothing for interviews, 138, 249n46
coding
    categories for, 147, 149–155
    conceptual, 153–155, 160
    qualitative, 158, 163
    quotations and, 154, 185
    second-order, 159
    software programs for, 146, 154, 250n16
    systematic process for, 143
    textual, 147, 156, 158, 160
Cohen, Philip, 66
cold cognitions, 17, 247n22
Collins, Caitlyn, 48–49, 55
Comey, James, 76
comparative analysis, 26, 27, 160, 170, 171
Compton, D'Lane, 55
computer-assisted interviews. *See* online
        interviews
concepts
    analytic, 69–70, 148–155, 159
    creation through interview
        studies, 11, 12
    for interview guides, 68–70
    relationships among, 34, 75–76
    theoretical, 150, 159
conceptual categories, 14, 71, 121, 149–150,
        153, 162–163
confidentiality
    attribution of quotes and, 183

controversy surrounding issues of, 129
    in ethnographic research, 66–67,
        129–130, 243n3
    institutional review boards and, 67,
        133, 243n3
    recruitment process concerns
        regarding, 67, 108
    of transcripts and memos, 130, 133
Connell, Catherine, 37
consent
    examples of forms for, 199–201
    informed, 123
    in interview process, 110–111
    for recordings, 102, 111, 133
contradictory accounts, 20–21, 167–168
convenience sampling, 64
Cooper, Marianne, 175
couple interviews, 4
Cox, Amanda, 50
critical race theory, 22
cultural conflicts, 2, 13, 236n25
cultural norms, 18, 19, 177
cultural schemas, 115

data. *See also* analysis
    feeling for, 26
    generalizability of, 16, 46, 53, 240n4
    methods of gathering, 135
    preexisting, 65
    quantitative, 164, 177
    relationship with theory, 143
    rigor in collection processes, 67
    in theoretical saturation, 52
Davis, Murray, 36
debriefing sessions, 102, 136
deceptive practices, 122–123
deductive techniques, 27, 68, 119, 149
defensive individualism, 11
de Graauw, Els, 60
delegation of interviews, 136
dependent variables, 43, 69, 242n38
depth interviews
    appropriateness of, 34
    avoidance of bias in, 24
    characteristics of, 4–5, 71, 114, 164
    critiques of, 17
    diversity of formats for, 3–5
    ethnographic research compared to, 4, 5

flexibility of, 68
objectives of, 12, 14, 192
in research toolkit, 26
sampling for (*see* samples and
    sampling)
as science as art, 26–29
structure and organization of, 82
survey research compared to, 5
truthfulness in context of, 25
wording of questions in, 78, 79
writing up (*see* writing projects)
design. *See* research design
Deterding, Nicole, 143, 149
determinist bias, 13
diaries, 135
Dill, Bonnie Thornton, 17, 237n40
discursive consciousness, 94, 245n37
Dow, Dawn Marie, 7, 36
dress for interviews, 138, 249n46
Durkheim, Emile, 35, 146
Dycus, Sabrina, 246n10
dynamic processes, 2, 6, 12–14, 159, 183

Ecklund, Elaine Howard, 58–59
ecological validity, 236n19
Edin, Kathryn, 10, 39–40
Einstein, Albert, 252n32
Elder, Glen H., 244n25, 251n27
Emerson, Robert, 140
empathetic probing, 128
empathy wall, 126
empirical debates, 178
empirical puzzles
    forms of, 35–36
    as gaps in literature, 177
    interviews in resolution of, 9, 11, 14, 28, 34
    research questions on, 35–36, 43
    in writing projects, 175, 176
empirical research
    discoveries from, 150, 171
    findings related to, 26, 40, 41, 192
    patterns in, 148, 160
    qualitative interviews and, 1–3
    relationships in, 32
    trends in, 147
employment discrimination, 10–11
ethical challenges, 121–130. *See also*
    biases; confidentiality

consent, 102, 110–111, 123, 133,
    199–201
management of biases, 124–127
sensitive questions and upsetting
    conversations, 127–129
skepticism and social distance,
    122–124
in social sciences, 172–173
understudied groups and, 37
ethnographic research
    confidentiality in, 66–67,
        129–130, 243n3
    depth interviews compared to, 4, 5
    field notes in, 67, 140
    immersion in, 30, 39, 51, 61
    interviews in, 9, 30
    limitations of, 79
    timing of stages in, 238n72
    of understudied groups, 10
events. *See also* experiences; life histories
    chain of, 87, 88, 170
    coding categories for, 154
    empirical, 32
    future, 94–95
    interpretation of, 144
    non-events, 169, 170
    present, 90–93
    time order of, 171
    triggering, 145
experiences. *See also* accounts; events
    audio diaries of, 135
    of changers vs. non-changers,
        89–90, 168
    in life histories, 13, 82, 83, 87–90
    macro-micro influences on, 37
    social context in shaping of, 88, 114
    subjective dimensions of, 20, 146
    timing and duration of, 145
explanations
    accounts vs., 165–166
    alternative, 41, 49, 72
    for outcomes, 64, 70, 164–171, 181
    theoretical, 6, 28
    for trajectories, 170–171
explanatory questions, 164
explanatory theories, 240n28
extended case method, 40
external validity, 240n5

face-to-face interviews. *See* in-person
  interviews
false consciousness, 18, 145
feminist theory, 8, 17, 22
field notes, 67, 140
findings, unanticipated. *See* unanticipated
  findings
Fisher, Robert J., 237n36
flexibility
  gender-related, 170
  of interview guides, 27, 68, 87, 96–99
  of interview studies, 5–6, 9, 44, 68
  mental, 2, 26, 120
  of questionnaires, 68
  of research questions, 32
  in sampling, 5, 57, 65
  in scheduling interviews, 108
  structure and, 68, 97–98, 100
  in wording of questions, 79
focus groups, 3–4
Foley, Nadirah Farah, 79
follow-up questions
  baseline orientation and, 85–87
  in interview process, 114–115
  neutrality of, 126, 128
  open-ended, 17
  outcomes and development of, 71
  probes vs., 85
  wording of, 78
Friedman, Richard, 88

Geertz, Clifford, 14
general categories, 48, 149–151, 153–154
generalizability, 16, 46, 53, 240n4
General Social Survey (GSS),
  77–79, 244n15
gender, *see* race, class, and gender
Gerth, Hans, 19
Giddens, Anthony, 94, 245n37
Glaser, Barney, 2, 15, 46, 52, 121, 150
Goffman, Alice, 66, 238n59
Gonzales, Roberto, 13, 63
Gottlieb, Lori, 110
grounded theory, 27, 150, 247n24

Hagedorn, Annelise, 56
Haney, Lynne, 40, 140, 177
Hays, Sharon, 8, 20

Hertz, Rosanna, 236n22
heteronormative bias, 55
hidden populations, 60, 240n1
hindsight bias, 13, 247n16
historical analysis, 51
Hochschild, Arlie, 126
Hondagneu-Sotelo, Pierrette, 8
hot cognitions, 17, 247n22
Humphreys, Laud, 122

ideal types, 101, 162, 176, 182
immersion
  ethnographic, 30, 39, 51, 61
  in interview data, 146–148, 171
independent variables, 69
in-depth interviews. *See* depth interviews
individualism, defensive, 11
inductive techniques, 27, 69, 119, 149
informed consent, 123
initial immersion, 146–148
in-person interviews, 3, 57, 108, 119,
  131–132, 248n40
insider perceptions. *See* outsider vs.
  insider perceptions
institutional review boards (IRBs)
  confidentiality requirements of, 67,
    133, 243n3
  consent requirements of, 110
  legal mandate of, 248n37
  on post-interview contact, 117
  pre-test interviews and, 102
  on protected group interviews, 241n10
institutional structures, 9, 12–13, 16
internal validity, 240n5
intersectional perspective, 13, 37, 158
interview-based research
  advantages of, 9, 11–12, 30, 192
  confidentiality in, 129
  design of (*see* research design)
  flexibility of, 5–6, 9, 44, 68
  guides for (*see* interview guides)
  insight in, 26
  presentation of, 190–192
  questions for (*see* research questions)
  sampling for (*see* samples and sampling)
  theory building and, 2, 14, 177
  timing of stages in, 238n72
  writing up (*see* writing projects)

interviewees
    changers vs. non-changers, 89–90, 168
    consent to record given by, 102, 111, 133
    criteria for selection of, 47
    motivational awareness of, 115, 116, 144
    partnership with interviewers, 18
    privacy rights of (*see* confidentiality)
    rapport with (*see* rapport)
    recruitment of (*see* recruitment process)
    safety of, 67, 129
    skepticism of, 22, 37, 64, 104, 122–124
    social desirability bias and,
        16–18, 237n36
    subjective dimensions of experiences,
        20, 146
    tools for focusing thoughts of, 68
    truthfulness of, 24–25
interviewers
    biases of, 21–24, 33, 58, 123–127
    challenges for, 7
    discretionary freedom of, 70
    partnership with interviewees, 18
    safety of, 136–137
    skill requirements for, 31–32
    training opportunities for, 102
interview guides, 66–99. *See also* questions
    for background information, 99
    for baseline orientation, 85–87
    for charting trajectories, 87–90
    comprehensiveness and length
        of, 98–99
    concepts and categories for, 68–70
    conclusion section of, 95–96
    ethical standards and, 67
    examples of, 203–234
    flexibility of, 27, 68, 87, 96–99
    functions of, 14, 66
    for future events, 94–95
    imposing rigor into, 67–68
    introductory section of, 83–84
    for present events, 90–93
    pre-testing, 68, 100–103
    structure and organization of,
        82–83, 97–98
    theoretical considerations for, 73–77
    trade-offs in design, 96–99
interview process, 109–142
    active listening during, 109, 114, 115
    building rapport during, 111–112
    closure of, 120–121
    clothing for, 138, 249n46
    collaborative relationships in, 109–111
    ending individual sessions in, 116–117
    ethical challenges during, 121–130
    gathering momentum during, 118, 120
    as learning experience, 141–142
    location considerations, 130–138
    materials for, 138–140
    mishaps during, 141
    oversimplification of, 17
    post-interview follow-up, 117–118
    probes in, 85, 114–116
    questioning strategies during, 112–114
    safety considerations, 67, 129, 136–137
    unanticipated findings in, 119, 120
interviews
    analysis of (*see* analysis)
    appropriateness of, 31–32, 34
    challenges related to, 15–25, 32, 118
    with couples, 4
    critiques of, 16–17, 249n4
    delegation of, 136
    depth (*see* depth interviews)
    diversity of formats for, 3–5
    in ethnographic research, 9, 30
    field preparation, 100–109
    focus groups, 3–4
    guides for (*see* interview guides)
    in-person, 3, 57, 108, 119,
        131–132, 248n40
    life history (*see* life histories)
    one-on-one, 4, 32, 136
    online, 3, 107–108, 131–135
    open-ended, 3–4, 30
    pre-test, 68, 100–103
    process for (*see* interview process)
    purpose of, 6–14
    qualitative (*see* qualitative interviews)
    questionnaires for (*see*
        questionnaires)
    question types suitable for, 34–42
    recording (*see* recordings)
    scheduling, 108, 131, 135, 137
    as science as art, 26–29, 100, 172–174
    structure and organization of,
        82–83, 97–98

interviews (*cont.*)
  survey research compared to, 5,
    118, 244n24
  telephone, 3, 107–108, 117, 119, 131–135
  time-ordered, 12–13, 82–83, 87–88
  writing up (*see* writing projects)
interview studies. *See* interview-based
    research
IRBs. *See* institutional review boards
iterative questioning approach, 31,
    244n22, 247n17

Jack, Anthony Abraham, 50–51
Jacobson, Heather, 18, 51
Jerolmack, Colin, 16–17, 129
journals, writing for, 174, 176, 178, 179

Kang, Miliann, 9
Kanter, Rosabeth, 73–74
Kaplan, Sarah, 67
Kasinitz, Philip, 236n17
Kefalas, Maria, 10
Khan, Shamus, 16–17
Klinenberg, Eric, 48, 55
Kuhn, Thomas, 41, 177, 240n27

Ladner, Joyce, 17, 22
Lamont, Ellen, 20
Lamont, Michelle, 249n46
Lareau, Annette, 50
Lee, Kevin, 10
life histories
  circumstances in, 83, 87, 90
  developmental paths in, 13, 90, 159
  experiences in, 13, 82, 83, 87–90
  as narratives, 87
  social contexts and, 13–14
  as time-ordered interviews, 12–13,
    83–84, 87–88
  trajectories in, 13, 87–90, 159, 168–171
  in writing projects, 182
Lipsky, Michael, 8
listening, active, 109, 114, 115, 245n1
literature review, in writing projects, 178
logic of discovery, 12
logic of inquiry, 26, 28
long-distance interviews. *See* online
    interviews; telephone interviews

Lubet, Steven, 66
Luker, Kristen, 2, 19, 25, 33, 46, 60,
    124–125
lumping and splitting process, 158, 163
Lyman, Stanford, 115, 237n42

marshmallow test, 21–22
Martin, John Levi, 17
matrices, 155–158, 160
McCabe, Janice, 176, 182
McMillan Cottom, Tressie, 38, 39
Mead, George Herbert, 238n64, 246n8
Meadow, Tey, 88
memos
  in analysis, 143
  composing, 118, 140, 146
  confidentiality issues and, 130
  reviewing, 121
  summary, 155, 156, 158
mental categories, 165
mental flexibility, 2, 26, 120
Merton, Robert, 2
methodological codes, 154
Miller-Idriss, Cynthia, 61
Mills, C. Wright, 19, 26, 37
mixed-methods projects, 1, 38
Moore, Mignon, 10, 62
motivation
  for actions, 18, 19
  interviewee awareness of, 115, 116, 144
  investigation through interviews,
    1, 10, 11
  for research studies, 173
  vocabulary of motive, 19
  of volunteers, 64
Murphy, Alexandra, 129

narratives
  analytic categories from, 155
  construction of, 25, 140
  layered, 25
  life histories as, 87
  question development and, 76
  in writing projects, 182–183
Nelson, Timothy, 39–40
nested questions, 31, 76, 80–82, 87, 92
Newman, Katherine, 125
non-relationships, 166–167, 171

norms
  conformity to, 13, 14
  cultural, 18, 19, 177
  gender, 75
  social, 16, 37, 165, 168
note-taking, 67, 140, 141, 147

objectivity of researchers, 22
one-on-one interviews, 4, 32, 136
online interviews, 3, 107–108, 131–135
open-ended interviews, 3–4, 30
open-ended questions, 17, 68, 78–79, 115
original categories, 162–164
outcomes
  conceiving, 160–164
  explaining, 64, 70, 164–171, 181
  future aspirations as, 94
  observation of, 9
  question development and, 27, 34, 70–72
  research design and, 42–43
  sampling considerations and, 47,
     49, 52, 64
  systematically biased, 8
  variation in, 72–73, 181
outsider vs. insider perceptions, 8, 22, 80,
     141–142
oversampling, 55, 61

Parreñas, Rhacel, 74
Parsons, Talcott, 240n26
participants. See research participants and
     respondents
Patterson, Sarah, 181
payments for participants, 104, 107,
     139, 246n9
Pedulla, David, 11–12, 38, 39, 79
personal accounts, 115–116, 166
Pfeffer, Carla, 36
phone interviews. See telephone interviews
Poniewozik, James, 115
Popper, Karl, 240n28
positionality, 21–24, 145–146, 238n59
practical consciousness, 245n37
Pratt, Michael, 67, 129
predictive analysis, 14
presentations, 190–192
pre-test interviews, 68, 100–103
privacy. See confidentiality

probability sampling, 46
probes
  accounts captured with, 18
  baseline orientation and, 85–87
  empathetic, 128
  follow-up questions vs., 85
  in interview process, 85, 114–116
  open-ended, 17, 83
  purpose of, 8–9
  systematic approach to, 31
promissory structure of talk, 94
publication bias, 166, 251n26
publishing, 55–56, 166, 240n4
Pugh, Allison, 19, 25, 72–73, 115–116

qualitative coding, 158, 163
qualitative interviews. See also depth
     interviews
  advantages of, 4–5
  as complement to quantitative
     research, 34, 38
  deceptive practices in, 122–123
  empirical and theoretical
     contributions, 1–3
  strategies for, 2–3
qualitative research. See also ethnographic
     research; qualitative interviews
  analysis in, 158, 161, 164, 250n9
  confidentiality in, 66–67
  methodological rigor in, 173
  pioneering approaches to, 2
  significance tests in, 239n5
  underlying principles of, 69–70
quantitative research
  analysis in, 69, 173
  biases in, 24
  challenges related to, 32, 118
  limitations of, 10
  lingua franca of, 69
  qualitative interviews as complement
     to, 34, 38
  timing of stages in, 238n72
quasi-statistics, 185
queer methodology, 55
questionnaires, 9, 19, 27, 68–69. See also
     interview guides
questions
  closed-ended, 16, 17

questions (*cont.*)
  explanatory, 164
  follow-up (*see* follow-up questions)
  generation of, 23
  iterative approach to, 31,
      244n22, 247n17
  nested, 31, 76, 80–82, 87, 92
  nonresponses to, 111–112, 128
  open-ended, 17, 68, 78–79, 115
  outcomes and development of, 27,
      34, 70–72
  probes (*see* probes)
  research (*see* research questions)
  sensitive, 79, 96, 111, 127–129
  theoretical (*see* theoretical questions)
  timing and placement of, 76, 111
  wording of, 69, 77–80
quotations
  in analytic context, 183–185
  coding, 154, 185
  confidential, 108
  in numerical context, 184–185
  recording of, 139
  selection of, 182–186, 191

race, class, and gender, 8, 13, 23, 54–55,
    79, 123
Ramirez, Michael, 159
random sampling, 46, 51, 58–61, 65
rapport
  building, 31, 111–112
  importance of, 4, 100
  maintenance of, 126
  in online interviews, 133
  sensitive questions and, 127
  wording of questions and, 80
recordings. *See also* transcripts
  audio quality of, 134
  interviewee consent for, 102, 111, 133
  malfunctions related to, 141
  of post-interview conversations, 96, 117
recruitment process, 103–108
  challenges related to, 55, 103, 123
  common questions and concerns
      during, 106–108
  confidentiality and, 67, 108
  initial contact script in, 104–106
  introductory letters in, 103–104, 195

master list for calls and follow-ups,
    196–197
  record of contacts in, 104, 195–196,
      246–247n11
  rejections during, 32
  sampling procedures and, 60, 63, 103
  screening forms in, 195–196
  script and eligibility sheet, 253–254n1
reflexivity, 23
Reich, Jennifer, 35
relationships. *See also* unanticipated
      findings
  action-mental state, 20
  among concepts, 34, 75–76
  in empirical research, 32
  non-relationships, 166–167, 171
  statistical, 10, 32, 34
  substantive, 85–87
reliability, 15, 64, 68, 76
representative samples, 12, 46, 58
research
  design of (*see* research design)
  empirical (*see* empirical research)
  ethnographic (*see* ethnographic
      research)
  inquiry and, 26, 28, 66, 71, 87, 94
  interview-based (*see* interview-based
      research)
  mixed-methods projects, 1, 38
  in private sphere, 8
  qualitative (*see* qualitative research)
  quantitative (*see* quantitative research)
  questions for (*see* research questions)
  sampling for (*see* samples and sampling)
  strategies for, 2–3, 23
  survey (*see* survey research)
research design
  clarification of, 178–179
  comparisons in, 27–28
  incorporation of unanticipated findings
      into, 100
  outcomes and, 42–43
  positionality and, 21–22
  selection of, 31, 44
  theory as guide for, 41, 42
  in writing projects, 178–179
research participants and respondents. *See
    also* interviewees

criteria for inclusion/exclusion, 47, 48, 52
disclosure of identity debates, 67
minimum number of, 53
motivation of, 64
payments for, 104, 107, 139, 246n9
privacy rights of (*see* confidentiality)
rapport with (*see* rapport)
recruitment of (*see* recruitment process)
selection of (*see* samples and sampling)
social context and, 4, 5
unmasking of, 129
volunteers, 58, 64, 101, 243n44
research questions, 30–42
avoidance of bias in, 23
development of, 26, 32–33
on empirical puzzles, 35–36, 43
evolution of, 30, 32
framing, 39–40, 113, 119, 176
on macro-micro links and interactive processes, 37–39
positionality in relation to, 24
in presentations, 190, 191
shaping to fit research design, 31
"so what?" test for, 33
suitability for interviews, 34–42
theoretically based, 26–28, 30, 35, 39–42
turning interests into, 32
on understudied groups, 36–37
in writing projects, 175–176
research toolkit, 26
respondents. *See* research participants and respondents
Rickey, Branch, 26, 238n70
Risman, Barbara, 102
Rivera, Lauren, 140
Robinson, Laura, 31, 244n22, 247n17
Roth, Louise, 40
Royster, Deirdre, 49–50, 60–61
Ryder, Norman, 241n22

safety considerations, 67, 129, 135–137
samples and sampling, 45–65
avoidance of bias in, 23
boundaries for, 47–49
challenges related to, 45, 57–58
comparisons in, 28, 47, 49–52, 55, 56, 240n4

controls in, 47–48, 52
convenience, 64
criteria for, 47, 48, 52, 241n6
flexibility of, 5, 57, 65
from known universe, 60–62
opportunistic, 52, 56, 64, 65
oversampling, 55, 61
population for, 46, 51, 54–60
probability, 46
random, 46, 51, 58–61, 65
representative, 12, 46, 58
size of, 5, 15–16, 36, 52–56, 54*t*, 241–242n26
snowball, 37, 61–63, 240n1, 242n35
sources for, 51, 53, 58–60, 65, 242n29, 243n44
strategic, 48–52
systematic approach to, 27
theoretical, 46–48, 52, 60–62, 65
variation in, 48–57, 240n4
sampling bias, 64, 134
saturation, 15, 52–57, 97, 121
scheduling interviews
flexibility in, 108
in-person, 131
long-distance, 135
safety considerations in, 137
schemas, 53, 115
Schilt, Kristen, 13, 63
Schulz, Jeremy, 31, 244n22, 247n17
science, interviews as, 26–29, 100, 172–174
Scott, Marvin, 115, 237n42
second-order coding, 159
selection bias, 15, 46, 62, 63, 65
self-disclosure, 28, 110
self-presentation, 18, 132, 249n46
self-reports, 16–19, 115, 144
self-selection bias, 58
sensitive questions, 79, 96, 111, 127–129
sequential ordering principle, 87–88
Sharone, Ofer, 177, 182
Shedd, Carla, 38–39
Sherman, Jennifer, 180–182
Sherman, Rachel, 180
Small, Mario, 46, 53, 143, 240n4
Smith, Dorothy, 17, 22
Smith, Sandra, 10–11

snowball sampling, 37, 61–63,
    240n1, 242n35
social contexts
    accounts shaped by, 18–19, 165
    changes to, 94, 171
    experiences shaped by, 88, 114
    interactive processes and, 37, 164, 183
    layers of meaning in, 25
    life histories and, 13–14
    participant information regarding, 4, 5
    statistical relationships and, 10
    in summary memos, 155
social desirability bias, 16–18, 237n36
social facts, 35, 44, 146, 239n6
social groups. See also
        understudied groups
    dynamics of, 170, 172
    intersectional analysis of, 158
    quantitative studies on, 10
    sampling procedures for, 57, 60
social life
    action-mental state relationship in, 20
    domains of, 74
    as dynamic process, 159
    qualitative descriptions of, 171
    research questions in relation to, 33, 73
    structures and processes in
        shaping of, 37
    time-ordered interviews and, 12
    universal patterns in, 188
    unobservable dimensions of, 8
social norms, 16, 37, 165, 168
social patterns
    analysis of, 158
    clarification of, 12
    discovery of, 6, 9, 14, 42, 64
    interviewer biases in study of, 22
    sampling sources and, 51
social science, 39, 59, 172–177, 249n5
social structures, 5, 25, 29, 37, 173, 192
sociologese, 188, 253n37
sociological imagination, 26, 37
Soto-Márquez, José, 51–52
"so what?" test, 33
Stanford prison experiments, 122
statistical analysis, 15, 164
statistical relationships, 10, 32, 34
Stinchcombe, Arthur, 16, 240–241n5
Stone, Pamela, 239n9

strategic comparisons, 15, 27–28, 49–52
Strauss, Anselm, 2, 15, 46, 52, 121, 150
structural conflicts, 2, 13, 236n25
structure
    agency and, 12–14, 88, 155, 170–171,
        183, 192
    flexibility and, 68, 97–98, 100
    institutional, 9, 12–13, 16
    for interviews, 82–83, 97–98
    invisible, 6, 8–9
    processes and, 29, 37
    social, 5, 25, 29, 37, 173, 192
substantive codes, 154
summary memos, 155, 156, 158
surprising findings. See unanticipated
        findings
survey research
    American Community Survey, 46
    closed-ended questions in, 16, 17
    General Social Survey, 77–79, 244n15
    hidden populations in, 240n1
    interviews compared to, 5, 118, 244n24
    limitations of, 10, 16
    validity and reliability in, 15
    wording of questions in, 77–79
Swidler, Ann, 237n50, 251n25
systematic analysis, 16, 47, 121, 143,
        145–148, 171
systematic bias, 8, 58

Tavory, Iddo, 9, 94, 247n16, 247n24
telephone interviews, 3, 107–108, 117,
        119, 131–135
textual coding, 147, 156, 158, 160
Thébaud, Sarah, 11–12, 79
theoretical approaches
    evaluation of, 27, 73–74, 178
    extended case method for, 40
    range of, 119
    reorientation of, 9, 12
theoretical arguments, 42, 121, 143, 155,
        176, 183
theoretical breakthroughs, 41, 43, 47,
        150, 160
theoretical categories, 55, 149
theoretical codes, 154
theoretical concepts, 150, 159
theoretical debates
    adjudication of, 47

clarification of, 41
deductive approach to, 27
engagement with, 43, 69, 72
interdisciplinary, 40
in presentations, 190
research questions and, 30, 35, 39
resolution through interviewing, 34
in writing projects, 176, 178
theoretical explanations, 6, 28
theoretical frameworks, 39–44, 54, 167
theoretical insights, 1, 44, 46, 65, 112, 118
theoretical paradigms, 41, 177, 178
theoretical questions
adjustment of, 43
deductive approach to, 27
explanatory factors and process, 74–75
inspiration and, 26
interview guides and, 72
logic of inquiry and, 28
in research process, 41, 143, 192
sample considerations and, 48
in writing projects, 175
theoretical sampling, 46–48, 52, 60–62, 65
theoretical saturation, 52, 55, 121
theory
building, 2, 14, 27–28, 177, 241n5
critical race, 22
discoveries explained through, 27
Einstein on, 252n32
explanatory, 240n28
feminist, 8, 17, 22
grounded, 27, 150, 247n24
relationship with data, 143
reorientation of, 10–12
research design guided by, 41, 42
thick description, 14
Thomas, Kevin, 7
Thomas, William and Dorothy
Swaine, 20
time-ordered interviews, 12–13,
82–83, 87–88
Timmermans, Stefan, 247n24
tokenism, 73–74
trajectories
categories for, 159
charting, 13, 87–90, 168–169
explaining, 170–171
transcripts. See also analysis; coding
confidentiality of, 130, 133

framework for reading, 146
length of interviews and, 15
process of transcription, 139, 250n9
truthfulness, 24–25
Tuskegee syphilis experiment, 122

unanticipated findings
aha moments and, 97, 119, 120,
150, 171
analysis of, 161
incorporation into research design, 100
insights about social world from, 1, 12
inspiration in search for, 26
openness to, 2, 97
recognition of, 34, 43, 70, 115
reflexivity and, 23
research question reframing due
to, 30, 32
understudied groups
ethnographic research of, 10
hidden populations as, 60, 240n1
reluctance to participate in
interviews, 37
research questions on, 36–37
sample size for, 36
unexpected findings. See unanticipated
findings
unmasking research participants, 129
upsetting conversations, 112, 127–129
Utrata, Jennifer, 50

Vaisey, Stephen, 17, 247n22
validity
assessment of, 129
of contradictory accounts, 20, 21, 167
ecological, 236n19
internal vs. external, 240n5
of quantitative analysis, 173
saturation and, 53, 121
in survey research, 15
variables
dependent, 43, 69, 242n38
independent, 69
statistical relationships among, 10, 34
variation
in categories, 149
explanations for, 165
in outcomes, 72–73, 181
in sampling, 48–57, 240n4

Vaughn, Diane, 9
virtual interviews. *See* online interviews
Viscelli, Steve, 51
visual schemas, 53
vocabulary of motive, 19
voice recognition technology, 139, 250n9
volunteers, 58, 64, 101, 243n44
von Pfetten, Verena, 245n1

Wade, Lisa, 35
Warikoo, Natasha, 20
Waters, Mary C., 143, 149, 241n17,
    242n26, 249n2, 250n12, 250n13
web-based interviews. *See* online
    interviews
Weber, Max, 146, 176
Weininger, Elliot, 50
Weiss, Robert, 2, 85, 115, 116
Whitaker, Elizabeth, 74–75
Whittington, Richard, 67
Whooley, Owen, 177
Williams, Christine, 73–74

Wingfield, Adia Harvey, 6–7, 62, 73–74
word clouds, 115, 116
wording of questions, 69, 77–80
writing projects, 174–190
    analysis and presentation of findings in,
        179–183
    argument presentation in, 179–182
    completion of, 189–190
    conclusion section in, 186–187
    introduction section in, 175–178
    literature review in, 178
    quotations in, 182–186
    research design clarification in,
        178–179
    resources for, 174
    style as substance in, 187–188
    theoretical and empirical debates in,
        176, 178

Yukich, Grace, 177

Zerubavel, Eviatar, 158, 251n29